D1476984

Western Daughters
in Eastern Lands

Western Daughters in Eastern Lands

British Missionary Women in Asia

Rosemary Seton

 PRAEGER

AN IMPRINT OF ABC-CLIO, LLC
Santa Barbara, California • Denver, Colorado • Oxford, England

Copyright 2013 by Rosemary Seton

Library of Congress Cataloging-in-Publication Data

Seton, Rosemary E.
  Western daughters in Eastern lands : British missionary women in Asia / Rosemary Seton.
    p. cm.
  Includes bibliographical references (p.   ) and index.
    ISBN 978-1-84645-017-4 (hardcopy : alk. paper) — ISBN 978-0-313-09729-4 (ebook)
1. Women missionaries—Great Britain—Biography.   2. Women missionaries—China—
Biography. South Asia—Biography   3. Missions—China. Missions—South Asia   I. Title.
    BV3703.S48   2013
    266'.0234105082—dc23   2012026337

ISBN: 978-1-84645-017-4
EISBN: 978-0-313-09729-4

17   16   15   14   13   1   2   3   4   5

This book is also available on the World Wide Web as an eBook.
Visit www.abc-clio.com for details.

Praeger
An Imprint of ABC-CLIO, LLC

ABC-CLIO, LLC
130 Cremona Drive, P.O. Box 1911
Santa Barbara, California 93116-1911

This book is printed on acid-free paper ∞

Manufactured in the United States of America

For DRS
and in memory of my parents

Contents

List of Illustrations

PERMISSIONS

Figures 3.2, 4.1, 5.1, 5.3, and 6.3 by permission of MMS Collection at SOAS ©
Trustees for Methodist Church Purposes; Figure 1.1 by permission of the Victoria
University Library (Toronto); Figures 2.1 and 7.3 by permission of OMF International (United Kingdom); Figures 3.1 and 4.2 by permission of the United Reformed Church; Figures 3.3, 5.2, and 7.2 by permission of SOAS Library; Figures
3.4 and 6.2 by permission of the Royal Free Archives Centre, Ludhiana Medical
College Collection; Figure 6.1 courtesy of the Council for World Mission; and Figure 7.1 by permission of the Trustees of the National Library of Scotland.

NOTE ON PLACE NAMES

I have rendered place names as Britons overseas knew them. The modern equivalent is given in parentheses after the first mention.

Acknowledgements

During my researches for this book I have received splendid service at a number of archives and libraries. I am particularly grateful to staff in the Asian and African Studies Reading Room in the British Library, and to colleagues of the Archives and Special Collections at SOAS. I am greatly indebted to Renate Dohmen, Valerie Griffiths, Paul and Jennifer Jenkins, Emily Manktelow, Steven Maughan, Laura Rivkin, Rhonda Semple, David Seton, Helen Wang, and Frances Wood for kindly reading and commenting on draft chapters. The book has been immeasurably improved as a result. I am most grateful to Audrey Salters for allowing me to quote from her parents' letters in *Bound with Love,* and to Vanessa Wood for permission to publish extracts from the letters of her great-aunt Myfanwy Wood.

List of Abbreviations

BFSS	British and Foreign School Society
BMS	Baptist Missionary Society
BZM	Baptist Zenana Mission
CEZMS	Church of England Zenana Missionary Society
CIM	China Inland Mission
CMAI	Christian Medical Association of India
CMS	Church Missionary Society
EIC	East India Company
FES	Female Education Society, also known as SPFEE
FMC	Foreign Missions Committee (of the Presbyterian Church of England)
IFNS	Indian Female Normal School and Instruction Society
IMC	International Missionary Council
LMS	London Missionary Society
LSMW	London School of Medicine for Women
NAC	Nurses' Association of China
PCE/WMA	Presbyterian Church of England/ Women's Missionary Association

PCI/PWA	Presbyterian Church in Ireland/Presbyterian Women's Association
SCM	Student Christian Movement
SOAS	School of Oriental and African Studies
SPCK	Society for Promoting Christian Knowledge
SPFEE	Society for Promoting Female Education in the East, also known as FES
SPG	Society for the Propagation of the Gospel
SVMU	Student Volunteer Missionary Union
WCC	Women's Christian College, Madras
WMC	World Missionary Conference
WMMS	Wesleyan Methodist Missionary Society
ZBMM	Zenana Bible and Medical Mission

Introduction

The lofty skill of Western lands has been bestowed by honoured hands.
How should such love and kindly grace come nigh my pitiable race?
My son, like winter, dead I bring, to rise as birds wake in the spring

In 1931, Sister Gladys Stephenson, a Wesleyan Methodist missionary in central China, had been temporarily drafted in to supervise emergency hospitals set up after the dreadful Yangtse floods of 1931. She recorded in her memoirs the lines above penned by a grateful father.[1] The sentiments confirmed Stephenson's elevated view of her calling, purpose, and status. In another country and decade, the more humble-minded Annie Small agonized that the Christian religion she represented "was so obviously remote from any concern, need or desire of these dear people with whom otherwise I had become most happily intimate."[2] These brief extracts provide contrasting insights into an ambitious and complex undertaking that, supported by ardent networks of women at home, propelled many hundreds of British women eastward, participants in a unique venture of Christian womanhood.

Comparatively little has appeared in recent years about the history of an enterprise that mobilized "the largest mass movement of women in Britain in the nineteenth century."[3] By contrast, a proliferation of works published about the North

American women's missionary movement testifies to its size and importance, while studies of Continental women's missionary efforts have also appeared.[4] Helen Barrett Montgomery, a zealous leader of American women's missions, brought out *Western Women in Eastern Lands* in 1910 to mark the 50th anniversary of the first American Women's Board of Foreign Missions. It sold more than 100,000 copies. Yet what Montgomery describes as "perhaps the most important afternoon tea in history" occurred in the vestry room of a church in Bloomsbury, London in July 1834. Here, "a little company of ladies" formed the first society dedicated to the task of sending women missionaries overseas, setting a precedent emulated in Continental Europe, North America, and Australasia. During the next three quarters of a century, Britain sent more missionaries overseas than any other country, and, by the end of the century, well over half were women.

HEROINES OF THE MISSION FIELD

A rich literary legacy of heroism and martyrdom in the form of published memoirs and biographies commemorates the early efforts of these women.[5] Especially popular were single volume collections of short biographies, often destined as prizes for Sunday school pupils, or distributed through networks of missionary supporters as money-raising ventures. Among the earliest to appear was *Memoirs of British Female Missionaries* by Jemima Thompson. Published in 1841, it set out to correct the impression that only men could be celebrated in this way.

> Many excellent women have adorned, and still adorn, our foreign missions;—full of love to the perishing Heathen, and of zeal for the honour and glory of the Saviour of men. Missionary biography ought not, therefore, to be limited to Schwartz, Henry Martyn, Drs. Morison, Milne, Carey, and such laborious and apostolic men.... Women, possessing those indispensable qualifications which have conferred imperishable honour and shed such sacred lustre on the cause of the Redeemer, are needed to accompany the servants of Christ in their evangelical missions.[6]

The women Thompson wrote about were almost all the wives of missionaries, and their names have little resonance more than a century and a half later. An outline of the life of Margaret Wilson (1795–1835) provides a flavor of the sort of life portrayed—pious, self-sacrificing and industrious despite physical frailty—and a premature death in the midst of her labors! Later on appeared colorful titles like *Heroines of Missionary Adventure: True Stories of the Intrepid Bravery and Patient Endurance of Missionaries in Their Encounters with Uncivilized Man, Wild Beasts and the Forces of Nature in All Parts of the World* by E. C. Dawson and Emma Raymond Pitman's *Heroines of the Mission Field*. These promoted more independent and active role models: Fanny Butler, Britain's first female medical missionary; Irene Petrie who had "every advantage of birth, education and breeding" yet chose to become a missionary at Srinagar in Kashmir; Hannah Mullens who spoke, taught, and wrote in fluent Bengali; and the traveler and explorer Isabella Bird Bishop, a convert to the missionary cause.[7]

Latterly, British women missionaries have fared less well in terms of memorials. Although a tiny few like Mary Slessor, Amy Carmichael, and Gladys Aylward have become well known, attracting a fair quota of biographies, and in the case of Aylward, a popular and glamorized film version of her life, the lives of countless others remain hidden or obscured.[8] In part, this is due to what can only be described as a collective act of forgetfulness, for reasons that are not hard to discover. Belief in Christianity has been in decline for decades in Britain, playing a far less important role in people's lives than in previous generations. That for more than 150 years, thousands were engaged in a global enterprise to convert Hindus, Muslims, Buddhists, and adherents of less well-known faiths strikes current opinion as essentially wrong-headed, something to disregard, disavow, and to condemn as an episode connected to and tainted by Britain's colonial past.

ASSESSING WOMEN'S MISSION

Yet to deny this history—to make no attempt to understand or unravel its various strands, or how it evolved over the years—is to omit a fascinating, complex, and critical chapter of our fairly recent past. The encounter between missionaries from Britain's towns, cities, and villages with people in Asia, Africa, the Pacific, and elsewhere was an unusually close and prolonged association, requiring careful scrutiny to assess its cultural significance and impact. It was a role identified with colonialism, yet detached from it. Missionaries could be, and were, just as critical of their fellow British as of indigenous society. The part played by women in the missionary movement, present in small numbers at the beginning but later the predominant force, awaits thorough investigation. What were the assumptions and motives driving their mission and how did these change over time and in the light of experience? From what social, educational, and religious backgrounds did they come? How were they trained, organized, and supported? How far did the goals of women's mission—for much of the period specifically directed to the spiritual, educational, and physical welfare of women and girls overseas—differ from, or coalesce with, those of their male colleagues, and the missionary movement's predominantly male leadership? Many of the women were single. How did they manage to live and work, often for decades, far from familiar home circles? How were they viewed by indigenous societies and what, if any, was the impact of their work? The women's missionary movement was a transnational one. What comparisons can be drawn between British women and those from other parts of the Western world? How did the women's missionary movement connect with developments in church and society at home?

Such rich and rewarding areas of research have only relatively recently begun to interest scholars, notably those engaged in examining connections between religion, gender, and empire. Over the last two decades, there has been a welcome flurry of books, articles, essays, and theses by both British and overseas scholars.[9] But as yet, there has been no comprehensive published study of the subject. My book attempts a broad overview of the contribution made by British women to the overseas missionary enterprise between the start of the 19th century and the midpoint of the 20th century, illustrated by a number of localized and historically specific case studies. Women served in all major mission fields—Africa, Asia, South America, the Caribbean, and the Pacific—but I have chosen to focus on two regions that saw the highest concentration: the Indian subcontinent and China. Indeed, by the early 20th century, missionary women there outnumbered their male colleagues by nearly 20 percent.[10] The missionary movement was not monolithic; there were many differences in emphasis between the various groups, in methods of working, and in the way women missionaries were regarded. The women I describe came from a variety of denominational backgrounds, both high and low-church Anglican, Baptist, Congregational, Methodist, and Presbyterian; and also from interdenominational groups like the China Inland Mission and the Zenana Bible and Medical Mission. In what is a short book, there are some regrettable omissions—among them Anglican sisterhoods, Roman Catholic orders and societies, Quakers, and the Salvation Army.

ARCHIVAL LEGACY

The fact that women did not have a leadership role in the British missionary movement is reflected in that movement's archival legacy. Their doings, particularly those of married women, lack prominence in the formal record. Their personal papers can also be hard to find. A recent survey of holdings in British institutions identified 237 manuscript collections of male missionaries, 43 family collections, and only 69 collections of the papers of single women missionaries.[11] For this study, I have utilized a wide range of published and unpublished sources, including missionary society archives, private manuscript collections, memoirs, histories and biographies, and the many magazines that promoted women's work. This approach has also enabled me to recover and assess the lives and contribution of a number of individual women, hitherto largely unknown, who went out to India and China determined to make a difference to other people's lives, and in so doing enormously change their own.

NOTES

1. Gladys Stephenson, Unpublished memoir, "The Glory of the King in Central China" (1935), 17, MMS Archive, MRP Box 7a.

2. Annie H. Small, "The Making of a Missionary," *International Review of Missions* viii, no. 31 (July 1919): 386.

3. Mary Taylor Huber and Nancy C. Lutkehaus, eds., *Gendered Missions, Women and Men in Missionary Discourse and Practice* (Ann Arbor, MI: University of Michigan Press, 1999), 18.

4. Amongst these are R. Pierce Beaver, *All Loves Excelling: American Protestant Women in World Mission* (Grand Rapids, MI: William B. Eerdmans Pub. Co., 1968) revised as *American Protestant Women in World Mission: History of the First Feminist Movement in North America* (Grand Rapids, MI: William B. Eerdmans Pub. Co., 1980); Jane Hunter, *The Gospel of Gentility: American Missionaries in Turn-of-the-Century China* (New Haven, CT: Yale University Press, 1984); Patricia Hill, *The World Their Household: The American Woman's Foreign Mission Movement and Cultural Transformation* (Ann Arbor, MI: University of Michigan Press, 1985); Patricia Grimshaw, *Paths of Duty: American Missionary Wives in Nineteenth-century Hawaii* (Honolulu, HI: University of Hawaii Press, 1989); Ruth Compton Brouwer, *New Women for God: Canadian Presbyterian Women and India Missions, 1876–1914* (Toronto, ON: University of Toronto Press, 1990); Dana L. Robert, *American Women in*

Mission: A Social History of their Thought and Practice (Macon, GA: Mercer University Press, 1996); Maina Chawla Singh, *Gender, Religion, and "Heathen Lands": American Missionary Women in South Asia, 1860s-1940s* (New York: Garland Publications, 2000); and Barbara Reeves-Ellington, Kathryn Kish Sklar, and Connie A. Shemo, eds., *Competing Kingdoms: Women, Mission, Nation, and the American Protestant Empire, 1812–1960* (Durham, NC: Duke University Press, 2010). Ulrike Sill, Line Nyhagen Predelli, Rita Smith Kipp, and others have published on women in Continental missions.

5. See discussion on " 'Christian Psychobiography' and the Early Female Missionary Memoir," in Clare Midgley, *Feminism and Empire: Women Activists in Imperial Britain, 1790–1865* (London and New York: Routledge, 2007), 99–108 and Judith Rowbotham, " 'Soldiers of Christ'? Images of Female Missionaries in Late Nineteenth-Century Britain: Issues of Heroism and Martyrdom," *Gender & History* 12, no. 1 (April 2000): 82–106.

6. Jemima Thompson, *Memoirs of British Female Missionaries* (London: W. Smith, 1841), ix.

7. E. C. Dawson, *Heroines of Missionary Adventure* (London: Seeley, Service & Co., 1925) and Emma Raymond Pitman, *Heroines of the Mission Field* (London: Cassell & Co., 1880).

8. *The Inn of the Sixth Happiness* (Beverly Hills, CA: 20th Century Fox, 1958).

9. The most relevant are listed in the Select Bibliography.

10. Jeffrey Cox, *The British Missionary Enterprise since 1700* (New York and London: Routledge, 2010), 269. Africa was not really considered a safe mission field for single women missionaries until the 20th century. There were some notable exceptions, including Mary Slessor who served in West Africa from 1876 until her death in 1915.

11. The survey was carried out between 1999 and 2002. Its results can be seen at http://www.mundus.ac.uk.

1

—〜—

The Making of the British
Female Missionary

*In general I should think it best that they [missionaries] should be married men, and
to prevent their time from being employed in procuring necessaries, two, or more, other
persons, with their wives and families, might also accompany them, who should be
wholly employed in providing for them.*[1]

When William Carey, often thought of as the first British Protestant missionary,
left for India in June 1793, he traveled as a married man, accompanied by his wife
and children. This was very much a last-minute decision. At the start, Dorothy
Carey had been obdurately against the notion of going overseas. As Carey's friend
and mentor, Andrew Fuller, explained:

> When he had made up his mind to engage in missionary labours, he ex-
> pected Mrs Carey and his family to accompany him; but to this for a long
> time she was utterly averse. This was a heavy trial to him, and to the society,
> who could not but foresee that though men are allowed to leave their wives
> and families for a time in mercantile and military expeditions; yet, in reli-
> gion, there would not only be a great outcry against it from worldly men,
> but even many religious people, who had thought but little on the subject,

1

would join in the general censure. He determined, however, to go; and if Mrs Carey could not be persuaded to accompany him, he would take his eldest son with him, and leave the rest of his family under the care of the society. She might afterwards be persuaded to follow him; or, if not, he could but return after having made the trial, and ascertained in some measure the practicality of the undertaking.[2]

Both parties stuck to their resolve. Carey, with fellow missionary John Thomas, and Carey's son, eight-year-old Felix, took berths in the East Indiaman, the *Earl of Oxford*, in April 1793, traveling without official permits; meanwhile the heavily pregnant Dorothy Carey remained in Northamptonshire with the rest of the family. Delayed at the Isle of Wight—war with France necessitated waiting for a convoy—the ship's captain discovered that he had persons onboard who had no permit to land in India. The mission party was put ashore. Journeying to London, Carey ascertained that an India-bound Danish ship, with sufficient cabin space for his entire family, would shortly call at Dover. He returned home by overnight coach to renew his plea to his wife that she and the rest of the family, including their new infant, now accompany him. This time she gave way, on condition that her younger sister came too. Doubtless she was swayed by the general conviction that "the Lord prevented their departure in the first instance, that Mr Carey's family might accompany him, and that all reproach on that score might be prevented."[3] From Dorothy Carey's perspective, however, her departure did not seem so providential. During the first half of the voyage she, like Lot's wife, constantly looked back to the home she had left forever, and she was full of anxieties as to what should befall them in an alien land.[4] Their first months in India realized her fears to the full. With no settled dwelling, they moved from Calcutta (Kolkata), which her husband considered too expensive a base, to the Sundarbans, a forested area in the Ganges delta. Finally, in August 1794, they reached Mudnabatti (Madhabbati) in present-day Bangladesh, where it was proposed that Carey take charge of an indigo factory, the family being allocated a brick house with an extensive garden. Here Carey planned to set up schools and commence evangelistic work in addition to his salaried duties. Illness, in the form of dysentery, had by this time afflicted most of the family. In October 1794 one of their younger sons died, the Careys having to bury him themselves since their Hindu and Muslim laborers refused to do so. A few months later, Dorothy Carey lapsed into an insanity that proved permanent. She had not wanted to leave her native land and was coerced into doing so. She had no real understanding of or sympathy with her husband's mission, and, prior to falling into the psychotic state to which her experiences doubtless contributed, constantly blamed him for all the family's discomfort and deprivations. Small wonder that William Carey would later stress the absolute necessity "for the wives of the missionaries to be as hearty in the work as their husbands."[5]

BACKGROUND TO CAREY'S MISSION

The founding of what became known as the Baptist Missionary Society (BMS) in 1792, and the departure the following year of its agent William Carey to inaugurate the mission in Bengal, is often thought to mark the commencement of the British Protestant overseas missionary movement. However, two important societies closely associated with the expansion of Protestant Christianity overseas had been founded nearly a century earlier. These were the Society for Promoting Christian Knowledge (SPCK) in 1698 and the Society for the Propagation of the Gospel in Foreign Parts (SPG) in 1701. Both had come about largely through the energy of one man, Rev. Thomas Bray, with the aim of spreading the influence of the Anglican Church both at home and in British territories overseas. In December 1735 a young Anglican clergyman, John Wesley, accompanied by his brother Charles, sailed for America. He had been engaged to serve as an SPG chaplain in Savannah, Georgia. His mission there to settlers and Native Americans was not a success, and he returned to England after less than two years. This abortive mission was, however, to have momentous consequences for both his own spiritual development and that of his native country.

Wesley's encounter with Moravian Brethren, German Protestant missionary pioneers, during the voyage and in Georgia, led him radically to reevaluate his religious beliefs, and he experienced, shortly after his return to Britain, an evangelical conversion. He came to be a leading figure in that heightened phase of Protestant religious activity of the 18th century known as the Evangelical Revival. While the movement had various strands, both within and without the Anglican Church, a central belief was the assurance of personal salvation through Christ's act of atonement on the Cross, and to communicate the knowledge of that salvation as widely as possible. It was also accepted as axiomatic that the Bible, as the sole repository of Christian truths, should be put in the hands of all, however uneducated: for the evangelical movement was broad-based, cutting across the deep class and sectarian divides of 18th-century Britain. Even women were for a time permitted an active role, by leading in prayer or in exhortation at evangelical meetings.[6] Some now saw it as essential to take the gospel message to those who lived beyond Britain's shores. Foremost among these was William Carey from Northamptonshire, a Baptist minister and shoe mender. In his *Enquiry into the Obligations of Christians, to Use Means for the Conversion of the Heathens,* he urged the necessity on Christian ministers not to stay comfortably at home "while so many are perishing without means of grace in other lands."[7]

Providentially, as it seemed to many evangelicals, the world was opening up in the late 18th century to the possibility of overseas missionary enterprise. Public interest in the Pacific islands, Australia, and New Zealand had been aroused by the publication, between 1773 and 1789, of James Cook's account of his voyages. On becoming acquainted with Cook's description of the Pacific islands, the influential clergyman Thomas Haweis persuaded himself that the South Seas offered a most promising area for Christian expansion. He was instrumental in deciding that the first mission of the London Missionary Society (LMS) in 1796 be sent to Tahiti and the neighboring islands. Elsewhere, Methodist missionaries had been active in the Caribbean since 1786, and Baptist missionaries arrived in Jamaica in 1813. The LMS sent a missionary to Cape Colony in 1799. It was, however, the populous subcontinent of South Asia, where British power and prestige had been growing for the past century, that was to become the main focus of British missionary effort during the 1790s and throughout the 19th century.

Influential Anglican evangelicals had by the 1780s begun to find their way to India as chaplains to the East India Company (EIC). Under a charter granted by the Crown, the Honorable Company exercised both administrative and military rule in British-occupied areas. While the Company accepted the need for chaplains, and had also admitted some SPCK-sponsored missionaries earlier in the century, its officials were wary of and hostile to the idea of more Christian missionaries, fearing that they would provoke disaffection, or worse, among their Hindu and Muslim subjects. When David Brown, a chaplain in Calcutta, together with the influential Company official Charles Grant, published in 1787 *A Proposal for Establishing a Protestant Mission in Bengal and Bihar,* a paper that would have ensured government patronage for the development of Anglican missions in those areas, they received scant support from official quarters. In 1793 however Grant, now a member of the Company's Home Administration, together with his ally, the parliamentarian and evangelical campaigner William Wilberforce, sought to introduce a clause into the EIC's charter, then under review, specifically mentioning missionaries:

> Whereas such measures ought to be adopted for the interests and happiness of the native inhabitants of the British dominions in India, as may gradually tend to their advancement in useful knowledge, and to their religious and moral improvement … the Court of Directors [of the EIC] … are hereby empowered and required to send out from time to time … fit and proper persons … as schoolmasters, missionaries, or otherwise.[8]

The proposal to insert the clause met with prolonged and vociferous opposition, and the government withdrew it, much to the disgust of Grant and Wilberforce. William Carey meanwhile reached Bengal that same year. He had at first contemplated a mission to the South Seas, inspired by Cook's *Voyages,* but after meeting with fellow Baptist John Thomas, who had spent 10 years in India and spoke Bengali, decided to sail with him to Calcutta. They did not sail purely on their own initiative. They were agents of the Particular-Baptist Society for Propagating the Gospel among the Heathen (later the BMS), which Carey, Andrew Fuller, and others had been instrumental in founding at Kettering in Northamptonshire the previous year. The independent voluntary association or society, modeled on and developed from the Baptist exemplar, came to be a pattern for later missionary efforts and was closely followed by the formation of other societies in the 1790s, for example the LMS, at first simply known as the Missionary Society, in 1795 and the Society for Missions to Africa and the East, later known as the Church Missionary Society (CMS), in 1799.

But the efforts of missionaries from these newly formed societies to reach India were still being impeded by the hostility of the EIC. Company officials were particularly mistrustful of missionaries from the dissenting churches whom they suspected of being politically radical. In 1813 the Company's Charter was again due for renewal and an effective campaign was mounted by evangelicals of all persuasions to ensure that this time a pro-missionary clause was inserted.[9] The campaign was led by William Wilberforce who considered that "next to the slave

trade, the foulest blot on the moral character of our country" was that the pop-
ulace of India should be left without the beneficent influence of Christianity.[10]
Outside Parliament pamphlets were circulated and hundreds of petitions written chiefly by members of dissenting missionary societies who felt particularly
discriminated against. This time there was qualified success for the reformers.
A pious clause was inserted that avoided the word "missionaries" but stated that
"persons desirous of going to and remaining in India for the purpose of accom-
plishing ... benevolent designs" were to be permitted to enter.[11] In the years following, although the Company did not refuse admittance to missionaries, their
movements and activities remained restricted until 1833 when such regulations
were finally withdrawn.[12]

HANNAH MARSHMAN, THE FIRST
WOMAN MISSIONARY?

Hannah Marshman journeyed to India with her husband, Joshua, as members of a party of reinforcements for the Baptist mission begun by Carey. Like
Dorothy Carey, Hannah Marshman was initially reluctant to leave her home,
but religious zeal in the end persuaded her. The party set sail from Portsmouth
in May 1799. After an uncomfortable voyage, during which she was frequently
unwell, partly due to her pregnancy, they reached Calcutta in October of that
year. Unable to land because the Company's ban was still in force, they established themselves at Serampore (Shrirampur), then a Danish settlement,
a few miles up the River Hugli. In January 1800, the party was enlarged by
the arrival of Carey, his wife—in a dangerous mental state often requiring
confinement—and their four unruly sons. Hannah Marshman took firm
charge of the domestic arrangements for the whole settlement of 10 adults
and 9 children, who, imitating the example of Moravian missionaries and to
save costs, decided to live communally. One of her letters describes a meal for
60—"four very large dishes of boiled rice piled up in a heap; four dishes of
curry, three or four joints of meat, sometimes eight or nine large fish, seven or
eight dishes of vegetables from our own gardens, three tureens of soup with
bread.... We make tea in two large urns." Nor were mealtimes prolonged, sociable affairs, Marshman claiming that "we scarcely ever sit more than twenty
minutes at breakfast or tea."[13]

Her activities ranged beyond her domestic responsibilities, great as these were. As part of a fund-raising enterprise for the mission, she and her husband ran schools for Eurasian boys and girls. Later on, schools for Indian children were also opened at Serampore including, in 1807, one for girls.[14] These flourished, impressing the pioneer American missionary, Ann Judson, when she visited in 1812. "I hope no missionary will ever come out here, without a wife, as she, in her sphere, can be equally useful with her husband. I presume Mrs Marshman does more good in her school than half the ministers in America."[15] Despite her initial fears, Marshman, who was to survive until her 81st year, dying in India in 1847, seems to have taken to missionary life with gusto. She described herself on the eve of her 36th birthday as "well in health, and sound in constitution, I may also add as full of activities and spirits, as at any time in my life. Had I been born in India, the country and climate could not have suited me better; nor the work more congenial with my spirit than I find it."[16]

A MISSIONARY COUPLE IN INDIA, 1830s–1840s

Not all missionary wives proved as resilient as Hannah Marshman. In her *Letters from a Missionary's Wife Abroad to a Friend in England* published in 1843, Martha (later known as Mary) Weitbrecht, wife of CMS missionary John James Weitbrecht, wrote of "that peculiar tendency to melancholy induced by an Indian climate." It was a struggle sometimes to possess "a cheerful, contented spirit."[17] She might have added that climate was not the only trouble; she herself lost her first husband after seven weeks of marriage; at least three of her children by Weitbrecht died young, and he himself died suddenly of cholera in robust middle age. John James Weitbrecht had been born in Württemberg in 1802 and embarked on a missionary training course at the Missionary Seminary in Basel in 1825. In 1828 he began a further course of training at the CMS training center at Islington; on arrival he felt better able to converse in Latin than in English! By 1830 he was a CMS agent stationed at Burdwan (Barddhaman) in Bengal, and three years later married Martha Higgs, widow of an LMS missionary, who lived in nearby Chinsurah. He assured his family that his friends thought him "happy and blessed in having found a suitable and devoted companion, who possesses the qualities so much needed in a missionary's wife."[18]

Hannah Marshman had shown that there was work for missionary wives beyond the mere domestic. In the first half of the 19th century such work was almost entirely educational. Missionary wives were active in setting up day schools for infants and girls, and establishing boarding schools for the daughters of Christian converts, orphans, and others. Instruction was usually given in the vernacular, the missionary wife acting as superintendent rather than as routine instructor. Education for both sexes was viewed, certainly by those in the mission field, as an essential accompaniment, if not precursor, to the premier missionary task of preaching in order to convert. As one missionary commented, there was "no hope of doing any good until we establish schools." The people were so ignorant "it is as if we were literally speaking to stones."[19] A dual effort by both missionary and wife was judged essential if progress was to be made.[20] There was no doubt, however, as to who was the senior partner. In her *Letters* Weitbrecht set out how she juggled her days to meet all that was required of one who occupied "so elevated a standing in the church as a missionary wife."[21] Her first responsibility was the "judicious, prudent care" of her husband. Her day revolved around his needs, and those of her children and household, as well as of her schools. In the memoir of her husband, she outlined his daily routine, which set the framework for hers:

> When at Burdwan, Mr Weitbrecht commonly sallied forth at six in the morning, on an elephant supplied to him by the [young and newly installed] Rajah, which carried him often several miles to a school, where he spent two hours in examining and preaching, and returned home by ten or eleven to breakfast. He then attended to the secular business of the mission, and to study till two, when a palanquin and bearers arrived from the palace, to carry him to instruct the Rajah. On returning from thence he dined, then gave a singing lesson to the boys, and at sunset went to preach again. After tea, he read or wrote letters, or his journal.[22]

Back at the mission house his wife based her own "diligent activity" around his. It was necessary to have "a thorough knowledge of household economy" despite the existence of servants. Indeed, these could prove a trial with their "cheating, lying, pilfering, and deceitful habits."[23] Then there were her schools for orphans and young Indian girls to be managed. A typical day for a wife should also start early. She might go out, and look around the garden, giving directions to the gardener, and proceed to the Infant or other School to observe, that all is commenced in time and going on in order. Ask a few questions, indiscriminately. . . . Return to the house, examine and direct the bathing and dressing of the children . . . give the children their breakfast—when your husband comes in from his preaching, sit down to breakfast, and immediately after, proceed to the storeroom, and with the assistance of the girl training in that department, weigh out the articles required for the day, and make them over to the cook, and order dinner. Then attend to domestic business, after which your presence is very desirable in the School, where the girls are employed from ten till two in needlework, embroidery, etc. with an interval of a quarter of an hour's recreation after twelve. The Christian women come during this time to bring their work and receive directions. . . . After dining at two, a little time must be given for rest. At four the girls assemble for afternoon reading, and at five all classes close with prayer.

An outing follows, and then "tea at seven when your husband comes in from evening preaching." During the evening, there are quiet activities such as reading, writing, or sewing. At nine there are family prayers, after which all retire to bed.[24] By this account, the life of a missionary wife was based almost entirely around the home. Evangelistic endeavors carried on in pulpit, street, or market square were strictly the work of the ordained male and his colleagues. In Weitbrecht's view, missionary wives should attend to their household and visit only their schools and local Indian Christian families. They might attend missionary meetings, although she prudently recommended that they should not come forward with "advice and opinions," especially "in the presence of the other sex, unless we are expressly solicited to do it." As for mixing in wider European society, they should never forget their "position as missionaries to the heathen" however attractive "the fascinating society of the polished and agreeable, among our fellow countrymen," might appear.[25]

THE FIRST SINGLE WOMAN MISSIONARY

One of the campaigners for the greater involvement by women in the missionary enterprise, above and beyond that rendered by wives, was William Ward, another Serampore missionary. His best-known published work, *An Account of the Writings, Religion, and Manners of the Hindoos,* made him "one of the most widely-read commentators during the first quarter of the nineteenth century."[26] In language that was always highly colored and at times inflammatory, Ward furnished descriptions of Hindu rites and practices, always emphasizing what he saw as the evils of Hinduism—its idolatry, its immorality, its harsh usage and neglect of women, and its cruel and barbarous ceremonies, especially the custom of widow-burning or *sati*. On completing a campaigning visit to Britain in 1820–1821, he wrote a series of well-publicized farewell letters. In one of these he appealed to the women of Britain and America to save the victims of *sati* by providing "the means of affording education to their sex in India."[27] Through the pages of the *Missionary Register*, a journal founded to publicize the work of Protestant missionaries, an appeal was launched to send "a Female, well qualified to superintend a School for training Native Female Teachers" to Calcutta. In May 1821 it was reported that the necessary sum had been collected and that "a Female of superior qualifications, agreeable manners, benevolent temper, and unfeigned piety" had been appointed. The *Register's* November issue reported that Miss Mary Ann Cooke had sailed for India in the company of the returning Serampore missionaries, Hannah Marshman and William Ward. Cooke, at 37, was a mature woman of some position—she had been a governess in the family of the Earl of Mulgrave—and this undoubtedly eased her entry into Calcutta society. Her abilities, energy, and good judgment ensured success in her pioneering educational work with girls, which she began immediately on arrival. She continued her work after her marriage in 1823 to Rev. Isaac Wilson, a CMS missionary, and she became an inspiration to later women workers. But for the next decade no single women followed in her footsteps. It was the involvement of wives and spinsters in work among Chinese and Malay communities, in the newly established British colonies of the Malay Straits, which led to the next stage in the evolution of the British female missionary. For that development, it is now necessary to look to the beginnings of the Protestant mission to China.

FIRST PROTESTANT MISSION TO CHINA

Robert Morrison was the first Protestant missionary to reach China in 1807. Here, even greater restrictions faced him than those imposed in India. At the beginning of the 19th century China was a country almost entirely closed to the outside world. Foreigners were only permitted to reside on a narrow stretch of shoreline at Canton (Guangzhou) or in the Portuguese, largely Roman Catholic, enclave at Macao. As a Protestant, Morrison's preferred base was Canton, although foreign residents were only permitted to remain there for six months in each year. He initially also faced the hostility of the EIC, which had a monopoly of trade with China. Fortunately he was able to find accommodation with the aid of sympathetic American traders. He lived a lonely, reclusive life, in two small rooms with little in the way of comfort. Even if he had had a wife, she would not have been permitted to accompany him to Canton, and when he did marry in 1809 his wife and family remained in Macao. His efforts to learn Chinese were impeded since this too was prohibited. How he to a degree circumvented this latter obstacle he confided to his journal, writing that

> All of the Europeans here have one servant, at least, who waits on them at table—makes their beds, etc. With this I am under a necessity of complying. I shall however endeavour to make him useful in teaching me the vulgar tongue of Canton; and as prudence may dictate, teach him the English language and things of higher meaning.[28]

Despite these difficulties he persisted in his task of acquiring the language, gaining such proficiency that the Company appointed him an official translator in 1809. By 1813 he had completed a translation of the New Testament. Mary, his first wife, does not seem to have played a role of any significance in these endeavors. For health reasons she and her surviving children spent the years between 1815 and 1820 in England. She returned to Macao in August 1820 and died of cholera the following year. But Morrison's new LMS colleagues William Milne and Walter Medhurst, arriving in the East in 1813 and 1816 respectively, brought with them wives who expected to engage in the work from the outset. Because of the impossibility at the time of developing a Christian mission on the Chinese mainland, a strategic decision was taken to develop a center at Malacca (Melaka), in the Malacca Straits, where there was a sizable Chinese community. Here the LMS were able to purchase land, set up a printing press, and build a college "for the purpose of teaching English, and the principles of the Christian religion to Chinese youth, and particularly for the purpose of instructing missionaries and others in the language and literature of China."[29] Morrison, and Milne who initially presided over the college, saw it as a training ground for missionaries, both European and Chinese, who could when that became possible take the Gospel message openly into China.

"FEMALE USEFULNESS"
IN THE STRAITS SETTLEMENTS

With Malacca at the center of their activities, other LMS agents opened stations at Penang and Singapore. The three settlements, known collectively as the Straits Settlements, were assigned to Britain under the Anglo-Dutch Treaty of 1824. Missionary wives such as Eliza Medhurst, Abigail Beighton, and Maria Dyer worked alongside their husbands, setting up day schools, giving instruction in English and Malay, and taking in boarders as a way of raising money.[30] Samuel Garling, the resident councilor at Malacca, and his wife, Caroline, showed considerable interest in and support for the LMS presence. Morrison now urged the LMS to give "grave and serious consideration" to the sending of "some unmarried ladies of experience and education ... with the design of teaching English and the principles of our religion to pagan girls." In England, between 1824 and 1825, he followed this up by teaching Chinese to a "class of ladies" interested in this object.[31] One was Mary Ann Aldersey, the daughter of a prosperous wholesale stationer, and another was Maria Newell. The LMS, reluctantly and only after a substantial donation from Aldersey (herself tied by family responsibilities), agreed to send Newell and another of Morrison's students to Malacca. In the event, Newell sailed alone, her companion withdrawing after suffering a breakdown brought on, it was thought, by the stress of studying Chinese. Newell did not find her Chinese lessons as useful as she had anticipated. She complained not long after her arrival that "all my Chinese goes for nothing. Malay and Portuguese are most wanted and I am studying both."[32] During the two years of her service, she started a number of schools for different language groups, including Chinese girls, and was soon begging for assistance since she could not be everywhere. Aldersey now gathered sufficient funds to send a second agent to support her, obtaining 100 pounds sterling from the LMS and the same amount from the British and Foreign School Society. Mary Wallace was sent out officially to run the girls' side of the government free school, which secured her an income: but also with the intention of conducting schools for Chinese girls in which Christian teaching would figure on the curriculum.

Despite losing her colleague in 1829, when Newell married the missionary pioneer Karl Gützlaff and went off with him to explore the new missionary area of Siam (Thailand), Wallace seems to have made considerable progress. She was soon running several schools for Chinese girls in Malacca, alongside her paid duties in the free school. LMS missionary Samuel Dyer was sufficiently impressed to write home that "Sister Wallace was a true missionary." She had succeeded in forming and conducting schools for Chinese girls and had shown "strong faith, under most discouraging circumstances."[33] By the early 1830s, educational work for Portuguese and Tamil-speaking girls had begun. Associated with this work was Martha Edwardes, the future Mrs. Weitbrecht, who traveled out from England under the protection of the Garlings in 1831 and almost immediately started her educational work.[34] When the American missionary David Abeel visited Malacca early the following year, he found it a positive hive of female industry. There were "one hundred Chinese girls under the instruction of Miss Wallace . . . and about two hundred more, principally Tamul and Portuguese, in charge of ladies belonging to the Resident's household, and one or two others of a kindred spirit." All told they presented, he thought, a fine spectacle of "female usefulness." He became convinced that "co-operation and influence of ladies was . . . greatly needed in evangelising the heathen."[35] However, the sustainability of the work developed at Malacca remained precarious, dependent on personal fund-raising initiatives, uncertain official support, and occasional handouts from the LMS. Indeed, not long after Abeel's visit, the efforts begun by Newell, and carried on so energetically by Wallace, seem to have ground to a halt. The government had refused to fund Wallace's work at the Malacca Free School. Overburdened and underfunded, she left Malacca in 1833 or 1834, while her replacement, Mary Wanstall, who arrived in 1833, remained there only a matter of months before becoming the second wife of Karl Gützlaff and leaving Malacca. Martha Edwardes, after disputes with Mrs. Garling, left too on her all-too-brief marriage to Rev. Thomas Higgs, an LMS missionary from Bengal.[36]

THE FIRST WOMEN'S MISSIONARY SOCIETY

These brave attempts by single and inadequately supported women in Malacca may have proved short-lived but were not without a positive legacy. David Abeel, following his tours of inspection of missions in China and the East Indies, returned to America via Europe. While in London, and in conjunction with the

influential evangelical clergyman Rev. Baptist W. Noel, he launched "an Appeal to
Christian Ladies on behalf of Female Education in China and the adjacent Countries."[37] A meeting was arranged at Noel's church, St. John's Chapel, Bedford Row,
in July 1834, and the Society for Promoting Female Education in China, India,
and the East, later known as the Society for Promoting of Female Education in
the East (SPFEE), came into being, the first such society in the Western world.[38]
Abeel hoped, on returning home, to fire American women in the same way. Indeed, Sarah Doremus, the organizer of much philanthropic and charitable activity
in New York, arranged for him to speak there at a specially convened meeting.
However, officials of the American missionary societies, particularly Rufus Anderson, the most powerful U.S. mission administrator of his day, firmly opposed the
idea. Writing in 1836, he declared that though he had received requests for unmarried women to go out as teachers to the mission field, few had sufficiently taken
into account the "difficulties of placing the single female in circumstances to live
and labor happily in pagan lands."[39] He considered that only those who had close,
preferably natural ties with a missionary family should so be sent. Not until 1861
was a woman's missionary society founded in the United States.

"A YOUNG WOMAN IS . . . THE LEAST INTENDED
TO STAND ALONE"

The SPFEE, from now on referred to by its alternative title, the Female Education Society (FES), concentrated on building up schools in India and further
East. "Pious and well-educated persons" were selected to go out as superintendents to train and encourage "subordinate native teachers." While "useful
knowledge" might be imparted, the chief end in view was to bring pupils at
their schools "to an acquaintance with Scripture truth, and to a belief in Christ
as their Saviour."[40] Mary Ann Wilson née Cooke advised that such women
should be "sensible" and "middle-aged" and if they had had experience as
a governess this would "answer extremely well."[41] Mary Weitbrecht felt that
those recruiting single females for missionary work should bear in mind "that
a young woman is of all persons, the least calculated, and the least intended
to stand alone." Only "superior persons in every respect" should be sent out,
and even they required the utmost protection.[42] Opposition to the very idea of
single women missionaries came in 1842 from a most authoritative quarter,

namely Daniel Wilson, the bishop of Calcutta, who in a much quoted letter declared:

> I object from my experience of Indian life, and indeed upon principle, to ladies coming out unprotected to so distant a place with a climate so unfriendly and with the utmost certainty of marrying within a month of arrival. . . . I imagine the beloved Persis, Tryphena and Tryphosa, Julia and others who "laboured much in the Lord," remained in their own neighbourhood and families, and that no unmarried female would have thought of a voyage of 14,000 miles to find out a scene of duty.[43]

The bishop's view that young unattached women had only to appear in India to attract a marriage proposal was well substantiated. Indeed in its early years, the FES was jokingly referred to as the Bachelor's Aid Society.[44] The society—realizing that their agents were likely to meet with offers as soon as they set foot in Calcutta, Madras, Malacca, or any other colonial town or city, if not on the voyage out—made them sign a pledge prior to sailing. This required repayment of a proportion of travel and other costs if they resigned before completing five years' service. Rosa Anne Woodman, sent out to Madras in 1840, incurred the society's wrath when she married the widowed Rev. John Michael Lechler "after only two days' acquaintance and while on the way to her mission station." The society's committee minutes recorded "their unqualified censure of a proceeding so repugnant to every feeling of female delicacy, of Christian propriety, and even of common honour, and so calculated to draw down reproach on the operations of this society and on the cause of missions generally."[45] Her new husband, reporting the matter to his own society, the LMS, hoped that the pledge would not apply, since as his wife she would still be in the thick of the work. If it did, he added,

> and the money has to be refunded, I have ventured to take the responsibility upon myself being confident that the worthy Directors of the London Missionary Society will gladly come to my help rather than see an important Mission destitute or one of their missionaries necessitated to leave his work and station and perhaps proceed to Europe to obtain a suitable partner. . . . I am happy to say that Mrs Lechler has taken charge already of

the adult female school and the Girls' school on the mission premises and if the Lord gives health and means an orphan Girls' school will be commenced shortly.[46]

He was mistaken. The FES demanded that the debt be paid, and the LMS did not come to his rescue. In 1850 the Lechlers were still paying off the 170 pounds demanded, though the matter seems to have been resolved shortly after. The reaction of the society, if understandable, seems heavy-handed. Rosa Lechler served ably and zealously as a teacher alongside her husband. At the time of her death in 1896, her obituary noted that she had been "connected with work at Salem for fifty-five years."[47]

WOMEN MISSIONARIES ENTER MAINLAND CHINA

Until the 1840s China had been largely closed to foreigners. Defeat at the hands of Britain in the First Opium War and the Treaty of Nanking, signed in August 1842, meant that the ports of Amoy (Xiamen), Canton (Guangzhou), Foochow (Fuzhou), Ningpo (Ningbo), and Shanghai were opened up to Western merchants and other residents, while the island of Hong Kong was ceded to Britain. Taking advantage of the situation, the resourceful Mary Ann Aldersey, who had finally gone out independently of any society to Batavia (Jakarta) in 1837, transferred herself and her school to Ningpo, becoming in doing so the first woman missionary to reach China proper. In 1860 the Treaty of Tientsin, concluding the Second Opium War, was ratified by the Chinese government and opened up 11 further ports to foreign settlement, permitted travel by merchants and missionaries throughout the country, and called on local authorities to guarantee their protection. These treaties, later dubbed "the unequal treaties," were to become a source of embarrassment to missionary opinion. In the mid-1800s, however, they were seen as providential. In his *China's Spiritual Need and Claims,* published in 1865, the founder of the China Inland Mission (CIM), James Hudson Taylor, alerted devout Christians to the needs of a country where "Every day tens of thousands, every three months 2,000,000 subjects of the Chinese Emperor pass into Eternity without ever having heard the Gospel."[48] In including nine unmarried women in his first party of missionaries to China in 1866, he was also in the forefront of those who demonstrated that women's spiritual qualities could and should be

Figure 1.1. Facsimile of a painting of Miss Aldersey's school at Ningpo, by a Chinese artist. Printed in colors for the Society for Promoting Female Education in the East. (London: George Baxter, 1847) (By permission of the Victoria University Library, Toronto.)

used in the missionary enterprise, particularly in a country where women were perceived as living degraded and neglected lives. He wrote that "at home our sisters have free access to the women in their own homes. . . . There is every reason to believe that female labour . . . the 'missing link,' as it has been well-called at home—will prove to be no less indispensable and no less successful here."[49]

THE EXPANSION OF WOMEN'S WORK IN INDIA

Missionary attention in India turned in the mid-19th century to the supposed plight of women and girls sequestered in the closed apartments or *zenanas* of many Indian homes. Originally a Muslim tradition, the custom of secluding women was also observed in high-caste Hindu homes, particularly in Northern India or where, as Janaki Nair has pointed out, "Mogul influence had been most direct and sustained."[50] Attempts by missionaries to teach Indian girls in schools had been largely unsuccessful. They had failed to persuade respectable families to allow their girls to attend. Partly this was because of objections to Christianity, but the custom of early marriage was also a factor. Since girls, in those days, married at the age of eight, and sometimes younger, attending school above that age was out of the question. As early as the 1820s and 1830s some missionary wives had taught wives and daughters of liberally minded Indians in their homes: one such was Mary Bird, the sister of R. M. Bird, commissioner of Gorakhpur, who taught there and in Calcutta. Such visits, the *Calcutta Christian Intelligencer* urged, must be "performed quietly and noiselessly (as indeed ought to be all the duties of a woman's sphere) but in this one to create a stir, or to have it known that such a one receives visits from a Christian lady... would cause a scandal, and so many taunts, as few among them have strength sufficient to withstand."[51]

In the 1850s zenana missionary work, as it was later known, became much more widespread largely through the efforts of two missionary wives in Bengal: Elizabeth Sale (the wife of John Sale, a Baptist missionary) and Hannah Mullens (the wife of Joseph Mullens of the LMS). Julius Richter, professor of missions at Berlin, attributed the founding of the zenana system to Rev. John Fordyce of the Free Church of Scotland who, after dispatching Miss Toogood "a clever Eurasian lady" and a "Bible woman named Rebecca" to the house of "Babu Kumar Tagore" in 1854, proclaimed "the beginning of a new era for the daughters of India." Whatever the truth of their origin, the development of zenana missions now led to a reversal of the previous policy: a huge expansion in the numbers of unmarried women accepted for missionary service in the latter part of the 19th century.

Why did the zenana movement acquire such momentum? A possible factor was the renewal of enthusiasm for missions in the wake of the great rebellion in India that broke out in 1857 and was not suppressed until the following year. An American missionary, Rev. Julius Ullman, writing in the pages of the *Female Missionary Intelligencer*, saw definite proof in the "active part... taken by the wife of the ex-King of Delhi, the Ranee of Jhansee, and the Begum of Oudh, in this great rebellion" that "idolatry and superstition, with all their concomitants, can only be found in their most perfect form among the female portion of the heathen or Mahommedan population." All the more reason, he thought, to secure those female "exertions, which hitherto have been employed on the side of darkness and superstition, for the propagation of Christianity."[52] Three women's missionary organizations were founded in the years immediately following the Indian Mutiny: the Ladies' Committee for the Amelioration of the Condition of Women in Heathen Countries, Female Education, etc. (an auxiliary of the Wesleyan Methodist Missionary Society) in 1858; the Woman's Union Missionary Society of America for Heathen Lands in 1860; and the Indian Female Normal School and Instruction Society (IFNS) in 1861—a development that seems not without coincidence. Hannah Mullens, abroad between August 1858 and December 1860, detected on her return to India a much greater willingness by progressive Indian householders to open their *zenanas* to women evangelists. It was a development she attributed to the "great advance in Native Opinion . . . just after the Mutiny, the inaugurator of so many other vital changes."[53]

Of more long-lasting import however was the realization that after several decades of missionary activity in India the results, in terms of the advance of Christendom, were meager indeed. A consensus began to emerge among mission supporters that it was Indian women who were holding back progress. Oxford University's Boden Professor of Sanskrit, Sir Monier Monier-Williams, asserted that "until a way is opened for the free intercourse of the educated mothers and women of Europe . . . with the mothers and women of India in their own homes . . . Christianity will make little progress either among Hindus or among Mahommedans."[54] Even government lent its weight to the denunciation of the evil influence of the *zenana*, which was "in very many instances, never eradicated, and much of the good learnt by a boy at school and college, is neutralised by the habits of his domestic circle."[55] Access to the *zenanas*, those previously impenetrable domains, was a task that only women could carry out, a fact that led directly to the wider deployment of missionary women. Moreover, the denizens of *zenanas*, regarded as a species of prisoner, became the object of fascinated and appalled concern to missionaries and their supporters alike. Periodical articles, papers, and books were written about their putative plight; hymns and appeals were penned; and meetings called. In church congregations and societies, there could scarcely have been a woman unaware of the supposedly wretched, enslaved circumstances of her Indian sister dwelling in "unfurnished, or semi-furnished . . . very small rooms" only reached after passing through "dirty courtyards, dark corners, breakneck staircases, filthy outhouses and entries."[56] British women were assured that

in every Hindu dwelling . . . the *worst* and most ill-furnished apartments are those set apart for the women. In some there is no accommodation for sitting, but a mat on the ground; in others, a wooden bedstead and perhaps a broken chair or two expelled from the gentlemen's sitting-rooms. Anything more dreary than their homes one can scarcely imagine, and they are but too true a picture of their sad and dreary lives.[57]

Frequent appeals for additional female laborers now appeared in missionary periodicals, including those of the main denominational societies, hastening to join in the new work. Ladies' associations or auxiliaries were formed during the late 1860s and 1870s by the SPG, the BMS, the LMS, and the English Presbyterian Mission. In 1880, the Church of England Zenana Missionary Society (CEZMS), one of the largest British zenana missionary societies, came into being. By the end of the 19th century, Julius Richter could report that "nearly every great English and American Missionary Society had a women's auxiliary."[58]

MEDICINE AND EVANGELISM

The 1870s also saw the beginnings of medical work performed by women missionaries. The more orthodox Hindu and Muslim homes had proved largely resistant to the zenana education movement. However it had been discovered that offering medical advice and assistance in unpromising areas often provided a way of rendering mission work acceptable. Medical missions had only recently come of age in Britain. Previously considered a dangerous distraction from the main evangelistic task, they had come to be welcomed "as a valuable auxiliary to the direct work of the gospel."[59] Dr. William Elmslie, a pioneering CMS medical missionary in Kashmir in the mid-1860s, found that his medical work was welcomed, whereas preaching the Gospel provoked a violent and hostile reaction. He became convinced that female medical missions would be invaluable, particularly in zenana work.[60] Already zenana missionaries had begun treating the sick women they came across with simple remedies and advice, so his appeal accelerated a trend that had already begun. Elmslie's call was picked up and promulgated by missionary propagandists such as Mary Weitbrecht and Emma Raymond Pitman, the latter's *Indian Zenana Missions* written to justify widening the remit of IFNS to include medical work. Soon, practically all the major missionary societies were sending out women agents who had been partly or fully trained to carry out medical work. In 1880 Dr. Fanny Butler, one of the first students to attend the London School of Medicine for Women, became Britain's first fully qualified woman missionary doctor in India. She was to be followed by many others trained at London, Edinburgh, and other medical centers that had begun to admit women students in the last quarter of the 19th century. The opening of mission hospitals and dispensaries at many centers in India and China, and the consequent need for nurses, sisters, and hospital matrons to run them, led to a large influx of nursing staff. A Nurses' Missionary League was founded in 1903, but many nurses were directly recruited by missionary societies.

The wider acceptance of an evangelistic role for women was another factor leading to an increase in the numbers of female missionaries, a development that has been described by one authority as "the crucial breakthrough" for women missionaries.[61] In the wake of the religious revivals that swept much of Britain during 1859 and 1860, and again in the 1870s and 1880s, there had been a deepening of religious experience. This led not only to renewed enthusiasm for the cause, but also to a greater awareness and acceptance of the spiritual agency of women. Among proponents of the revival were the American evangelists Phoebe Palmer and her husband, who toured Britain during 1859 and 1860, and Robert and Hannah Pearsall Smith, who visited in 1874 and 1875. Both wives spoke eloquently and effectively at the outdoor and tent meetings characteristic of the revival movement. Palmer also influenced Catherine Booth, herself an accomplished public preacher and speaker, and cofounder with her husband, William, of the Salvation Army. Moreover, as Olive Anderson explained, female preaching had by the 1860s become a more ladylike activity, very different from the earlier " 'primitive female preacher' who 'puts off her bonnet and shawl and goes at it like a ranter ... says some good things, but without order or arrangement and shouts till the people jump.' "[62] She also points out that the revivals, and the Holiness movement that developed out of them, placed an emphasis on "perfect love" and "purity of heart," areas of religious experience in which women were thought to be particularly competent, enabling men to feel less difficulty in accepting feminine exhortation.[63] At the center of the Holiness movement were the great annual conventions "for the promotion of practical holiness" held in the romantic setting of the English Lake District at Keswick. The convention's watchword—"All one in Christ Jesus"—had a particular resonance for women. At a missionary meeting held at Keswick in July 1887, women responded in some numbers to an appeal made directly by a CMS missionary based in Palestine for "Christian ladies with private means who are attending the Convention, and who could come out here and work among the Moslem women."[64] It is not without significance that the two societies that saw the greatest influx of women missionaries at this time—the CMS and the CIM—had close connections with the Keswick movement.

MORE WOMEN THAN MEN

In the closing decades of the 19th century, all the societies began to send large numbers of unmarried women into the mission field. This abrupt departure from earlier practice led in the 20th century to numerical domination by women, taking into account both married and single women. In his *British Missionary Enterprise since 1700*, Jeffrey Cox tabulates a female preponderance in the mission field as early as 1889.[65] Statistics produced at the time of the World Missionary Conference in 1910, and confirmed the following year, clearly demonstrated the numerical superiority of women in most of the Protestant mission areas, especially in Asian countries. Both in the Indian subcontinent and in China some 60 per cent of British missionaries were women.[66] The female predominance does not seem to have been generally apparent. Hierarchies in home and overseas councils and secretariats were overwhelmingly male. Moreover, reportage and historiography gave prominence to the central missionary tasks of preaching, converting, educating, and training an indigenous male clergy, and building and establishing new churches. The teaching of girls, the training of women evangelists, and the provision of medical services for women and children were seen as contributory, not central, to the essential enterprise. The title of the three-volume CMS centenary history, the *History of the Church Missionary Society: Its Environment, Its Men and Its Work* published in 1899 suggests little regard given to women's input. Perhaps it is not altogether surprising that its author, Eugene Stock, a leading CMS administrator as well as historian, could write as late as 1917 that "it is a fact little realized that there are more women missionaries in the field than men."[67]

CONCLUSION

At the start of the Protestant missionary enterprise in the late 18th century, little thought was given to a role for women. The presence of wives was considered necessary for the sake of propriety and because women were essential to the domestic support and comfort of husbands, fathers, and brothers engaged in the work. As time went by, educational work by women in the mission fields acquired importance, with missionary husbands and wives playing complimentary roles—always, however, with the husband as senior partner and the wife arranging her own missionary work around his needs. In practice, the domestic role of married women frequently took precedence over any missionary tasks. At various times, the need for more female workers was made known but their deployment was controversial. The presence of single women on the mission field was considered problematic by many until changing mission strategies in the 1870s and 1880s required their being sent out in larger numbers. Who these women were, and how they were selected and prepared for missionary work, must next be considered.

NOTES

1. William Carey, *An Enquiry into the Obligations of Christians to Use Means for the Conversion of the Heathens* (Leicester: Ann Ireland, 1792), 73.

2. "Fragment of Memoir etc. from the Hand of Mr Fuller," in *Memoir of William Carey, D.D.*, ed. Eustace Carey (London: Jackson & Walford, 1836), 76–77.

3. Carey, *Memoir of William Carey*, 77.

4. James R. Beck, *Dorothy Carey, the Tragic and Untold Story of Mrs William Carey* (Grand Rapids, MI: Baker Book House, 1992), 89.

5. Letter to Andrew Fuller, quoted in John C. Marshman, *The Life and Times of Carey, Marshman, and Ward, Embracing the History of the Serampore Mission* (London: Longman, Brown, Green, Longmans, & Roberts, 1859), 1, 78.

6. David W. Bebbington, *Evangelicalism in Modern Britain* (London and New York: Routledge, 1995), 25–26.

7. Carey, *An Enquiry*, 73.

8. Quoted in Stephen Neill, *History of Christianity in India 1707–1858* (Cambridge: CUP, 1985), 148.

9. Brian Stanley, *The Bible and the Flag* (Leicester: Apollos, 1990), 99.

10. Quoted in William Hague, *William Wilberforce: The Life of the Great Anti-Slave Trade Campaigner* (London: Harper Perennial, 2008), 408.

11. Andrew Porter, *Religion versus Empire? British Protestant Missionaries and Overseas Expansion* (Manchester and New York: Manchester University Press, 2004), 74.

12. Stanley, *Bible and the Flag*, 100.

13. Sunil Kumar Chatterjee, *Hannah Marshman, the First Woman Missionary in India* (Hoogly: S. Chatterjee, 1987), 48.

14. Mary Weitbrecht, *The Women of India and Christian Work in the Zenana* (London: James Nisbet & Co., 1875), 146.

15. Ann Judson in an 1812 letter quoted in Dana L. Robert, *American Women in Mission: A Social History of Their Thought and Practice* (Macon, GA: Mercer University Press, 1996), 44.

16. Chatterjee, *Hannah Marshman*, 51.

17. Mary Weitbrecht, *Female Missionaries in India: Letters from a Missionary Wife Abroad to a Friend in England* (London: James Nisbet & Co., 1843), 55.

18. Mary Weitbrecht, *Memoir of the Rev. John James Weitbrecht, Compiled from His Journal and Letters by His Widow* (London: James Nisbet & Co., 1854), 101–102.

19. John Michael Lechler, LMS missionary in Salem, Letter to William Ellis, November 22, 1841. CWM/LMS Tamil Incoming Correspondence, Box 8b.

20. See Clare Midgley, "Can Women Be Missionaries? Imperial Philanthropy, Female Agency and Feminism," in *Feminism and Empire*, ed. Clare Midgley (London and New York: Routledge, 2007), 95.

21. Weitbrecht, *Female Missionaries*, 55.

22. Weitbrecht, *Memoir of Rev. John James Weitbrecht*, 102–103.

23. Weitbrecht, *Female Missionaries*, 68.

24. Weitbrecht, *Female Missionaries*, 58–59.

25. Weitbrecht, *Female Missionaries*, 61, 74.

26. Geoffrey A. Oddie, *Imagined Hinduism: British Protestant Missionary Constructions of Hinduism, 1793–1900* (New Delhi, Thousand Oaks, London: SAGE Publications, 2006), 160.

27. William Ward, *Farewell Letters to a Few Friends in Britain and America, on Returning to Bengal in 1821* (London, 1821), 83.

28. Quoted in Christopher Daily, "From Gosport to Canton: A New Approach to Robert Morrison and the Beginnings of Protestant Missions in China" (PhD diss., University of London, 2009), 170–71.

29. Letter from Robert Morrison, November 14, 1820, to the LMS Directors, quoted in Daily, "From Gosport to Canton," 251.

30. C. Doran, " 'A Fine Sphere for Female Usefulness': Missionary Women in the Straits Settlements, 1815–45," *Journal of the Malaysian Branch of the Royal Asiatic Society* 69, no. 1 (1996): 100–111.

31. Letter from Robert Morrison, September 7, 1824, CWM/LMS, South China Incoming Correspondence, Box 2.

32. Valerie Griffiths, *Not Less than Everything* (Oxford: Overseas Missionary Fellowship, 2004), 43.

33. Letter from S. Dyer, June 26, 1831, CWM/LMS, Malacca Incoming Correspondence, Box 3.

34. "In Memoriam Mrs Weitbrecht," *India's Women* 8, no.45 (May–June 1888): 113–118.

35. David Abeel, *Journal of a Residence in China and the Neighbouring Countries from 1830–1833* (London: James Nisbet & Co., 1835), 246, 358.

36. Higgs died seven weeks after their wedding, on the way back to Bengal.

37. Appendix A, *History of the Society for Promoting Female Education in the East, etc.* (London: Edward Suter, 1847), 261–265.

38. *History of the Society for Promoting Female Education,* 7.

39. Quoted in R. Pierce Beaver, *American Protestant Women in World Mission* (Grand Rapids, MI: W. B. Eerdmans Publishing, c. 1980), 61.

40. *History of the Society for Promoting Female Education,* 275.

41. Extract from letter published in the *Annual Report* of the Society for Promoting Female Education in China, India, and the East, December 1835.

42. Weitbrecht, *Female Missionaries,* 141–142.

43. Quoted in C. F. Pascoe, *Two Hundred Years of the SPG: An Historical Account of the Society 1701–1900* (London: Society for the Propagation of the Gospel, 1901), 617.

44. William Arthur, *Woman's Work in India* (London: T. Woolmer, 1882), 11–12.

45. Margaret Donaldson, " 'The Cultivation of the Heart and the Moulding of the Will … 'the Missionary Contribution of the Society for Promoting Female Education in China, India and the East," *Studies in Church History, Vol. 27, Women in the Church,* eds. W. J. Shiels and Diana Wood (Oxford: Basil Blackwell, 1990), 436–437.

46. Letter from J. M. Lechler, August 3, 1840, CWM/LMS, Tamil Incoming Correspondence, Box 8A.

47. *Chronicle of the London Missionary Society* (June 1896): 124–125.

48. J. Hudson Taylor, *China: Its Spiritual Need and Claims,* 5th edition (London: Morgan & Scott, 1884), 38.

49. Taylor was here referring to the work of Ellen Ranyard's Bible women in London. See C. P. Williams, " 'The Missing Link': The Recruitment of Women Missionaries in Some English Evangelical Missionary Societies in the Nineteenth Century," in *Women and Missions: Past and Present, Anthropological and Historical Perceptions,* eds. Fiona Bowie et al. (Providence, RI and Oxford: Berg, 1993), 47–48.

50. Janaki Nair, "Uncovering the Zenana: Visions of Indian Womanhood in English-women's Writings, 1813–1940," in *Cultures of Empire*, ed. Catherine Hall (Manchester: Manchester University Press, 2000), 227.

51. Behari Lal Singh, *The History of Native Female Education in Calcutta* (Calcutta: Baptist Mission Press, 1858), 54.

52. Julius Ullman, "Importance of Female Education in India," *Female Missionary Intelligencer*, New Series no. 14 (February, 1859): 23–24.

53. Paper by Joseph Mullens, *Report of the Punjab Missionary Conference 1862–1863* (Lahore: 1863), 64.

54. Quoted in Richard Lovett, *History of the London Missionary Society* (London: Oxford University Press, 1899), ii, 716.

55. Quoted in David Savage, "Missionaries and the Development of a Colonial Ideology of Female Education in India," *Gender & History* 9, no. 2 (August 1997): 211.

56. Mary Weitbrecht, *The Women of India and Christian Work in the Zenana* (London: J. Nisbet & Co., 1875), 105.

57. Mrs Weitbrecht, *The Women of India, and Zenana and Educational Work among Them* ([London]; Indian Female Normal School and Instruction Society, [1878]), 16.

58. Julius Richter, *A History of Missions in India* (Edinburgh: Oliphant Anderson & Ferrier, 1908), 339.

59. Minute, Conference on Missions held at Liverpool in 1860 quoted in C. Peter Williams, "Healing and Evangelism: The Place of Medicine in Later Victorian Protestant Missionary Thinking," in *Studies in Church History, Vol. 19, The Church and Healing*, ed. W. J. Sheils (Oxford: Basil Blackwell, 1982), 275.

60. W. J. Elmslie, " On Female Medical Missions for India," *Indian Female Evangelist*, 1, no. 5 (January 1873): 193–206.

61. C. P. Williams, "The Recruitment and Training of Overseas Missionaries in England between 1850 and 1900" (M.Litt. diss., University of Bristol, Bristol, 1976), 314.

62. Olive Anderson, "Women Preachers in Mid-Victorian Britain: Some Reflexions on Feminism, Popular Religion and Social Change," *The Historical Journal* XII, no. 3 (1969): 471–472.

63. Anderson, "Women Preachers," 477.

64. Eugene Stock, *The History of the Church Missionary Society: Its Environment, its Men and its Work* (London: Church Missionary Society, 1899–1916), 3, 289.

65. Jeffrey Cox, *The British Missionary Enterprise since 1700* (New York and London: Routledge, 2010), 270.

66. James S. Dennis, Harlan P. Beach, and Charles H. Fahs, *World Atlas of Christian Missions* (New York: Student Volunteer Movement for Foreign Missions, 1911), 86–91.

67. Eugene Stock, *Beginnings in India* (London: Central Board of Missions and SPCK, 1917), Project Canterbury.

2

—⁓—

Responding to the Call: Motivation, Selection, Training, and Preparation

Do you think you have the elasticity of spirit and energy of character which can "endure hardness" and cheerfully meet difficulties and adapt yourself to the ways of others?[1]

"GOD AND NATURE INTENDED YOU FOR A MISSIONARY'S WIFE"[2]

It was at a missionary meeting in Manchester when she was a girl that Mary Smith felt the germ of her desire to be a missionary. She had attended "the first missionary meeting to be held in our part of the country.... My mind was powerfully affected. I was very young and had not the slightest prospect of joining the missionary band but I felt the cause was worth a thousand lives."[3] Smith was 11 or 12 years of age when the missionary association in Manchester was formed in 1807. The eldest child and only daughter of a prosperous nursery gardener, her interest in missions had first been aroused through hearing stories about the early Moravian missions at her school, part of the Moravian Settlement at Fairfield. "It was the custom in that institution, to read among the young ladies the short monthly reports of what God was doing in the dark places of the earth, principally by means of Moravian mission workers."[4] Since missionary societies did not at that time accept female applicants, a missionary vocation for Smith would have been out of the question had she not met in January 1816 her father's gardener, Robert Moffat, who was studying part time for missionary service. By the end of the year he was on his way to South Africa as an ordained agent of the London Missionary Society (LMS), leaving Smith behind since her parents would not hear of her joining him. Finally she overcame their objections and booked her passage to Cape Town, where in December 1819 the couple duly married. They went on to establish at Kuruman a center of LMS influence in the region, a huge pioneering work in which, despite her frequent childbearing, Mary Moffat was jointly involved until ill-health forced them to return to England in 1870. Smith's Moravian background might be considered untypical, but her enthusiasm for missions was felt by other devout young women in the ever-expanding evangelical circles of the early 19th century. A number succeeded in finding husbands who shared their zeal.[5] *The Youthful Female Missionary,* published in 1840, memorialized the life of Mary Ann Hutchins née Middleditch, who had attended frequent meetings and read and reread the memoirs of the American pioneering missionary wives, Ann Judson and Harriet Newell, long before she met her husband. She confided to a close friend that a "sentence ... in Mrs Newell's diary as to affording comfort to one of God's dear Missionaries is constantly on my mind." In a letter to her father in August 1833, she wrote that she longed "to go as a Missionary more and more." She "would rather go to Jamaica than dwell in England with every comfort." In November 1833, she wrote again to say that she had accepted "an offer to one who is so eminently the Lord's" and beseeching her parents to let her go—"Could your Mary Ann be happy ... if she refused to devote herself to missionary work?" Parental agreement obtained, she married Rev. John Hutchins, who was designated as a Baptist missionary to Jamaica the day before his wedding in February 1834, and immediately embarked with him for the Caribbean.[6]

Missionary societies soon realized they needed to take steps to ensure the suitability of marriage partners who would be playing a significant if subordinate role in the work. The LMS drew up a document entitled "Considerations and Regulations Respecting Missionaries in Connection with the Missionary Society" as early as February 1811 that each missionary was expected to sign prior to departure. More than half of the document related to the position of missionary spouses. Each agent appointed was required "not to make any declaration of his partiality to any female, with a view to marriage, till he has communicated the matter by letter to the Directors and has received their concurrence." As for the missionary wives, the society recognized that "by that relationship they had been brought into connection with this Society, and into a situation of considerable influence in promoting or retarding the success of the Missionaries themselves." It had thus become necessary for "the Directors to examine and to judge whether they possess the views and qualifications which are suitable to the services in which they are to be engaged, and the stations they are likely to occupy."[7] A list of "confidential questions to pastors concerning the intended wives of missionaries" was devised requiring satisfactory responses to the following:

> Is her Christian zeal, in promoting in some way the cause of Christ, such as to justify the conclusion that she has a true Missionary spirit?

> Has her religious history been such as to foster the conviction that she would prove a faithful co-worker in a foreign field as a Missionary wife?

> Is her disposition amiable, and is her general bearing so conciliatory and Christian-like as to encourage the hope that she would be "wise to win souls"?[8]

Increasingly, departing missionaries went as married rather than single men. Of 11 newly ordained LMS agents in 1815, 8 married shortly before they left these shores.[9] If a suitable male was not available, some unmarried women went out as sisters or other relatives. In 1816 Martha Cobden joined her sister Eliza Reeve, a missionary's wife in Bellary, India, where her domestic skills were greatly needed, not only in the Reeve family due to her sister's ill-health, but also by the family of Senior Missionary John Hands, whose wife had recently died.[10] Mary Bird, often referred to as one of the earliest pioneers of zenana missionary work, made full use of her position as companion to her widowed brother R. M. Bird, commissioner at Gorakhpur. Having studied Hindustani on the voyage out in 1823, she soon set up a school for girls. Moving later to Calcutta to join another brother, similarly afflicted, she began visiting and teaching Indian women in their own homes. Martha Edwardes was the daughter of a Welsh Congregational minister recently moved to London. With no missionary fiancé in sight and no relation to claim in the mission field, she was introduced early in 1831 to Samuel Garling, resident councillor at Malacca, and his wife Caroline, who were in England on leave. Less than a week before their return voyage, she obtained parental permission, made her preparations, and sailed with them.[11] She began Christian education work with Eurasian girls shortly after her arrival, the start of a lifelong commitment to the missionary cause.

LADIES—"FREE FROM THE CARES AND TOILS OF HOME AND FAMILY DUTIES"

When female missionary work expanded in the second half of the 19th century, there seems to have been an initial assumption that there was an untapped supply of refined, cultured, and unmarried ladies, who "free from the cares and toils of home and family duties" could devote their lives to the work of teaching, visiting, and ministering to the women and children of faraway lands.[12] Self-supporting, honorary missionaries were, in particular, sought after. It was the more solidly middle-class Anglican societies that were able to recruit in any numbers at this privileged level which did not however prevent other societies from making the attempt, as an appeal in *Our Indian Sisters*, published by the Baptist Zenana Mission shows:

> Are there not many ladies of culture and refinement who, with small incomes of their own, have no special home claims? . . . In the work of the Zenana Mission they would find a noble vocation, a sphere that would give abundant scope for all their powers . . . the best that the Christian Church has is needed for our work.[13]

Wesleyan Methodists too appealed for "educated, cultured" ladies who could go out to the mission fields "without cost to the Society."[14] It soon became clear that the source of well-educated, middle-class English spinsters in the 1880s and 1890s could not meet the many appeals for more missionaries to work in the mission fields "white to the harvest in India and China."[15] The January 1890 issue of *Grain of Mustard Seed: Or Woman's Work in Foreign Parts*, published by the Society for the Propagation of the Gospel's (SPG) Ladies' Association for the Promotion of Female Education among the Heathen, revealed that there was "scarcely a SPG mission-station that would not gladly accept help in female work if the Association were but in a position to offer it."[16] The 1890s was a peak period for recruitment of single women from Britain, part of the rapid expansion of the missionary movement as a whole. The number of female recruits was not as great as was hoped. By 1899 more than 1,600 single women in Britain had been appointed overseas; by 1916 there were around 2,500, with perhaps half that number again having been rejected.[17] Compared however to the total number of around 200 who had been sent out by the pioneering women's societies before 1875, the increase is striking.

"THE MASTER NEEDS ME IN HIS FOREIGN FIELD"

Women's responses to the appeals reveal an awareness of the power of religion and a commitment to Christian compassion, perhaps difficult in our own more secular times to fully appreciate. Some candidates had experienced an intensification of religious experience under the influence of the Keswick movement, and saw missionary service as a way of fully consecrating themselves to God's purpose. Many were humbly aware of their inadequacy for such a high calling, yet were assured that "He who has called will also qualify." One wrote in her letter of application that "I do not feel to have one quarter of the qualities of the ideal missionary. However, I comfort myself with the thought that if the Master needs me in His Foreign Field he will prepare me for it and help me to overcome all difficulties." A powerful and widespread motivation was a deep concern for the pitiful state of women's lives in heathen lands as portrayed in the mission literature of the period. Ellen Horton felt that while she could "never teach from the love of teaching and do not like it in itself, the thought of those poor women in India, their darkness and ignorance, the greatness of the work and the need of workers makes me feel I could do anything or give up anything to save and help them."[18] Some saw the work as essentially evangelistic—"to go forth and make disciples of our sad and suffering sisters in distant lands."[19] Others were attracted by the thought of being able to use their skills or abilities through missionary service. Elsie Baker, a trained and qualified nurse, could not "possibly go and preach a sermon" but still wished to "show something of God's great love in a life of work and service."[20] Few articulated the sense of imperial responsibility, expressed by Sarah Hewlett of the Church of England Zenana Missionary Society (CEZMS), that "India has a claim upon every English subject, because so many of her people own the sway of the British sovereign," although others may have felt something similar.[21]

The attraction of a "definite sphere of work and usefulness" and "of the many open doors for female labourers" in mission work undoubtedly encouraged some to come forward at a time when there was popularly understood to be a surplus of women of marriageable age in the British Isles.[22] This information had been extracted from the 1851 census, which had for the first time enquired about the age, sex, and conjugal status of each individual. Articles such as that by Harriet Martineau published in the *Edinburgh Review* in 1859 and another in the *National Review* by W. R. Greg in 1862 drew attention to the fate of such women who could not hope to "marry and be taken care of."[23] Although this interpretation was later shown to be flawed, the imbalance being mainly among older women, there remained until the turn of the century a generally held view that many young British women could not look forward to marriage and should make other plans for their lives and livelihood. Nor was the salary for a single woman missionary uncompetitive, at around 100 pounds sterling a year plus accommodation and the prospect of a pension. Salary for school mistresses at home varied between 90 and 120 pounds, depending on qualifications and seniority, while that for a nurse was usually around 50 pounds per annum.[24] Unimpressed by some LMS women missionaries in the field, Wardlaw Thompson, LMS secretary from 1881 to 1914, felt constrained to comment that there was "a strong impression among many who know something of the market for women's work that the prospect of a salary of £100 a year and house-room really becomes a temptation to many women to enter upon mission work who ought never to go into it."[25] Many women missionaries, however, were either wholly or partly self-supporting, and those entering the China Inland Mission (CIM) could expect no salary at all. A combination of obedience to Christ's teaching, a desire to engage in a "mission of sisterhood" to heathen women, and an awareness of the nobility and self-sacrifice of a calling seemed to have been the strongest motivations.[26] Alice Clark wrote in offering to serve as hospital matron in China that the "love of ambition, home and friends called me to stay at home, and so I tried to put it on one side but it was not to be."[27]

EDUCATIONAL BACKGROUND

During the 1890s it became clear that if missionary societies were to recruit sufficient numbers of women, they would either have to lower their standards or provide better training. Otherwise promising candidates often lacked the required social, cultural, and educational standards. Between 1875 and 1907 the LMS rejected more than 180 candidates, about 46 percent of applicants.[28] The Ladies' Committee of the Wesleyan Methodist Missionary Society was shocked at the low educational standards of its first 25 applicants, only 8 of whom could be taken seriously. The committee commented "it would save some trouble if friends and advisers would bear in mind that a year's training at Westminster cannot make up the deficiencies of an entirely neglected early education."[29] The Church Missionary Society (CMS), while continuing to recruit around 20 percent of its female candidates who were self-supporting, established a college at Highbury in London in 1892 to remedy educational gaps for those who came "from socially and educationally defective backgrounds." Around 15 percent of the CMS female intake attended Highbury College during this period.[30]

It is hardly surprising that so many candidates were found lacking in educational attainments. The provision of secondary education for girls in Britain lagged far behind that for boys in the 19th century, while colleges at the tertiary stage were almost nonexistent at the start of this period. Girls from upper- and middle-class homes were often taught at home; others attended private day or boarding schools of varying standards. For the urban and rural laboring classes, there were only the schools established by the National School Society or the British and Foreign School Society, providing a rudimentary education for children in by no means all towns and villages. The emphasis for many middle-class girls lay in the acquisition of accomplishments such as drawing, embroidery, and music, while teaching of academic subjects was often sporadic and superficial in the extreme. The shortcomings of the existing provision for girls were laid bare in 1864 by the Taunton Commission, which cataloged "want of thoroughness and foundation . . . inattention to rudiments; undue time given to accomplishments and those not taught intelligently or in any scientific manner."[31] Secondary schooling for girls markedly improved in the second half of the 19th century, commencing with the pioneering efforts of Frances Mary Buss, Dorothea Beale, and others in the 1850s and the founding of schools under the Girls' Public Day School Company in the 1870s. More than one-third of early 20th-century recruits to the LMS had attended high schools or schools like Milton Mount College, Gravesend, for the daughters of congregational ministers, opened in 1871. Whereas college education for girls in the United States was not uncommon in the mid-19th century (Mount Holyoke College in Massachusetts was founded as early as 1837), university education was closed to girls and women in Britain until the early 1870s, although some institutions had been founded to provide teacher training. In 1869 Emily Davies and Barbara Bodichon started a small college at Hitchin in Hertfordshire, which was moved in 1873 to Girton, just outside Cambridge. Thereafter the expansion of higher education for women was rapid, and by the early 1880s, women's colleges had been established at Cambridge, Oxford, and London. However, only between seven and eight percent of LMS women candidates in the period 1875–1914 had received a university or college education, while Eugene Stock lamented the very few CMS applicants coming out from "the women's colleges at Oxford and Cambridge."[32] In 1910 a report, compiled for the World Missionary Conference, deplored the intellectual unpreparedness of many women candidates, a deficiency attributed to the fact that "it is still comparatively rare for girls to continue any regular disciplined studies after school age."[33]

HEALTH, AGE, AND FAMILY CIRCUMSTANCES

The health of aspiring missionaries was an important consideration, since only the "strongest and best fitted to service abroad" could be appointed.[34] An LMS pamphlet emphasized the need for candidates to be physically strong and resilient. "The hot climates of India, China and Africa, etc., are more-or-less trying to all Europeans; and the anxiety, fatigue and exposure that must necessarily be involved in the daily hard work of an earnest and energetic Lady Missionary cannot but prove a serious strain on physical health and strength."[35] In the 19th and early 20th centuries, the good health of candidates could not be taken for granted. Missionary records reveal the unhealthy family background of many of the applicants with "multiple deaths of siblings from measles, scarlet fever, and other then common childhood illnesses," and a history of tuberculosis running through many families.[36] All candidates were subject to searching medical examination and those found to have worrying symptoms were ruled out, however suitable their other qualifications might be.[37] Sometimes societies erred on the side of caution. The LMS were initially delighted to receive an application in January 1911 from Dr. Constance Cousins, daughter of an LMS missionary who had served in Madagascar for many years, since they were seeking a suitable female medical missionary for their new hospital in South India. However, following an examination by the society's medical adviser for women candidates, Cousins was found to be suffering from latent epilepsy, a diagnosis supported by a specialist. She was informed that it was out of the question for her to serve in the tropics. Bitterly disappointed, she took up an unpaid post in Almora in northern India, where she died in service 33 years later without ever having suffered an epileptic attack.[38] Temperament was also important. Mrs. Weitbrecht had considered that it was "impossible for what is commonly called a passionate or bad-tempered person, to enjoy good health in India." A "sweet, even temperament was much to be preferred."[39] Missionary applicants with any record of mental instability or any hint of a family history of insanity were usually ruled out at an early stage. Ralph Wardlaw Thompson, LMS secretary, was highly suspicious of Agnes Frédoux, since both her mother and aunt (the daughters of pioneering missionaries Robert and Mary Moffat) were "to say the least *very peculiar*, and it would be a grievous misfortune if one were sent to a tropical climate who had any tendency to brain trouble."[40] Despite all precautions missionaries persisted in falling ill, particularly in the early years of service. Ella McTavish—declared by Dr. Mary Scharlieb, medical examiner to the LMS, to be "a very good candidate, her age is suitable [she was 26] and her organs in all respects are in good working order"—fell ill almost as soon as she arrived in Hong Kong in the autumn of 1904. She returned to England on medical advice and resigned.

Great emphasis was placed on age. Medical opinion took the view that women were less able to adjust to difficult climatic conditions after the age of 30. The Scottish Free Church considered "the best age for going to India" to be "about twenty-five years of age, after the character and constitution are formed, and before either the power of languages and the capacity for acclimatisation are lost."[41] However, Sara Billing, appointed to India in 1881 at the age of 34, quoted her doctor's opinion that women of her age had a more settled constitution and were "more likely to bear the strain of climate than if younger." Billing was accepted, but it was rare for women of her age. The CIM was more relaxed about age restrictions. Between 1880 and 1895, 19 percent of their female recruits were 30 or above, while Ella Webber was appointed in 1887 when she was only 18.[42] Mainstream societies applied less stringent rulings to self-supporting missionaries. Charlotte Maria Tucker, who had written many works for children under the pseudonym of A.L.O.E. (A Lady of England), went out to India in 1875 under the auspices of the Indian Female Normal School and Instruction Society at the age of 54. Finding herself finally free of family responsibilities, she decided to "devote the Evening of her life" to the missionary cause. It is extremely unlikely that she would have been accepted for missionary service if she had not entirely paid for her own passage and keep. Despite being considered both frail and delicate, she worked in India for the remaining 18 years of her life.[43]

Family responsibilities were a crucial consideration in the application process, reflecting the centrality of family to the lives of all women, married or single. In December 1897, the LMS Ladies' Examination Committee approved a revised list of the questions to be answered by candidates. At the top of the list after giving the place and date of their birth, applicants were required to state whether their parents still lived and if they were in any way dependent on the support of the applicant. As Rhonda Semple indicates, the concern about family responsibilities partly reflects the reality of family obligations prior to state welfare.[44] Mary Ann Aldersey delayed for several years her departure for China to take care of her brother's children who suddenly became motherless. Missionary documents also demonstrate the subordinate role of daughters in the late 19th and early 20th centuries. Women candidates were often asked if their parents knew of their wish to become a missionary.[45] But parental disapproval did not always stop women going ahead. Semple cites the case of Emily Blomfield who sailed to India in 1882 despite her parents' inability to reconcile themselves to the prospect of "giving up their child."[46] In other cases, one gains the impression that women were lent to the missionary cause until such time as family need required their return. Stephen Massey, a senior director of the Manchester engineering firm B. & S. Massey, visited China in 1893 and determined to found a women's hospital at Wuchang. That same year his daughter Ruth commenced her medical studies at Edinburgh. By 1899 she was on her way to Wuchang where, financially supported by her father, she spent the next 29 years as a medical missionary. In 1928 she resigned in order to nurse her now dying parent, an eventuality accepted as very proper by her family, the LMS and, seemingly, herself. However, Elspeth Hope-Bell, a hospital matron in China since 1911, was most reluctant to leave China, when she was summoned home to look after her elderly parents 18 years later. She also worried about forfeiting her pension, until her brother Fred, loudest in reminding her of family duty, undertook to "see" to her future.[47]

SOCIAL BACKGROUND

Eugene Stock was impressed by the socially eminent and relatively wealthy background of the first female recruits to the CMS. Ten of the first seventeen candidates were able to go out as self-supporting missionaries. One of them, Alice Wardlaw Ramsay, was "a niece of the great Marquis of Dalhousie." Other early recruits were Mary Bird, "a grand-daughter of the great Anglo-Indian Civilian, R.M. Bird and cousin of Mrs Isabella Bird Bishop"; Miss A.C. Bosanquet was a "daughter of a Northumberland Squire"; and Miss Maxwell "daughter of a Scottish baronet."[48] Yet Stock seems to have been ready to accept, after the first heady years, that recruitment could not, and should not, be limited to young women of the middle and upper classes. He supported the setting up of Highbury College in 1892 to provide general educational courses for candidates from less-privileged backgrounds, on the grounds that "God does not commit his work in the world to one class only. He can use persons of all classes."[49] In a report of 1896, he implied that it had been proved possible for a factory girl to be trained as a missionary.[50]

It is doubtful whether such a candidate would have been welcome in more socially conservative and less evangelically inclined societies. In its pamphlet *What Are the Qualifications Needed for a Lady Missionary?* the LMS required its candidates to be "ladies of some education, culture, and refinement" since they would be required to visit zenanas of families in "the higher classes of Hindu and Mohammedan society." Several quite promising candidates were rejected on grounds of unsuitable background. Twenty-five-year-old Agnes Lancaster, from Canning Town, Essex, having been a Sunday school teacher there for 11 years, impressed the Ladies' Committee in 1878 "by her energy and force of character. Her parentage and associations were, however, such as to render it unlikely that she would prove a suitable agent for work either in India or China."[51] Lily Medland's surroundings in her hometown of Plymouth shocked Ladies' Committee member Ada Browne in July 1904: "She lives in a working man's house ... The front room was about as simple and bare as possible, not even a carpet, and when I asked whether that was Miss Medland's room, the woman replied "oh no she lives along with us." However, another visitor was more favorably impressed, having discovered that Medland's lower than desired living standards were due to her having been left in very straitened circumstances following the death of her father, a Congregational minister. She was accepted.[52] Constance Long seemed an ideal applicant. Her interviewer wrote: "I like the girl . . . she is ladylike, refined, and I think most intelligent and there was withal a diffidence and forgetfulness of self which much pleased me."[53] Whatever their ladylike qualities, the background of most successful LMS candidates was not that of the wealthier and leisured middle classes. Many had, or chose, to work for a living. Around 28 percent of accepted candidates between 1875 and 1914 were teachers or governesses, 12 percent were nurses, while others worked in offices, or as dressmakers or milliners, or were engaged in paid home mission work.[54]

One mission that looked for spiritual qualities in its aspirant missionaries, regardless of education, class, and gender, was the CIM. Its founder James Hudson Taylor—partly from conviction, but also because of reluctance to conflict with other societies—sought missionaries of both sexes from outside the usual social bracket. He looked for "willing, skilful labourers" from all classes for whom "God has his own universities."[55] He was also a keen advocate for the wider use of women missionaries particularly in the interior provinces of China. Since "men were all too few to work the central stations why should not women trained and gifted for such service, fill the gap?"[56] However, an analysis of the CIM female intake between 1881 and 1895 reveals a close similarity with the class and occupation basis of the LMS group: 23 percent were teachers or governesses, with the next larger group, 20 percent, having no stated occupation. Eight percent were dressmakers or milliners, with roughly similar numbers employed as nurses, shop assistants, or engaged in home missions. Smaller numbers were engaged in clerical work and domestic service. Four were factory workers.[57] It is true that the CIM probably recruited from a broader range of classes than did other missions, with members of the educated upper and middle classes, attracted by the success and spiritual charisma of Taylor, and influenced by Holiness and premillenarian zeal, making some notable but perhaps unexpected additions to the mission's workforce in the 1880s and 1890s.

PROFESSIONAL VERSUS VOCATIONAL

The initial intensive phase of recruitment of women missionaries in the years before World War I coincided with profound and quite rapid developments in the professionalization of women doctors, nurses, and teachers. Specialized knowledge and skills were still at the turn of the century viewed as accomplishments—"the art of teaching, a knowledge of sick-nursing, of the art of medicine, of music and singing, of needlework, drawing and domestic economy" as the LMS recruitment pamphlet had it.[58] From the 1880s, however, British missionary societies had begun to send out fully qualified women doctors who had been through the new women's medical schools at London or Edinburgh, and this process extended to nurses when formal qualifications for nurses and midwives came into being in the early 1900s. The missionary societies, initially blamed for sending poorly quali-fied personnel lacking appropriate experience, increasingly required well-trained staff to be hospital matrons or to set up courses to train indigenous nurses. For these purposes properly qualified staff were required. The same professionaliz-ing process can be seen in education. By the early years of the 20th century the societies were recruiting missionary educators who had a degree or attended a recognized course at a teacher's training college. Of 80 women recruited by the LMS between 1914 and 1923, 56 were graduates or had a professional qualifica-tion or training as teachers, doctors, or nurses.[59] Eugene Stock might bemoan the low number of CMS female recruits coming from the older universities of Cambridge and Oxford, but more candidates were emerging from the vari-ous London colleges. Westfield College in Hampstead, founded in 1882, whose motto was "Behold the handmaid of the Lord," sent 50 graduates to the mis-sion field between 1883 and 1913, the greater number of whom became teachers in mission schools.[60] Between 1880 and 1910, the London School of Medicine for Women produced 95 medical missionaries, the peak decade being the 1890s, when 43 missionary doctors qualified.[61] There remained a place, however, for the general missionary whose versatile skills would allow her to combine some teach-ing with evangelistic work in towns and villages, and to be able to diagnose and apply simple remedies and medicines for the common ailments and conditions. Some considered this a more truly missionary role, there being "nothing so fatal to the success of Christian work" as "professionalism."[62]

Yet the women who had attended colleges or universities prior to applying for missionary service showed a strong sense of vocation. Indeed many had be-longed to the Student Christian Movement (SCM) or the Student Volunteer Missionary Union (SVMU) and had signed the SVMU pledge. As late as 1928, a decade during which student recruitment to the missionary movement declined, Marjorie Sykes, a Cambridge graduate and a trained and qualified teacher, could write that

> The call to missionary service formed an integral part of the experience which the SCM summer conference of that year [1924] crystallised, and since then intercourse with foreign students at Cambridge, detailed study of missionary work and personal intercourse with missionaries, have deepened the conviction that my work lay abroad. I joined the SVMU in the summer of 1925, believing that those not otherwise hindered by circumstances should help where the need seemed greatest.... My personal longing for foreign service was the result of Divine Guidance.[63]

Nor were missionary salaries and employment conditions as generous as those available to professionally qualified women at home. By the second decade of the 20th century opportunities for women's professional advancement at home were far greater than those attainable overseas. As Eleanor McDougall, principal of the Women's Christian College at Madras, pointed out:

> A University woman bred at one of the English residential colleges has a number of interesting and lucrative careers open to her at home in competition with which India with its trying climate, its distance from home, its scanty pay and limited possibilities of advance offers no attraction.... It is only a sense of vocation that brings out from England women of the best type, intellectual, moral and social, to take up the very trying work of a teacher in India.[64]

In her study of secondary school Headmistresses Joyce Goodman finds evidence that "colonial experience held the potential to enhance female careers in the metropolis."[65] However, most educational missionaries dedicated the whole of their working lives to the mission field. Shorter periods of missionary service when skills learnt could be transferred back to the home country were not common during the period of this study.

PREPARATION AND TRAINING
FOR THE MISSION FIELD

"It was difficult to get any but a few to believe in the training of women missionaries at all," commented the secretary of the Women's Foreign Missions of the Free Church of Scotland, looking back in 1911 over a quarter of a century.[66] While missionary societies required women candidates entering the mission field after 1870 to have some relevant training and experience, they were mostly vague about what exactly this should comprise. They were also at pains to ensure that the said training and experience should be acquired at no cost to themselves. Until the second decade of the 20th century, missionary societies thus largely deprived themselves of the opportunity to provide systematic preparation for candidates. They instead relied on existing centers or training institutions mainly involved in charitable work among the poor of Britain's towns and cities.

Extensive experience of practical Christian work such as Sunday-school teaching, district visiting, working in girls' clubs, sick nursing, and dispensing medicines was considered an absolute requirement for mission work. Applicants lacking such experience were required to spend some months at centers such as the London Bible Domestic Mission in the Strand, Miss Macpherson's Home of Industry in Bethnal Green, or the Bridge of Hope Mission in Ratcliffe Highway, East London. Emma Foggitt, a graduate from Leeds University and an experienced teacher going out to work in a mission girls' school in Shanghai, was obliged to spend several months at the Canning Town Settlement for Women Workers in East London before sailing in 1906. She found that the work "largely consists in visiting, addressing gatherings, working in the girls' clubs, holding children's services and doing dispensary work." She seems to have enjoyed the varied experience and wrote to tell the LMS so.[67] Work directed to the London poor did not always prove an adequate preparation for life overseas. One woman wrote from her mission station that she had "witnessed things that would never have cropped up in Kentish Town Mission."[68]

A high order of domestic skill was expected. Evangeline French, who had been educated in Geneva, was taken on arrival at the CIM Women's Candidates' Home in Pyrland Road, London to

a room divided by cotton curtains into four sections. In the corner allotted her was a small bed, one chair and a painted wooden wash-hand stand. A little later she was called down to take on her first job, which was the writing of labels to be pasted on a great array of jam pots.... In the middle of the night Eva realised with horror, that she had written them all in French, "Abricot," instead of English "Apricot." She felt this was a bad beginning, and when a few days later her bed, being unexpectedly inspected, the housekeeper exclaimed: "My dear, what would the Chinese say to a bed made like that?" she felt she had but slender hopes of passing the councils.[69]

French, who had been brought up in a comfortable middle-class home, considered herself "painfully undomesticated" compared to most other CIM candidates, but soon realized that she was required to show humility and a willingness to take on tasks she would normally consider a "bothersome duty." On a second visit to Pyrland Road, she wore a garment showing "unmistakable evidence of being home-made, and was sufficiently dowdy, even for a missionary."[70] Even the least skill familiar to those running a home could be put to a good purpose. As Charlotte Tucker commented:

> It is amusing to see in India what trifling pieces of knowledge will come to account. How to pack a box, or strap up a bundle, prepare arrowroot or quiet a baby, nail up a picture or knit a stocking, strum on an instrument or sketch a ground-plan, are scraps of knowledge not to be despised.[71]

In addition to practical experience, women candidates, especially those without teaching or medical qualifications, were expected to have spent time at an approved training institution. By 1910 there were "at least thirteen institutions" in the United Kingdom where missionary candidates were receiving training, "though only seven of those were solely dedicated to overseas missionary preparation."[72] Two, the Women's Missionary Training Institute in Edinburgh and a CMS institute at Highbury, were run by missionary societies. Others were private, run by sisterhoods, or were deaconess institutes catering for women to work in home or overseas missions.[73] Among the more pleasantly located was The Willows, "a lovely secluded mansion" set in a "beautiful park, with its old trees and well-kept gardens" forming part of the Mildmay Mission, founded by the Rev. William Pennefather, rector of St. Jude's Mildmay, and his wife in the 1860s.[74] It comprised a missionary training home, a deaconess home, a cottage hospital, orphanage, conference hall, and other buildings. At any one time 30–40 trainee missionary students would be in residence, chiefly destined for the mission stations run by the CEZMS and the CMS. Fees at The Willows were relatively high, about 50 pounds per annum, and most students were ladies from well-to-do homes, often going out at their own expense into the mission field. The CMS training home at Highbury by contrast was designed for those women "whose social position and previous education made them unsuitable for admission to the Willows."[75] After two years at Highbury, it was hoped to bring them up to a sufficient standard to benefit from a short period at The Willows before being sent off to the mission field.[76]

The LMS included The Willows in their list of recommended training institutes, but provided details of cheaper alternatives, among them Doric Lodge, part of the East London Training Institute for Home and Foreign Missions, founded by the revivalist leader Henry Grattan Guinness and his wife in 1873. The Grattan Guinnesses were close associates of James Hudson Taylor; connected even more closely after 1894 when their daughter Geraldine married his son, Howard. Their training institutes were utilized by the CIM: male students attending Harley House in Bow and the women, Doric Lodge. CIM recruits however received most of their training in the mission's training homes in China where they learned the language, were introduced to the Chinese classics and other literature, and practiced "street preaching, and mission-hall work."[77] Prior to acceptance, female applicants were first received and assessed at the Women Candidates' Home in Pyrland Road. There, under the eagle eye of the Superintendent Henrietta Soltau, their characters and missionary vocation were tested, and their training requirements assessed. Soltau had been drafted in by Hudson Taylor in 1889 when it became clear that the number of CIM female recruits was set to increase dramatically. Here, despite being initially oppressed by "the unutterable dreariness of the northern suburb and the dingy garden with smutty shrubs," she remained for 27 years, guiding and preparing more than 500 women for their work in China.[78]

It is difficult to find any detailed syllabuses: most training courses however seem to have followed a similar pattern. Bible study and lectures in the morning would be followed by practical Christian work in the afternoons, when the trainee missionaries assisted in schools, orphanages, soup kitchens, dispensaries, hospitals, mothers' meetings, and so on. At The Willows, the surrounding institutes and charities of the Mildmay Mission, including, from 1892, the Mildmay Mission Hospital in Bethnal Green, provided conveniently situated practical training centers. Intensive language-training for the most part took place in the mission fields, but The Willows did give some classes "in Hindostani and Bengali." Harriette Cooke, who wrote and published an account of Mildmay in 1892, also reported classes in bookkeeping—"one evening each week, so that each one may be able to keep her own accounts, lessons in cookery, in housekeeping and two evenings in sewing are given.... They are all taught to sing, and a very thorough drill in tonic-sol-fa." Old Testament and New Testament lessons in the mornings "given by men well-prepared for this work" do not seem to have been particularly challenging, except as a test of memory. The "young ladies" were "expected to write these lessons out from memory, and submit their notes for correction."[79] Students at The Willows would also be made familiar with the geography and history of the various mission fields and the peoples who lived there. There were also classes in doctrine and Christian evidences, so that the women could have a basic, if not profound, grasp of the faith they were going out to promote.[80] Time was also set aside for personal devotions and communal worship. All training institutes laid stress on the importance of character training, and considered personal and spiritual development and the experience of living in harmony with others during their residence to be key elements of the training.

The most mission-focused training course was that devised by former missionary Annie Hunter Small at the Women's Missionary Training Institute in Edinburgh, founded in 1894. Small claimed the syllabus was "designed to give to candidates neither general education nor definite professional instruction in medicine or teaching, but purely such preparation as they might require for the special work of the day." Instruction at the college included "advanced work" in Old and New Testament studies, comparative religion, sociology, the history of missions, as well as practical subjects such as voice culture and how to keep accounts in different currencies. A house guild gave practice in how to run meetings and there were opportunities for discussions and debates. Small had had to defend her beliefs when a missionary in India and wanted her students to have sufficient theological training and facility in debate to be able to hold their own in argument.[81]

Small was to have quite a hand in formulating the criticisms of the training of women missionaries made at the time of the World Missionary Conference at Edinburgh in 1910. She was a member of Commission V, which carried out a thorough investigation into "The Preparation of Missionaries." Generally, the commission found that insufficient attention was paid to preparing both male and female candidates for work overseas, especially in inculcating an understanding of foreign cultures, religions, and languages. Members considered the "work of training the character, the devotional life and habits of students, and developing their capacity to work with and for each other goes ahead fairly satisfactorily." But Bible studies, church history, dogmatics and apologetics, and comparative religion were taught superficially; most candidates were not made aware of "the modern situation in the mission-field" nor was there a full "realisation of the actual responsibilities and opportunities of a woman missionary."[82] The practical Christian work that women trainees carried out should be recast to make it more applicable to the realities of life on the mission field. Above all, it was felt that missionary societies should connect more closely with the training of missionaries. Feeling such criticisms rather keenly, a number of societies decided that they should take up the gauntlet. The Baptist Missionary Society, the LMS, and the Women's Missionary Association of the Presbyterian Church of England decided to take matters forward by setting up a women's college at Selly Oak near Birmingham. Carey Hall opened its doors in 1913, offering a three-year course in theology, Bible studies, education theory and practice, linguistics and phonetics, comparative religion, and psychology. For its female candidates the CMS purchased The Willows from the Mildmay trustees and renamed it Kennaway Hall, while SPG elected to place its college for women in Selly Oak. The College of the Ascension opened its doors to women students in 1923.

PREPARATIONS FOR DEPARTURE

If she was ill-prepared in some ways, the outgoing missionary was, on the whole, very well equipped. The CIM had as early as 1873 devised an outfit list for their women missionaries designed to cater both for the needs of the voyage and also for their first years in China. In fact, it was possible to have too much. Frances Abbey traveling out with Alice Gill in 1887 noted that "Miss Marris, the lady missionary with whom Miss Gill is to work, told her not to have too large a stock of linen, as the *dobies* [washermen] . . . were in the habit of letting people hire part of it one week and returning it to the rightful owner the next."[83] Claire Thomson was advised to take a generous supply of white stockings in silk and cotton. She packed 20 pairs but never wore them![84] Missionaries were recommended to take small quantities of medicaments such as Keating's powder, Vaseline, smelling salts, quinine, enema, carbolic powder, and castor oil. Possibly some of these could be found in the small medicine case for each outgoing missionary supplied by the pharmaceutical firm Burroughs Wellcome & Co. on presentation of a letter from their missionary society secretary. They were also advised to make sure they received appropriate vaccinations, and to have had their "teeth attended to by a dentist."[85]

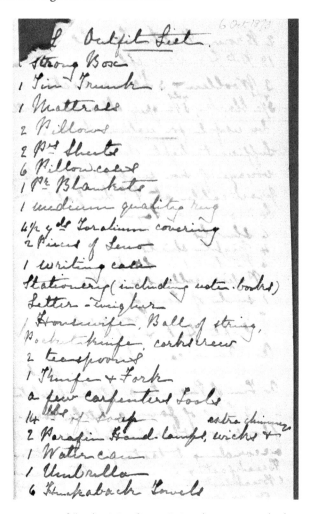

Figure 2.1. First page of "Ladies' Outfit List," October 6, 1873. The list was enclosed with a letter from James Hudson Taylor to the London Council of the China Inland Mission. (Courtesy of OMF International [United Kingdom].)

VALEDICTORY SERVICES

As the time approached for missionaries to depart, arrangements would be made for them to formally take their leave of their church community and to be sent on their way.

The type of service or meeting varied according to the nature of the church supporting them. Alice Gill, Leila Robinson, and Frances Abbey took tea in the

LMS museum before attending a meeting addressed by LMS Foreign Secretary R. Wardlaw Thompson, while a party of outgoing Baptist missionaries in 1891 held their farewell meeting in the library of Baptist Mission House.[86] By contrast, *India's Women* for November 1893 recorded an "outgoing band" of 33 CEZMS missionary ladies "and their friends, numbering more than two hundred, receiving Holy Communion in St Mary's Abbots Church."[87] Isabella Plumb also attended a service in the West Church, Aberdeen in October 1882. "The Rev James Cooper, East parish, conducted the service. After prayer and praise followed an impressive charge to the two ladies thus sent forth as assistants to Miss Bernard in her arduous work. The interest felt on the occasion was shown by the large number who assembled and by the subsequent hearty greetings to the two young women."[88]

On the day of departure, each outgoing missionary would be accompanied to the station and sometimes to the docks, by friends, relations, and supporters. Members of the CIM would gather at the dockside while the ship cast off, and then as it began to move, the parties, both onboard and ashore, would sing evangelical hymns such as "All Hail the Power of Jesus' Name." Myra Carpenter, traveling out on the S. S. *Naldera* in 1928, was in one such group of 10 women and 6 men. She describes how the CIM party was driven in two buses from the headquarters in Newington Green to Liverpool Street Station to take the boat train to Tilbury. "The boat train leaves there at 12.30 pm and we are due to sail at 2 pm." She wrote from Margate that "the finishing touch was when the CIM party began singing 'Jesus shall reign where're the sun' as the boat began to move off."[89] The lengthy ocean voyage that followed was often more dreaded than the final destination.

NOTES

1. PCE/FMC Series III, Box 31, File 3.

2. Charlotte Bronte, *Jane Eyre* (London and Glasgow: Library of Classics, n.d.), 493.

3. Mora Dickson, *Beloved Partner: Mary Moffat of Kuruman* (London: Gollancz, 1974), 180.

4. Emma R. Pitman, *Heroines of the Mission Field* (London, Paris, and New York: Cassell, Petter, Galpin & Co., n.d.), 42.

5. See Alison Twell, *The Civilising Mission and the English Middle Class, 1792–1850* (Basingstoke: Palgrave Macmillan, c. 2009), 119–121.

6. T. Middleditch, *The Youthful Female Missionary: A memoir of Mary Anne Hutchins* (London: G. Wightman, 1840).

7. "Considerations and Regulations Respecting Missionaries in Connection with the Missionary Society," 1811, CWM/LMS Home Odds, Box 34.

8. "Confidential Questions to Pastors Concerning the Intended Wives of Missionaries," CWM/LMS Candidates Papers passim.

9. James Sibree, *Register of Missionaries, Deputations etc.* (London: London Missionary Society, 1923), 11–16.

10. Jemima Thompson, *Memoirs of British Female Missionaries* (London: W. Smith, 1841), 50–54.

11. "In Memoriam Mrs Weitbrecht," *India's Women* 8, no. 45 (May–June 1888): 114.

12. Pitman, *Heroines,* 4.

13. *Our Indian Sisters: A Quarterly Magazine of the Ladies' Zenana Mission in Connection with the Baptist Missionary Society,* no. 3 (January 1886): 51.

14. C. P. Williams, "The Recruitment and Training of Overseas Missionaries in England between 1850 and 1900" (M.Litt. diss., University of Bristol, Bristol, 1976), 309.

15. *What Are the Qualifications for a Lady Missionary* (London: London Missionary Society, 1895), 1.

16. *The Grain of Mustard Seed: Or Woman's Work in Foreign Parts,* no. 109, (January 1890): 5.

17. Steven Maughan, "Regions Beyond and the National Church: The Foreign Missions of the Church of England in the High Imperial Era, 1870–1914" (Ph.D. diss., Harvard University, Cambridge, MA, 1995), 364 and Jeffrey Cox, The *British Missionary Enterprise, since 1700* (New York: Routledge, 2010), Table 1.

18. Bartlett, German, and Horton, CWM/LMS Candidates Papers, 1796–1899.

19. Lowe, CWM/LMS Candidates Papers (Unaccepted) 1796–1899.

20. Baker, CWM/LMS Candidates Papers 1900–1940.

21. S. S. Hewlett, *Daughters of the King* (London: Church of England Zenana Missionary Society, 1886), 1.

22. French, CWM/LMS Candidates Papers (Unaccepted) 1796–1899; and Baker, Candidates Papers 1796–1899.

23. Quoted in Lee Holcombe, *Victorian Ladies at Work: Middle-class Working Women in England and Wales, 1850–1914* (Newton Abbot: David and Charles, 1973), 10.

24. Rosemary Seton, "'Open Doors for Female Labourers': Women Candidates of the London Missionary Society, 1875–1914," in *Missionary Encounters: Sources and Issues,* eds. Robert A. Bickers and Rosemary Seton (Richmond, Surrey: Curzon Press, 1996), 61.

25. Quoted in Norman Goodall, *A History of the London Missionary Society, 1895–1945* (London: Oxford University Press, 1954), 12.

26. See Jane Haggis, "Ironies of Emancipation: Changing Configurations of 'Women's Work' in the 'Mission of Sisterhood' to Indian Women," *Feminist Review* 65 (2000): 108–126.

27. Baker, CWM/LMS Candidates Papers 1900–1940.

28. Seton, "Open Doors," 56.

29. *Ladies' Committee for Ameliorating the Condition of Women in Heathen Countries, Female Education etc.,* Occasional Paper No. 8, March 1861, 149–150.

30. Williams, "Recruitment," 304–305.

31. Philippa Levine, *Victorian Feminism 1850–1900* (London: Hutchinson, 1987), 27–28.

32. Eugene Stock, *The History of the Church Missionary Society: Its Environment, its Men and its Work* (London: Church Missionary Society, 1899–1916), 3, 371.

33. World Missionary Conference (WMC), *Report of Commission V* (Edinburgh and London: Oliphant, Anderson & Ferrier, 1910), 83.

34. Georgina H. Endfield and David J. Nash, " 'Happy is the Bride the Rain Falls on': Climate, Health and 'the Woman Question' in Nineteenth-century Missionary Documentation," *Transactions of the Institute of British Geographers* 30 (2005): 373.

35. *What Are the Qualifications Needed for a Lady Missionary?* (London: London Missionary Society, 1913), 7–8.

36. Rhonda A. Semple, *Missionary Women: Gender, Professionalism and the Victorian Idea of Christian Mission* (Woodbridge: Boydell, 2003), 30.

37. Endfield and Nash, "Happy is the Bride," 374–378.

38. Bryan Papers, Box 2, File 12.

39. Mary Weitbrecht, *Female Missionaries in India: Letters from a Missionary Wife Abroad to a Friend in England* (London: James Nisbet & Co., 1843), 31.

40. Fredoux, CWM/LMS Candidates Papers 1796–1899.

41. Semple, *Missionary Women*, 27–28.

42. Register of China Inland Mission Missionaries 1853–1895, CIM, Box 11.

43. Agnes Giberne, *A Lady of England. The Life and Letters of Charlotte Maria Tucker* (London: Hodder & Stoughton 1895), 174, 215.

44. Semple, *Missionary Women*, 39.

45. CWM/LMS, Ladies' Examination Committee, Minutes, Tuesday, December 14, 1897.

46. Semple, *Missionary Women*, 40–41.

47. CWM/LMS China Personal, Box 12, Elspeth Hope Bell, undated note [1930].

48. Stock, *History*, 3, 368, 370.

49. Stock, *History*, 3, 672.

50. C. P. Williams, " 'The Missing Link': The Recruitment of Women Missionaries in Some English Evangelical Missionary Societies in the Nineteenth Century," in *Women and Missions: Past and Present, Anthropological and Historical Perceptions*, eds. Fiona Bowie et al. (Providence, RI and Oxford: Berg, 1993), 58.

51. Lancaster, CWM/LMS Candidates Papers (Unaccepted) 1796–1899.

52. Medland, CWM/LMS Candidates Papers 1900–1940.

53. Long, CWM/LMS Candidates Papers (Unaccepted) 1796–1899.

54. Seton, "Open Doors," 61.

55. Geraldine Guinness, *The Story of the China Inland Mission* (London: Morgan & Scott, 1893), 1, 235.

56. Guinness, *Story*, 385.

57. Register of China Inland Mission Missionaries 1853–1895, CIM, Box 11.

58. *What Are the Qualifications?* (1895), 6.

59. Sibree, *Register of Missionaries*, 163–170.

60. Janet Sondheimer, *Castle Adamant in Hampstead: A History of Westfield College 1882–1982* (London: Westfield College, University of London, 1983), 67.

61. Ruth E. M. Bowden, *Royal Free Hospital Missionaries, 1880–1910* (n.d.), Appendix 1, RFH Archives.

62. Miriam Young, *Among the Women of the Punjab: A Camping Record* (London: Carey Press, 1916), 117.

63. Sykes, CWM/LMS Candidates Papers; and Clifton J. Phillips, "Changing Attitudes in the Student Volunteer Movement in Great Britain and North America, 1886–1928," in *Missionary Ideologies in the Imperialist Era 1880–1920*, eds. Torben Christensen and William R Hutchison (Arhus: Aros, c. 1982), 140.

64. Quoted in letter from Lord Pentland, May 9, 1914, WCC Papers, Mss Eur F220/1.

65. Joyce Goodman, " 'Their Market Value Must Be Greater for the Experience They Gained': Secondary School Headmistresses and Empire, 1897–1914," in *Gender, Colonialism and Education: The Politics of Experience*, eds. Joyce Goodman and Jane Martin (London: Woburn Press, 2002), 177.

66. Quoted in Semple, *Missionary Women*, 69.

67. Foggitt, CWM/LMS Candidates Papers.

68. Goodall, *History*, 12.

69. Mildred Cable and Francesca French, *Something Happened* (London: Hodder & Stoughton, 1933), 31.

70. Cable and French, *Something Happened,* 33.

71. Quoted in Jennifer A. Morawiecki, " 'The Peculiar Mission of Christian Womanhood': The Selection and Preparation of Women Missionaries of the Church of England Zenana Missionary Society, 1880–1920" (Ph.D. diss., University of Sussex, Falmer, 1998), 194.

72. WMC, *Report of Commission V,* 85.

73. For more on Anglican sisterhoods and the deaconess movement, see Carmen Mangion, "Women, Religious Ministry and Female Institution-building," in *Women, Gender and Religious Cultures in Britain, 1800–1940,* eds. Sue Morgan and Jacqueline de Vries (London, New York: Routledge, 2010), 72–93 and Martha Vicinus, *Independent Women: Work and Community for Single Women, 1850–1920* (London: Virago, 1985), Chapter 2.

74. Harriette J. Cooke, *Mildmay; or, the Story of the First Deaconess Institution* (London: Elliot Stock, 1892), 123–124.

75. Williams, "Recruitment," 304.

76. Williams, "Missing Link," 60.

77. WMC, *Report of Commission V,* 58.

78. Mildred Cable and Francesca French, *A Woman Who Laughed: Henrietta Soltau* (London: China Inland Mission, 1934), 143.

79. Cooke, *Mildmay,* 127.

80. Morawiecki, "Peculiar Mission," 191–192.

81. WMC, *Report of Commission V,* 250–251.

82. WMC, *Report of Commission V,* 89.

83. James H. Brown, *Frances Brockway: Memoirs* (London: Unwin Bros., 1905), 52.

84. Thomson Papers, Mss Eur D1102/2, 144.

85. WMA, *Outfit List for Ladies Going to China* (London: The Harewood Press, n.d.), 10.

86. *Chronicle of the London Missionary Society* (December 1887): 523 and *The Missionary Herald of the Baptist Missionary Society* (October 1891): 413.

87. *India's Women* 13 (November 1893): 487.

88. *News of Female Missions in Connection with the Church of Scotland* (January 1883): 13.

89. Letter from Myra Carpenter, October 18, 1928, Carpenter Papers.

3

— ❦ —

Life on the Mission Field

The fascination of the East was opening in front of her, and she went out to it as a bride to her marriage.[1]

THE JOURNEY OUT AND FIRST IMPRESSIONS

Most travelers to India and China during the 19th and first half of the 20th centuries went by sea from Tilbury or Southampton, often in ships of the Peninsular and Oriental Steam Navigation Company. Prior to the opening of the Suez Canal in 1869, the sea route was usually via the Cape of Good Hope and the voyage took long, weary, and sometimes dangerous months. Some missionaries bound for China traveled via America or Canada. The Trans-Siberian Railway to Vladivostock, completed in 1916, was sometimes used, for reasons of economy or personal preference or because sea routes were considered unsafe. Only exceptionally would missionaries go first class, most traveling in second. By train, they traveled hard rather than soft. Standards of comfort onboard varied. Eva French, journeying out to China in 1893 in the S.S. *Britannia,* found the voyage "desperately uncomfortable." The boat was "old-fashioned, the cabins cramped and stuffy, the food unpalatable, and the whole party tormented by sea-sickness."[2]

Isabella Plumb, sailing for India in the autumn of 1882, felt similarly cramped, sharing a six-berth cabin with five other ladies. She also suffered from seasickness "and even more from home-sickness."[3] Illness of one sort and another was a common experience. Hannah Marshman, traveling to India with her husband and two small children in 1799, was ill almost throughout the four-and-a-half month voyage. Very thankfully indeed did she disembark at Serampore, a few miles up-river from Calcutta, and make for the comfort of Meyer's Hotel. A few months later she gave birth to her third child, and some of her discomfort and illness can be attributed to pregnancy.[4]

Frances Abbey, sailing in 1887 on the S. S. *Manora* to join her missionary fiancé in Bengal, as the ship went "breezily through the Mediterranean . . ., began to think a sea voyage not so bad after all" despite the "depth of our misery and woe" some days earlier. She appreciated the helpfulness of the gentlemen of the party, each of whom "seems to strive what more can be done to make the ladies comfortable." She ventured into the saloon and saw "black waiters in the blue and white turbans, brown clothes, with blue and white cords round their waists come into the saloon in a long line capering and dancing around in the funniest fashion."[5]

Once in the Mediterranean, sightseeing provided a source of interest, since ships often put in at Marseilles, Genoa, and elsewhere. Twenty-six-year-old Hannah Davies, bound for China, went "ashore at Malta" to see "the place where St Paul was wrecked—the place where two seas meet." At Brindisi, the English mail arrived and each of her party "hurried away to a quiet corner to be alone for a while with letters from loved ones far away." She was impressed by Port Said, "the largest coaling station in the world."[6] Dr. Isabel Mitchell was horrified by her brief visit ashore. She wrote home, "We went into Port Said this morning . . . It was my first peep of the real East. Somehow the whole place struck me as repulsive. Genoa was beautiful, and Naples was dirty but Port Said is wicked, wicked, wicked. . . . It made me feel I wanted to go and fight . . . that awful, visible evil."[7] Such cultural and spiritual sensitivity contrasted with Sister Gladys Stephenson's more robustly patriotic views on her journey out in 1915. She enjoyed her glimpse of Port Said, although she was not allowed onshore during the six hours it took to re-coal the ship. She saw some British soldiers riding by on mules—they waved their hats and "I waved back vigorously and wished I could have seen brother Jack among them." She thrilled "with pride to be a Britisher, as one sees the mark of British sovereignty everywhere." It was traditional for first-time, eastward-bound travelers to acquire sun helmets in Port Said. One of the men, allowed ashore, brought back two for her and for Miss Weaver. They were lined with green and, to her surprise, "quite becoming."[8]

From the departure of the boat train from Liverpool Street Station to Tilbury docks, the traveling missionary fraternity would have been readily identified by their fellow passengers. They would be accompanied to the station and some-times to the docks by friends, relations, and supporters. Fanny Woodman, sailing with her husband Fred to China in 1894, heard that other passengers referred to their group as the "Gospel Grinders." It amused her to see many passengers give them a wide berth, "while others allow us to chat and drop in the seed."[9] The independent-minded and self-supporting China Inland Mission (CIM) mission-aries, Mildred Cable and the French sisters, disparaged missionary exclusiveness during the voyage, writing in their joint memoir that "the sight of those sober young women holding prayer meetings and taking lessons in the Chinese language was certainly calculated to keep outsiders at bay."[10] After experiencing the long sea voyage through the Mediterranean, Suez Canal, Indian Ocean, and China Seas, they preferred to make their own outward and homeward travel arrangements, usually via the Trans-Siberian Railway. It was also the cheaper option. Ronald and Gwyneth Still, traveling to China in 1935, thought "missionary passengers have too strong a tendency to be cliquey" and regretted they had been booked to share most of their meals with other "mishes." "It's quite obvious which they are—they need no introduction." They were amused by one of their fellow passengers who, during a break ashore at Marseilles, joined them in a trip to the Château d'If. She confessed she "wouldn't have come with us had she known" who they were. She had thought that Ronald Still was an engineer, but had wondered about his wife as she used no face "paint or make up at all."[11]

Whatever the reason, parties of missionaries largely kept to themselves while onboard. This exclusiveness provided opportunity for shared Bible reading, prayer, and language tuition. Meals together allowed them to try out or brush up the language spoken in their mission fields. Gladys Stephenson reported that one group had begun speaking Chinese at mealtimes, until a late addition to their table put a stop to this. She herself was given lessons by a missionary in the party, returning after furlough. By the time she reached Sicily she could say "in the bath-room there is a chicken (= a can of water)."[12] Missionaries were concerned about the provision of general Christian services at sea and tended to agitate if these were not forthcoming. One missionary found an opportunity for testifying to fellow passengers that she had not bargained for. When Margaret Dryburgh sailed to China in October 1919 she was accompanied by Miss J. A. Lloyd returning from furlough. They found it "impossible to have a Sunday service on board" but joined by two male CIM missionaries they held "a daily Bible reading on the 2nd Class deck." They reported "there has been some discussion among the passengers on the efficacy of Christian Missions," and at the suggestion of an American major on his way to supervise Red Cross work, a meeting was convened at which Lloyd, as senior missionary aboard, would speak. She wrote later that she "did not expect many to be present, but . . . nearly if not all passengers gathered together. I felt terribly nervous for I had never spoken to such an audience but I was much helped. They listened attentively and afterwards many thanked me."[13] On a lighter note, healthy deck sports were activities in which missionaries could and did join, although there were moral considerations. Frances Abbey commented on how much she had enjoyed a tug-of-war between passengers and crew, in which missionaries participated, however, only after the proffered prize of a bottle of whisky was withdrawn. She commented favorably on the "fine specimens of Christianity on board amongst the young men—just two or three—whose influence over the rowdier set is indeed for good. It is through them that gambling has been abolished during the day, such healthy sports as those of yesterday have taken the place of sweepstakes and the like."[14]

Beyond Port Said was the heat of the Red Sea and "many weary days of continuous sea" before Bombay (Mumbai), the end of the voyage for many since, by the late 19th century, it was possible to travel by train to most Indian cities. The journey to Calcutta took four days. Gladys Minns, arriving in Bombay in May 1923 after a two-week voyage, found that it took a further three to four days, by train and a few miles by car, to reach the ladies' bungalow at the mission station in Medak, Hyderabad state. Almost immediately, heavy rain began to fall. She was startled when one of the inmates "ripped off her dress and vanished upstairs onto the roof. She came down rejoicing at being soaked through. It was June 1st the day we always expected the monsoon."[15]

After Bombay, for those still onboard, there might be a stop at Colombo in Ceylon (Sri Lanka). Here Gladys Stephenson was met by Nancy Hood, a friend from her training days, who had a small rowing boat to take her ashore. They took a rickshaw each to the Wesleyan Mission Compound and embarked on a tour of

Colombo "in a funny antiquated looking carriage like those we sometimes see old ladies driving in at Brighton and other places with a hood on it."[16] Frances Abbey also took the opportunity to do some visiting. She and other missionaries were "met by Mr Piggott of the Baptist Mission" and were taken to his house. She was impressed. "I wish I could describe it all to you: the short drive round a clump of Oleanders, Ceylon jessamine, yellow tulip-tree flowers, maiden hair and cocoa-trees, to the cool verandah, where comfortable, cane chairs were scattered all about." When the *Manora* finally tied up at Calcutta, she had the thrill of being met by her fiancé, William Brockway. She reported that "passengers take a keen interest in any young man on an approaching boat or launch who looks as though he might be a bridegroom." Her intended showed up looking very gaunt, having just recovered from a fever, despite which she was married three days later from her uncle's house in Calcutta.[17] Hilda Johnson, by contrast, found her arrival in Calcutta on Christmas Eve 1900 particularly bleak. She thought it "a desolate day… as the Golconda crept up the Hugli … contrasting so sharply with Christmas jollities at home." The home-loving Johnson had to fight homesickness during her five-week voyage. Despite the presence of other London Missionary Society (LMS) missionaries aboard, she had felt "awfully lonely sometimes." She could not help "being homesick, especially at night, and when we pass ships that are going home." Perhaps it was just as well that "promptly on January 1st she began to take Bengali lessons with a pundit."[18]

For the China-bound, there could be another couple of weeks at sea in the unpredictable China Sea. At 4 A.M. one morning Hannah Davies was shaken awake when "a huge roaring billow burst with a tremendous crash against the vessel. It was followed by a noisy clash of broken glass and china, and many shouts and screams from all parts of the ship…. Turning up the light we found our cabin a perfect wreck." They decided the situation was grave enough to join the missionary ladies in the next cabin in prayer.[19] Myfanwy Wood, enduring a similar experience in January 1909, went up on deck. "The sea was a peculiar livid green—with great mountainous waves—the sky one mass of grey clouds—we didn't see the sun all day and the wind was particularly cold and swept around the ship as if it would tear everything down. We were in the Formosan Channel and cross-currents and the monsoon were responsible for the rough weather." Earlier she had enjoyed the approach to Hong Kong, her first glimpse of China—entering "by quite a narrow gorge" with the sun "just rising a glorious boiled-red behind the Peak. We went very slowly & so smoothly. . . . On either side, tier upon tier rose, well-wooded hills and mountains. The yellow rock showed bare in patches, and the whole had a very beautiful effect of light and shade. The yellow patches looked like gleams of dazzling sunlight and the dark woods the shadow of the clouds".[20] Sister Gladys Stephenson thought Hong Kong lovely. The shops were full of beautiful things—British, French, and Chinese. She admired the strong and sturdy Chinese boatwomen, the coolies with their broad hats, and men wearing black or blue silk with fans sticking out of their suits at the back, used to shade them from the sun as they crossed the street. She and her companions lunched at the King Edward Hotel before going to the Peak, passing two women carrying an older relative with bound feet "no longer than my little finger."[21]

Most missionaries traveling to China finally disembarked at Shanghai, three days from Hong Kong, some like Eva French with exquisite relief. As Myra Carpenter's boat entered the harbor, she and her companions "began to pick the faces. Mr Hoste and Mr Gibb were the first ones we saw."[22] As at Calcutta, fiancées met up, in some cases very self-consciously. From the deck the sharp-eyed Carpenter soon spotted Mr. Johnston on the harbor-side looking very excited. "He is engaged to Devina Buchan but as he did not write and ask her until after he was in China, they do not know each other very well, and so Devina was feeling very nervous. Everyone has been teasing her unmercifully the last few days. Mrs Stark came to the rescue by lending her cabin, sending Devina there and then arranging for Mr Stark to take Mr Johnston there, and so get the first meeting over in private. They re-appeared a long while later, both looking very happy."

Once the CIM missionaries had been rounded up and reunited with their luggage—Myra Carpenter thought that the "Lord was very good to me as I escaped any duty"—they were taken by car to CIM headquarters in Woosung Road. Here they went straight to the dining room before going up to a room "full of flowers and fruit."[23] Gladys Stephenson spent her first night in China at the house, known as the 'Eavenly 'Ome, of an American missionary couple, Mr. and Mrs. Evans, before taking the riverboat for Hankow. She thought the boat a great improvement on the oceangoing ships. It was "simply lovely, very much like a fine houseboat on the Thames." The paint was all ivory white, and there were pretty curtains at the windows, and the Chinese servants brought a tray at breakfast time with hot buttered toast and tea. Best of all, they had the riverboat to themselves. There were Dr. Grosvenor, who had bought Gladys her sun helmet at Port Said, and his family; Mr. Helps, full of amusing anecdotes; Dr. Cundell, with whom Sister Gladys was to work; and Miss Weaver, whose curly hair had provoked censure from one of the Chinese passengers on their passage from Singapore. After dinner they went out on deck and experienced "the most heavenly moonlight night I have ever seen." The next day they reached Hankow and were driven in rickshaws to the mission compound.[24] The romance of the journey was over and the serious work for which she and others had traveled thousands of miles could now begin.

LEARNING THE LANGUAGE

In nearly all cases, the first of the newly arrived missionary's tasks was an intensive bout of language study. It was considered better to acquire the language of the area in which they were to work in situ and to be instructed by native speakers. Later on it became common practice to attend central institutions like the Darjeeling or Peking Language School, or to have a spell at the School of Oriental and African Studies (SOAS) before leaving Britain. Ronald and Gwyneth Still studied at the Peking Language School, although only for a term. The school catered not only for missionaries from many countries and denominations, but also for business people and others who came to live and work in China. According to the Stills, the students were a "jolly crowd," and there were extensive extracurricular activities.[25] For others, acquiring the language was a much less sociable experience. The CIM had its own language schools, one for men at Anking and one for women 200 miles away at Yangchow (Yangzhou). Hannah Davies described how language tuition occupied six hours a day, two hours of which were spent with a Chinese teacher. "The room is almost bare except for two tables, a form and a few chairs. Inside the room are two Chinese tutors, one at each table—untidy-looking men with sun-browned faces and shaven heads hidden under their black caps, from beneath which hang their long, black, pig tails; their clothes are well-padded and not over-clean; their finger nails are very long, and they dig them mercilessly into the books, leaving indelible marks. Opposite each teacher are two figures, who, in spite of all the Chinese garb, hair-dressing etc will persist in retaining an excessively 'foreign look.'"[26]

Many missionaries acquired their languages either on the mission station at which they worked or at a station in the same district. Hilda Johnson, who arrived in Calcutta in 1900, was sent almost immediately to a smaller, more rural station at Berhampur (Brahmapur), "in the midst of a simple Bengali life" where she was likely to become more proficient in the vernacular than in the hurly-burly of Calcutta—the capital of British India. She seems to have enjoyed the two years she spent here. She and fellow missionary Leila Robinson lived—together with several Bengali women teachers, Christian converts, and a number of orphans—in a large house, with porch and verandah, built for an army officer in the time of Robert Clive. The house, like other European-occupied houses, looked out onto the *maidan* (square or green) where "only Europeans or Indian gentlemen wearing European dress" were allowed. After six or seven hours of language study, Johnson took a break and cycled around the *maidan*. She also tried out her Bengali on the children in the mission school.[27] Some missionaries ended up having to acquire several languages. Isabella Plumb, sent to Poona (Pune) in 1882, spent five years learning and using Marathi. In 1887 the Church of Scotland decided to send her to Sialkot in the Punjab, where she was expected to learn three more vernaculars. We do not know how proficient she became, but in 1893 we learn of her success in passing "her second examination in Hindi and Hindustani and also an examination in Punjabi."[28]

Since success was regarded as critical, examinations proved a barrier for some missionaries. In his study of Society for the Propagation of the Gospel (SPG) women Jeffrey Cox notes the reason "too old to learn the language" being given as cause for dismissal.[29] Marjorie Rainey had nothing to fear from her second-year examinations held over two days in March 1918. She was faced by her senior colleague E. R. Hughes and two Chinese teachers. They examined her in character writing, in texts comprising Confucius' Analects and Matthew 1–13 in Chinese, on exercises from Baker's and the Republican Reader, in conversation, and in the delivery of an address. She obtained an average of 82.9 percent, her lowest mark being 77 percent on Matthew.[30] Gladys Minns, wrestling with Telegu at Medak in Hyderabad State, surprised herself and others by doing rather well in her language exams only five months after her arrival. She and a male colleague studied together, but since he was not allowed to stay at the all-women mission house he "made his home in the little church." For the written examination they both sat in the church, "he at the front and I at the back." They also journeyed on the same train to take their oral exam, but sat "in different parts of the train."[31] Complaints about the difficulty of the language were much more commonly voiced by those learning Chinese. Hannah Davies found the language "difficult, very difficult indeed."[32] Dr. Isabel Mitchell, who had left her drugs at the railway depot that she "might not be tempted to begin medical work before I had some grasp of the language," found that acquiring Chinese took all her energy. "Greek is no name for it! It is Chinese—and absolutely awful."[33] It is a moot point as to how well missionaries could speak fluently, or write well, in the vernacular. There was pressure on them to take up their duties as soon as possible, before they were truly proficient. Inevitably, there was a certain amount of learning on the job.

THE IMPORTANCE OF THE CHRISTIAN HOME

When asked what constituted her chief task in the mission, one wife commented, "I mind my missionary."[34] The entire domestic arrangements of the Baptist mission at Serampore in its early days rested in the capable hands of Hannah Marshman. She also kept the mission accounts. Mary Weitbrecht considered the position of a missionary wife essential, recalling that one zealous missionary had admitted to her that he "should have died long ago, if I had not been married." Not only should she take "judicious, prudent care" of her husband, timing meals to suit his convenience, but she should guard all members of the household against "the effects of climate, in the arrangements of the house, the accommodation, diet, and other particulars."[35] Timothy Richard, after nine years as a bachelor in China, felt "that I could do more effectively my work in this newly opened province (Shansi) if I were married."[36] He wrote home to his mother "I am very glad you have heard that I have a home at last." He had "been blessed with a very valuable wife. She is always at some work or other.... She is religious, good and of tender heart, learned, hard-working ... an unequalled help to me."[37]

Weitbrecht also saw that in attending diligently to the needs of her husband and household she was providing an example to "the native Christian women, which will influence them, more than direct exhortation."[38] Promoting the ideal of the harmonious Christian home with an industrious, pious wife and mother at its heart was a key element of 19th-century Protestant theory and practice, seen as greatly superior to the lifestyle of Roman Catholic and other celibate orders. Ralph Wardlaw Thompson, secretary of the LMS from 1881 to 1914, declared at the 1888 Missionary Conference that "one Christian mission home with a Christian wife does more to humanise, elevate and evangelise a race of people than twenty celibate men."[39] The expense of maintaining a family life on a European scale with the need for superior accommodation, increased living and travel costs, the expense of educating children, and so on, does not seem to have been a consideration in the early days. Criticism grew in the course of the 19th century, and in the 20th century, as did awareness of the contrast with "badly paid and badly housed" indigenous mission workers.[40]

The Protestant domestic construct of missionary, wife, and children proved difficult to sustain. In most cases missionaries observed the usual colonial practice of educating their children back in the homeland. Wives were placed in a dilemma. Should they remain on the mission field, minding their menfolk, or did their duty lie with the children? The expectation was that they should remain with their husband, perhaps accompanying their children to see them into the boarding schools that had been established for missionary children in Britain, before returning to the mission field. Baptist missionaries Timothy and Mary Richard were to experience many partings, not only from their children but also from each other. Timothy wrote to Mary in a low moment that he was "getting quite lonely and homesick without you. Others seem to have their homes, their wives and children with them while we are scattered and not to meet for several months."[41] The couple took their first furlough in Britain after their marriage in 1884. On their return they left their two elder daughters—one seven, the other six—at Walthamstow Hall School.[42] A letter written to the girls during the return voyage in October 1886 betrays their mother's anxious concern. In large, clear handwriting, she hopes that they will "remember all the good advice your dear father gave you about how you should behave to your teachers and playmates." They should ask for God's help in this and in doing their lessons well.[43] Many wives and mothers felt the loss of their children keenly. Gladys Bevan remembered how she was called over to spend some time with the wife of a medical missionary whose three daughters had all been sent off to school. She had "walked round and round the compound" with the grieving mother, desperately lonely without her daughters who "were *life* for her."[44]

HOMES FOR SINGLE WOMEN MISSIONARIES

Another departure from married domesticity was the arrival on the mission field of large numbers of young, unmarried women who, it was intended, should remain single, entirely dedicated to mission work. Practical arrangements had to be made, and swiftly, as to how and where they should be housed. An early solution, that they should have the protection of missionary families and form part of the household of a married male missionary, did not prove practicable. Not only did this give rise to domestic tension, but it also led to the suspicion among curious onlookers that a missionary had more than one wife! The answer in most cases was the erection of houses for lady missionaries, and by the early 1900s most mission compounds had such an establishment. To their surprise, some women were closely involved in the building process. "I had no idea," wrote one, "that missionaries had to draw out a plan of their own house, and estimate for bricks and timber."[45] In these homes, two or more women missionaries would live together for lengthy periods of service, since it was not thought suitable or desirable for a woman to be ever alone, that is, without another Western woman. Presumably this was for reasons of propriety, but the need for companionship seems to have been the prior concern. When Gladys Minns arrived in India in 1929, she was sent posthaste to rescue a woman missionary driven almost to breaking point by loneliness. "It was a lovely home and a boy looked after her every need but . . . Telegu did not come easily to her and no one else knew a word of English."[46] Interestingly, it does not seem to have been an issue that the woman in question had been living alone except for a male servant or boy. Jane Hunter comments that the unequal status between woman missionaries and servants guaranteed that "sexuality was not an issue."[47] But there must have been cases where matters were not so clear cut, especially if either party was young and attractive. And as Kenneth Ballhatchet points out, there was a presumption among British males in India that women were in permanent need of protection from "lascivious Indians."[48]

Successful living arrangements for single women were essential not only for the good of the mission, but also for the well-being of the individuals concerned. Yet it was asking a lot of women to live at very close quarters with a companion or companions, whom in most cases they had not chosen, in alien surroundings far from family and friends. The difficulties facing them seem to have been recognized. An SPG pamphlet warned would-be recruits that many "have confessed that their greatest trial has been in connection with life in a household of very earnest women of different temperaments."[49] Commission V reporting to the 1910 Mission Conference found that single women missionaries had "less privacy" than male missionaries, and that "uncongenial companionship" was not uncommon.[50]

Much depended on individual personalities and the willingness to make a successful life even in a remote outstation. Dr. Isabel Mitchell arrived at the market

Figure 3.1. Ladies' house in Amoy. House built for single women missionaries at Kulangsu Island, Fujian Province, China, c. 1895. (By permission of the United Reformed Church.)

town of Fakumen (Faku) in Manchuria in November 1905. The Irish Presbyterian mission there was small, consisting of Rev. Fred O'Neill, his wife Annie, their infant son, and one young woman, Sara M'Williams. She received a warm welcome. In a letter home, she told of "a very happy little family" who experienced "such a pleasant winter all together."[51] In February however the O'Neills departed on furlough, and she and Sara M'Williams were on their own. They evidently felt the loss, but kept busy: Sara teaching in the mission's schools and Isabel engaged in intensive language study. A decision as to their future would be made at the May meetings in Newchwang (Yingkou) of all the Irish Presbyterian missionaries in Manchuria. In the event, it was decided they would remain at Fakumen. The two enjoyed fraternizing with colleagues and singing "our dear old hymns and psalms once again." On the journey back, it was quite a wrench to put all that aside and to feel themselves "alone in the world again!" with no chance for many months of seeing "another English face!" Yet the knowledge that they "could now settle down and be at home" was reassuring, and Mitchell felt relaxed enough to enjoy the summer scenery on their way back. "The country was glorious . . . everything so tall and green, and all along the banks quantities of wild flowers that I had never seen, besides some familiar marigolds and meadowsweet." The next day she was so pleased to see "dear old Fakumen in the sunshine" and to tell "our people . . . that we were going to stay."[52]

They had to arrange to buy land and materials, engage labor, and start building a home for themselves, as well as a dispensary for Mitchell's medical work. In October 1907, she reported that the ladies' house was finished and that they had enjoyed their "first Sunday night in the new little grey house. It is so cosy."[53] The daughter of a manse, Isabel now saw herself as settled in one in Fakumen with her companion, referred to in her letters as Miss Mac or Sally, sometimes cast in playful make-believe as *husband.* Writing, once again on a Sunday, she expresses her pleasure at having her "*husband* home again. She was more than three weeks away (itinerating with Biblewomen), and glad indeed was I to see the little blue cart coming through the gate."[54] Mitchell's sense of humor came into its own in the garden too, over what she described as the "Lovers' walk." This greatly tickled the fancy of Sir Alexander Hosie, of the British Legation in Peking, who was traveling in the area and came to lunch with them. She gleefully recorded that "he thought we were remarkably happy all alone, and liked our house, and roared over the 'Lovers' walk.' " Isabel Mitchell, an extremely attractive youngish woman working in a remote location, had little chance of meeting a suitable marriage partner other than at infrequent missionary gatherings. But her strong vocational zeal as a female medical missionary makes it doubtful whether a marriage proposal would have diverted her. Nonetheless she continued to make metaphorical and amusing references to the married state as a way of contextualizing her situation. Thus when she had an old college friend to stay, it was "nice to have a wife," and when they went off together for a short holiday, it was "a honeymoon in Japan!" The basis of her existence in Fakumen was a companionable friendship, judiciously managed, with "Miss Mac." Returning from a month's holiday at Peitaiho (Beidaihe), a seaside resort in North China frequented by missionaries, she mentioned that others there had been amused to see how she and M'Williams "tried to keep away from each other, but we knew we should have the rest of the year in solitude and now we are enjoying each other tremendously."[55] Such wise accommodations to the reality of life in isolated locations are to be admired. It is however not surprising that they were seldom achieved.

LOVE AND FRIENDSHIP

In her study of American women missionaries in China, Jane Hunter considers it was "common for American women to develop deep friendships with those with whom they shared work and social rituals," and that this pattern was inevitable in the circumstances of missionary life in China. She likens life in the ladies' missionary home to that of a college dormitory, with its emotional closeness and opportunities for night-time confidences and even cuddles.[56] While there were close relationships among some of the women studied here, there does not seem to have been quite the physical and emotional closeness of the American sample, or, if it did arise, it was not so frequent. It could be that British women missionaries chose not to write about such feelings or contact in their letters home. In any case, fewer of them would have had the American college girls' experience of dormitory life to strengthen their notions of female bonding. There might well have been more reticence and more social distance in a British than in an American ladies' missionary home. In addition, in the early decades of the 20th century, there were some notions of danger about close relationships between women: not in reference to physical intimacy, about which there was much innocence then, but to obsessive and passionate friendships between one woman and another. Writing in 1929 about the situation of the unmarried woman, the physician, friend, and supporter of missions, Mary Scharlieb, advocated "wise and good friendships" between women that could allow for the development of both within the relationship. Such relationships should be "calm, deep and true, without the foam and fury of passion as generally understand."[57]

Several examples of enduring friendships can be instanced. One of the closest and most loving partnerships is revealed in the writings of Annie Buchan, an LMS missionary nurse in China. She had been escorted to Tilbury in February 1925 by her father and uncle. Here she met Margery Brameld, like her appointed to Siaochang (Xiaochang) in northern China. During the 20 years they spent in China, not always together, they were nonetheless looked on, despite a certain amount of teasing, as having a settled relationship in which each was the most important person in the other's life. They took holidays together, including one in the Canadian Rockies. When in 1942 Brameld fell terminally ill, Buchan demanded that she be allowed to look after her. She badgered the Japanese authorities in Tientsin, where she was based at the Mackenzie Memorial Hospital, into giving her a permit to join her friend at the LMS mission in Peking. Despite immense difficulties—all other missionaries had been interned, and security was an issue as was obtaining food—she remained devotedly with her friend, who suffered in the last months of her life from "paralysis of the brain and optical nerve and throat." When she died in February 1944, fellow missionaries testified to the loving and close relationship between the two, describing it as "a rare and very beautiful thing," and likening it to the biblical friendship of David and Jonathan.[58]

HOME SUPPORT

The assurance of the support of family and friends at home was of immeasurable importance to all women missionaries, but most particularly to those without families or loved ones on the mission field. The home link was most commonly represented by letters. As Georgina Smith wrote in 1894, "kind loving letters have cheered many a lonely hour."[59] It was a two-way process, frequently bedeviled by postal vagaries. Myfanwy Wood explained in an early letter home that

> My letters will come now quite regularly once a week—but you must not settle on any special day nor be worried if one is delayed. I learn that we have a mail bag of our own at Siaochang brought by hand (on a cart) up to Peking. Then from here it goes up to Vladivostock. Then by Russian mail to Berlin. Well you see there may be quite a lot of hitches on the way. So don't hold me responsible nor think anything has happened to me if my letter doesn't come when you expect it. I shall write every week & you must do the same. Just take it in turns & it won't be too much of a burden on you.

Postal delays were not infrequent. Wood wrote in March 1909, "I am sorry to think that my last two Peking letters will tell you how I longed for home news.... It is just splendid the way letters are all coming now (I've had one from Winnie Perry & Miss Scott & Mr Bailey as well as Mr C Kenward's & one from Gwen Rees besides my 'fat' home letter this week) & I feel quite easy about you all."[60]

Christmas was a doubly important time. There were special services in the churches, carol singing in the hospitals, and social gatherings. But it also brought a realization of how very far away home and loved ones were. Extra hopes were placed on the mail getting through. On Christmas Eve 1907, Isabel Mitchell wrote excitedly that her Christmas box had arrived that very day:

Yes, through all the snow and the storm, a nice bulky parcel for me, and one the very same size for Sally.... It was nearly dark, but I had two very sick patients to attend.... I tore down and saw them and saw that all was right in Hospital, and then I tore up again to the Manse, and with a big parcel under each arm, and with a sheaf of letters ... I arrived white with snow, no hair to speak of, and the remains of a hat, but Sally said I did a war dance round the dining-room table to think the parcels had come through after all.... I had not had a letter for so long ... and every one of these darlings sent me cards with their own writing on them.[61]

There was a constant cry from the mission field that letters did not arrive when they were most needed. Mitchell constantly read and reread old ones until the next batch got through. Their families, friends, and supporters at home equally needed to be reassured that they were safe and well, and that the work was going forward. Not all missionaries were as well-organized and regular in their letter writing as Myfanwy Wood who, busier and more laden with administrative responsibilities than most, wrote to her family once a week throughout 30 years of service.[62] A common excuse was that they were simply too busy. Hilda Johnson explained, in a letter from India:

I meant to have a quiet half-hour for writing, but interruptions keep coming—first a woman with a baby for medicine; the baby wouldn't take it from her, so she must needs bring it to me to be dosed; then two men from the Sunderbans bringing a child to school; then the pupil teachers for help with tomorrow's work; then a village woman wanting cotton-wool and a bit of flannel for a child with pneumonia then some of my babies [from the orphanage] with a longing for beads or something else to play with—all these since this letter began! The days are all like that from 6 in the morning till 9 at night. But I am ever so well and happy.[63]

MARRIAGE

The single women missionaries sent out in increasing numbers from the 1870s onward were of an age when in other circumstances they would have been getting married. As the LMS pamphlet put it, ladies should not "wait till the best years of life and strength are past" but apply for overseas mission work between the years of 21 and 28. Missions were thus sending out women who were young, unmarried, and of childbearing years to parts of the world where such women were in notably short supply. It is hardly surprising that quite a high percentage of them married, many of them within a few years of being appointed. For example, of the 230 single women appointed by the LMS during the period 1875–1914, no less than 34 percent married and had to resign. Myfanwy Wood, writing to a sister at home, deplored the fact that so many women sent out by the LMS have "sooner or later (mostly sooner) married.... I just cannot reconcile the satisfying of personal craving for happiness with the loss to the work. For when all is said and done, what a married woman can do does not amount to a quarter of that which a 'chiao shih' [unmarried teacher] can accomplish." She felt this put LMS women's work much behind that of American societies. "The American Congregationalists . . . have two ladies who have been out over forty years and several over twenty. They have done either women's or girls' work consecutively for the whole of that time. Imagine the difference in the LMS. Our senior single lady is Miss Livens who has been out six years!!!!!!!"[64]

Her views on the lack of commitment shown by many women missionaries were shared by the members of Commission V reporting to the World Missionary Conference in 1910, who noted "the frequent resignation of young women missionaries through marriage." They were quick to add that they were not attacking marriage as such, but were critical of those who sought marriage as a way out of a mistaken vocation, or were feeling a sense of failure, or were suffering because of unhappy relations in the mission house. Yet there are grounds for thinking that the male heads of the societies were by no means opposed to the young women marrying, particularly to fellow missionaries. And that was by and large the case. Just after arriving in India in 1929, Gladys Minns met Eric Bevan, an agricultural missionary in Hyderabad. Seven years later and completely out of the blue she got a letter from him proposing marriage. "We had never met otherwise and I just knew him as Mr Bevan who had a farm at Kamareddi. What a surprise. I laughed and went out in the garden and dug for a bit." Having talked it over with her chairman and prayed with him, she accepted Bevan's proposal.[65] Myfanwy Wood learnt that she was to receive a proposal of marriage from a fellow missionary in 1910, when she had been at work for less than two years. During a private conversation, Frank Hawkins, later LMS secretary, told her "I have reason to believe that the greatest gift in the world may be offered to you—love—and I want you not to reject it because of your work."[66] Her strong sense of dedication to "the cause of girls' education under the LMS in North China" led her to decline the offer. Women's associations and committees at home were not overjoyed to learn that recently appointed agents had received offers of marriage and wished to tender their resignations. Some took steps to fend off the danger. Amy Foster, wife of LMS missionary Arnold Foster, wrote to the secretary of the LMS Ladies' Committee to advise against sending single ladies to Canton for language study, on the grounds that they were more "likely to get married there than in Hong Kong. There are no batchelors [sic] in the latter place, while in Canton there are always young Wesleyans or American Presbyterians who have not yet married."[67]

On marriage, even to someone in the same society, women missionaries were required to resign from their posts. If they resigned within five years of taking up their appointment, they were expected to repay a proportion of the cost of their training, outfit, and passage. It was often contested by the individuals concerned, but most ladies' committees stood firm. This was not the only drawback to marriage. There was also the end to an independent income and a loss of status. In a piece entitled "An Old Friend with a New Name and a New Sphere," the former Lillie Ashburner, newly married to Rev. John Parker of the LMS mission to Mongolia, wrote of her dismay at seeing her name in "a list of those who have left the missionary service." She felt that missionary wives looked for "opportunities as great for serving the Master and our loved Society, in our present position ... as those we enjoyed as lady missionaries."[68] Not all married women missionaries found such opportunities, and often went through a period of painful adjustment. After marriage, Gladys Bevan found herself "crying and crying." She, who had been in charge of a training and boarding school, had now nothing to "give herself to."[69] Another wrote that it took her 10 years to reconcile herself to the loss of an "independent income" and the "freedom to act independently."[70]

HEALTH AND RECREATION

Missionaries were warned during the recruitment process that the "hot climates of India, China and Africa, etc are more-or-less trying to all Europeans; and the anxiety, fatigue and exposure that must necessarily be involved in the daily hard work of an earnest and energetic lady missionary cannot but prove a serious strain on physical health and strength."[71] Women were thought to be particularly suscep-tible to health breakdowns in tropical climates.[72] Not only were they considered constitutionally less able than men to bear the climatic conditions, but they were also less willing to break off from their work in order to take rest and recreation. A 1923 health manual urged the importance of taking some exercise every day, and the desirability especially for women of lying down "for at least half an hour in the middle of the day during the hot season." It was also feared that women would succumb more easily to mental stresses and strains in a difficult climate and alien surroundings, since they were more likely to be "anxious-minded," and "more given to tax their strength."[73]

The successful missionary possessed a strong store of physical energy, a sound constitution, and gave no hint of a nervous temperament or inclination to hys-teria. On beginning missionary work at the age of 40, Mary Ann Aldersey was advised to take great care of her health. She did so through regular exercise.

> The year round she was accustomed to walk on the wall at five in the morning . . . in wintertime she was preceded by a servant carrying a lantern. . . . In the summer . . . she would climb to the ninth storey of the lofty pagoda, and sit there through the long hours of the afternoon breath-ing in the wind that came from the sea.
>
> On taking her walks she would carry a bottle of spirits of hartshorn for headache and odours.[74]

As well as advice on medical and health matters, societies made more concrete provision. All missionaries were allowed furlough initially after seven years of ser-vice, and thereafter every four or five years. A furlough permitted a period of rest and recreation, and a renewal of family ties. It also enabled the missionary to re-port on and promote the work of her particular mission to auxiliary organizations around the country. After a couple of months' rest and recuperation, missionaries were expected to take part in a strenuous program, addressing meetings and con-ferences in a wide variety of places. In addition, they might find on their return to Britain that they were expected to shoulder family or domestic responsibilities, something Mary Scharlieb strongly deprecated. Women were "sent home to pre-pare for further service, not to wear themselves out by spending their strength on acting as nurse or parlour maid to family and friends."[75]

Usually, for a period of four or more weeks each year, missionaries took a vacation. This was a time to relinquish demanding responsibilities, recruit health in a beneficial environment, and immerse themselves in a familiar society, largely drawn from fellow missionaries. In India they repaired to one of the 80 or more hill stations in the very hottest weather of April and May, while in China they would be more likely to go to the seaside during August. Gwyneth Still describes the popular resort of Peitaiho in a letter home in August 1936. Staying there with her husband, Ronald, she found the "air so refreshing" and "there seems to be a sort of lovely cool breeze all the time." The sky was "a perfect clear blue and the sea the deepest of blues and the sand and grass so fresh and clean." The resort stretched for about 6 miles, with 600 or so well-spaced houses each with a view. The missionaries, "from all over China, some even from Hong Kong," were at one end, and the business community at the other, so that the holidaying community was very much an expatriate one.[76] No motorized vehicles were allowed, people got around on donkeys, bikes, and rickshaws. On arrival in July 1909, after a long, hot journey, Myfanwy Wood found she had "a six mile donkey ride" in front of her. She wrote home that she had "an awfully good animal but found the journey tiresome. There were no saddles—no roads—a track simply wound up and down, up and down through three ponds—one never knew which way to balance—still I stuck on—not going to be beaten by a donkey!! The view was exquisite (when I had time to look at it)."[77] There were very few Chinese shops, although Chinese peddlers came around the houses selling "fruit, cloth, embroidery, silk, cotton wool, flowers, etc.," and there were seasonal foreign shops. Picnics were a popular event, especially on the rocks, where cooks could find convenient places for their fires. The Stills also enjoyed the cinema, which was "just a put up thing for summer—no roof and matting walls—canvas seats." One evening they went to see "The Lives of a Bengal Lancer" and were looking forward to "David Copperfield" before the end of their holiday. They also enjoyed socializing with the wider missionary community, though Gwyneth found such exposure at first "overwhelming." At Chouts'un, their Baptist Missionary Society (BMS) station, on some days she only had her husband and her two servants to speak to. They both agreed that the experience had the healthy effect of blowing their "cobwebs" away.[78]

If Peitaiho was the holiday refuge for missionaries in North China, Kodaikanal in the Palni Hills served the same purpose for American and European missionaries in southern India. It had been founded in 1845 by American missionaries searching for a health resort high enough to be clear of malaria. The imperial gazetteer considered the climate to be "one of the best in India." It possessed other attractions. "The houses of the European residents are picturesquely grouped about a natural theatre of hills surrounding an artificial lake which has been constructed at the bottom of a beautiful little valley or on the cliff which overhangs the ghat road leading up from the low country."[79] It was a great favorite with missionaries of all denominations. They tended to dominate the place between April and June, outnumbering other Westerners, despite the uncomfortable and protracted journey up from the plains. Travelers would first alight at Kodaikanal Road on the Southern Indian Railway. From there, they normally went by *transit* (a covered wagon drawn by bullocks) to the Tope bungalow, a distance of 33 miles. The journey was usually made at night, when it was cooler, and took around seven hours. Visitors were urged not to linger at the bungalow, a malarious spot and where, according to a 1909 guide, the service was very inferior since the butler in charge was "not to be depended on." From here the rest of the ascent, about six hours, was "made in chairs or *doolies* [litters], or on wretched ponies, that have to be considerably assisted by shanks' mare." At the ninth milestone, it was possible to obtain some much needed sustenance, provided one had written beforehand "to Mr Tapp of the bakery at Kodaikanal … very welcome … at this stage of the journey, the eggs, butter, scones etc. being such a treat." The scenery made up for some of the journey's discomfort with its "clumps of feathery bamboo, flowering shrubs, and forest trees of all descriptions, creeping ferns and tree ferns, all growing in wild confusion … every turn … bringing changing views of forest and glen, hills and valleys … what a change, after the scorched up scenery of the arid Plains so lately left behind." One could also listen "to the weird song of the chair-bearers" or "be soothed and healed by the sound of water rippling through the ferns."[80] At the top, four roads met at Charing Cross and the traveler had arrived. There were no hotels; the usual practice was to rent a cottage (by 1909 there were more than 150). While golf, hunting, and fishing were popular pursuits with some, walking to the Silver Cascade or Bear Shola Falls and, if feeling more vigorous, climbing Mount Perumal were more usual recreations for missionary visitors.

Figure 3.2. A time of refreshing. A group of missionaries enjoying a rest at The Silver Cascade, Kodaikanal, South India. (MMS Collection at SOAS © Trustees for Methodist Church Purposes. Used with permission.)

BEYOND THE MISSION COMPOUND

Missionaries tended to form cliquey groups, segregating themselves even when traveling or on holiday. The development of large mission sites housing hospitals, schools, colleges, places of worship, and their families ensured that many spent most of their time within mission, hospital, or educational compounds, insulated from the world beyond. Like their fellow countrymen living overseas, most British missionaries failed to socialize across racial boundaries except on semiformal, rather constrained, occasions. Margaret Hunt, a young teacher arriving in Madras in the early 1930s, complained that when she was invited to missionary homes, she "did not meet … Indian colleagues except at tennis parties." She did not want to spend her "evenings eating English-style dinners and listening to 'mission' talk."[81]

In her study of Indian Christian women, Padma Anagol comments on the "insolence and arrogance" shown by Western women missionaries, particularly in the latter part of the 19th century.[82] This was at the height of the imperialist era, and the period when ill-prepared cohorts of young women—described contemporaneously as "the daughters of a ruling race"—began arriving in India eager to take education and Christianity to upper-caste women living in seclusion.[83] A paper on zenana missions by Sarah Joseph, herself India born, published in 1887, examines relations between the new breed of lady missionary and the existing mission workers, many of whom had been recruited in India. Its pages betray class divisions at work as well as those of race. Women recently arrived from Britain complained that they could not make friends with Eurasian coworkers because they could not discuss "books, or music, or any other subject" with them. Joseph deplored the "proud and overbearing" behavior of the British newcomers, contrasting them unfavorably with American women missionaries who were friendly and less prejudiced. An elderly Eurasian mission worker wrote to say how she felt undervalued by the new missionaries. One had told the mission's zenana pupils "that only she and the missionary's wife were Europeans, all the rest including myself were *desi log* [country-born] who were thought nothing of." The unhappy result as Joseph pointed out was that Eurasian agents then passed on to Indian Christian women the insults they themselves had received.[84]

A plea for friendship across racial divides made by the young Indian Christian V. S. Azariah, at the World Missionary Conference in 1910, resonated over the years in many missionary consciences. In a recent article Dana Robert claims that " 'world friendship' emerged as a mission focus after World War I" and instances a number of friendships formed by individuals across racial boundaries.[85] Equality in social interaction was particularly strong in international student circles. It was less easy to achieve in India where British missionaries, however reluctantly, were members of the ruling race. Marjorie Sykes had Indian friends at Cambridge in the 1920s. When in India, a teacher at an LMS school, she joined the Madras International Fellowship "devoted to subverting the social barriers that kept Europeans and Indians apart." Here she met C. Rajagopalachari and through him became acquainted with the ideas of Gandhi.[86] Margaret Hunt—a teacher at the Women's Christian College, Madras—shared accommodation with Indian colleagues, spent some of her leisure time at a Christian ashram, and noted the sympathies of friends like Nora Brockway, with the cause of Indian nationalism. Yet she confessed to never having felt at ease in Indian company.[87] It seems to have been much easier for Marjorie Rainey at an LMS school in Fujian Province. A colleague wrote that she had "a special gift of becoming the intimate of families, of knowing all the members even down to the cousins of the nth degree" and drawing around her "group after group of high school students."[88]

If some single women missionaries were able to form interracial friendships, it was more difficult for missionary wives, who at the larger missionary stations were expected to live and entertain in correct colonial style. In 1940 Eric and Gladys Bevan of the Methodist Missionary Society were posted to Medak in Hyderabad State, where they found themselves occupying a large bungalow necessitating an elaborate lifestyle and an array of servants. Finding the life intolerable, they requested permission to move to "small but comfortable living quarters at the end of a hostel down near Eric's gardens." Retaining one village boy as cook, the couple were still able to provide hospitality when it came to the annual gathering of Methodist district staff. They did their bit by inviting several visiting Indian ministers to eat with them. Curry was served, which their guests were free to eat with fingers, Indian style. Gladys Bevan felt that they had "broken lots of ice" on that occasion with the guests appreciating "our attempt to break away from the more strained and formal way of entertaining we had all endured."[89]

Women missionaries on itineration in the countryside often relished the opportunity, like Baptist Miriam Young, to "escape from the mission house and the mission compound; from the smelly, noisy streets of the city or town . . . leav[ing] behind organisations and institutions, conflicting claims and distracting duties,. . . to steep one's body and mind in the sights and sounds and smells of primitive country life." But these were short-lived interludes and, in the villages, an itinerant missionary was still a stranger, having "driven over in a foreign cart" and wearing "foreign clothes."[90] Young and a colleague tried the experiment of living in a Punjab village, along with an Indian woman and several children, "to model the externals of our daily life on those of our fellow villagers." They also hoped that "the fact of our foreign nationality might be overlooked." In this particular aim, they were not successful. At first exasperated, they later ruefully accepted that they simply could not escape the public gaze. Villagers stared "at our inexpert ways of managing the fire, grinding spices and kneading flour" and con-stantly visited unannounced. Nevertheless the experiment lasted three years and could not be wholly described as a failure.[91]

Missions were not slow to condemn and stigmatize single women missionar-ies who sought to push boundaries too far—particularly if, in so doing, they ven-tured into that totally prohibited area, intimacy with natives of the other sex. Mary Wallace arrived in Malacca in May 1829 with the aim of establishing girls' schools in association with the LMS. Fellow missionary Samuel Dyer was impressed by her efforts to set up schools for Chinese females "under most discouraging cir-cumstances" and wrote to tell the LMS so. He also approved of the way in which though "remarkably timid, modest and retiring ... among English people," she was "bold, undaunted and active among the natives."[92] However, circumstances deteriorated and Wallace was obliged to leave her labors in Malacca. By 1834 she was in Singapore attempting to run a small school based in a part of the mission house of American missionaries. It does not seem to have been a flourishing affair and the sole missionary in residence, Rev. Ira Tracy, had to help her out financially. He seems to have been perturbed about her in other ways and—taking advantage of the arrival of Peter Parker, a medically qualified missionary—paid her a visit early one morning in January 1835. The two decided she had become "deranged," an impression confirmed the next day when they found her "in a Chinese House barefooted, her hair loose, and in native dress." Thinking it "improper" for her to remain, they induced her to leave, putting her on a ship bound for Calcutta, which she left at Penang.[93] Eventually, a commission of lunacy was obtained and she was shipped home. Mary Wallace might very well have become insane; but the only evidence is the impression of two male missionaries and her being found in a Chinese house wearing native dress.

The case of Baptist missionary Bertha Scorseby is not dissimilar. She elected in 1915 to move out of the BMS compound at Bhiwani, about 70 miles from Delhi, to live and work among ordinary Indians. This seems to have been toler-ated by her colleagues. When, however, in the following January she attempted to marry a Christian *fakir,* they "resorted to kidnapping and drugging" her. Dr. Ellen Farrer reported that she had found her, after having been forcibly sepa-rated from Fakir Jitu, "lying on a *charpoi* in the yard guarded by the preachers and others, and still resisting everybody. She scratched me when I tried to get her to be reasonable, so I went home and fetched my boy, and administered a strong dose of morphine. Its comparatively slight effect rather confirms the idea that she is really mad now, and looks it too." Scoresby nevertheless succeeded in continuing a life of penurious independence, sharing this with another *fakir*, Mirza Amir Husain, whom she eventually married.[94] The most celebrated case of a single woman missionary marrying a foreign national had happened in China some years earlier. Anna Jakobsen, a pioneer CIM missionary, was appointed with Sofie Reuter to Huzhou in Shansi Province in 1886. In 1898 she announced her intention of marrying Cheng Xiuqi, a local Christian preacher, so that the two could carry out a joint mission. Most of her colleagues, and CIM senior staff including Hudson Taylor, were aghast. Such a transgression of interracial boundaries would bring disgrace on the mission. It also posed the threat that Jakobsen and Cheng Xiuqi might found and lead an indigenous Christian movement. Jakobsen resigned from the mission and following the marriage in 1898, which a few brave CIM colleagues attended, the pair commenced an independent mission in Xiangtan, Hunan Province, which continued until her death in 1911.[95]

Another relationship forged by a number of women missionaries was that with adopted children. Usually frowned on by mission authorities, partly for financial reasons, the adoption of one or more children was not uncommon. Looking after children orphaned by famine or other disasters, and also on occasion bought for cash, had been part of the missionary enterprise since the early 19th century. Such children were educated in mission orphanages and schools, with the intention of their forming part of the indigenous Christian community of the future. However, some women missionaries chose to make themselves personally responsible for the upkeep and education of one or more individual orphans, and usually went through some sort of adoptive process. According to Jane Hunter, most children adopted by missionaries in China did not become part of the missionary household, but were put to live with a local Christian family.[96] Not all followed this route. Sally Wolfe, a medical missionary at the Methodist Women's Hospital in Hankow between 1915 and 1951, adopted two children whose mother, a Bible woman, had died and a third orphaned by famine. She brought the three up in as close a family unit as she could manage, writing to her family at home about their doings and sayings in the most natural way. She appears to have maintained them entirely from her own resources, leaving them in China when she went on furlough so that the mission was not put to any additional expense. The undoubted bonds that existed between them ended abruptly in 1951 when all missionaries had to leave China. She was never to see or hear from her children again.[97] Marjorie Rainey virtually adopted Liao Hongying, a former pupil, arranging and part-funding her higher education in England. The two formed a close attachment. Letters survive among Hongying's papers, endorsed "from Mother," in which Rainey addresses Hongying as her "pearl-girl" and "my heart's own child." Rainey died shortly afterward and these letters have been lovingly preserved among Hongying's papers.[98]

Figure 3.3. Studio photograph of Marjorie Rainey, principal of Tingchow Girls' Primary School, and her former pupil Liao Hongying, c. 1927. The two formed a close bond, which only ended when Rainey died in 1931. (Bryan Papers, by permission of the SOAS Library.)

RETIREMENT FROM THE MISSION FIELD

Not many single women missionaries looked forward to retirement. Without families of their own and having, in many cases, outlived parents and siblings, there seemed no obvious place to which they could retire. After 30 or more years, overseas connections with Britain had, in many cases, become tenuous. Most retired missionaries, by the 20th century, were in receipt of pensions, but these were not generous and many struggled with high rents and heating bills. Some might have been more than happy to accept an offer of shared accommodation in a North Indian hill station, as did the fictional Barbara Batchelor in Paul Scott's *Raj Quartet*. Only late in the day were missionary retirement homes set up and then only by one or two societies. Lomas House in Worthing, for example, was founded in 1963, a retirement home for LMS missionaries. The home provided accommodation for up to 24 missionaries, mainly though not entirely women. Photographs in the LMS archive show an animated knitting group, residents working in the garden, as well as a group holding a singsong in the lounge.

For many, giving up the work to which they had dedicated their lives could be painful in the extreme. Edith Brown found the prospect of leaving the world she had created at the Ludhiana Women's Medical College and Memorial Hospital almost too unbearable to contemplate. The college was not only her office, but also her home—the chapel, students' residence, "the playground, *dhobie* [laundry] quarters, farmyard and dairy, servants' houses and kitchens," and, close by, the Memorial Hospital. Very reluctantly she agreed to retire as principal in 1941 at the age of 77, but remained firmly and very visibly at Ludhiana, as principal emeritus, causing no little difficulty to the new administration in doing so. Not until 1948 did she finally agree to leave the precious site of her life's work. She had been spending part of her time in Kashmir, where she had a houseboat named *Water Music,* moored at Srinagar, and this is where she spent her retirement years. She contrived to find fresh activities—running a Christian Reading Room and Bible correspondence course, making Gospel recordings in Kashmiri dialects, and engaging in agricultural experiments. But her heart remained at Ludhiana and, until her death at the age of 92, she made sure she returned each year for Founder's Day.[99] Others managed the transition into retirement more happily. Mary Ann Aldersey gave up her labors in Ningpo at the age of 64 and retired to McLaren Vale, Australia, where with her nieces she opened a school, known as Tsong Gyiaou (the Third Bridge). Feeling that she had been "a person of one idea in China" with "no time for flowers or butterflies," she enjoyed both in her new surroundings. She took her exercise by riding a donkey around the large grounds and in trying to grow the plants she had brought from China—her experiments in growing tea failed! She was more successful with her pupils; four girls at the school subsequently became missionaries, one of whom was her great niece Lois Cox.[100]

Figure 3.4. The reluctant retiree. A garlanded Dame Edith Brown photographed at her final retirement in 1948, Ludhiana, India. (Royal Free Archives Centre, Ludhiana Medical College Collection.)

NOTES

1. Lewis Johnson, *Hilda Johnson: A Memoir* (London: London Missionary Society, 1920), 18.

2. Mildred Cable and Francesca French, *Something Happened* (London: Hodder & Stoughton, 1933), 39.

3. Notebook containing autobiographical material, Plumb Papers, File 19.

4. Sunil Kumar Chatterjee, *Hannah Marshman, the First Woman Missionary in India* (Hoogly: S. Chatterjee, 1987), 36.

5. James H. Brown, *Frances Brockway:Memoirs* (London: Unwin Bros., 1905), 32–33.

6. Hannah Davies, *Among Hills and Valleys in Western China* (London: S.W. Partridge & Co., 1901), 16–17.

7. F.W.S. O'Neill, ed., *Dr Isabel Mitchell of Manchuria [Letters]* (London: J. Clarke & Co., [1917]), 35.

8. Sister Gladys Stephenson, *Diary of Journey out to China,* September 1915, MMS Special Series, Biographical, China.

9. A. Hodges, *Love's Victory: Memoirs of F Woodman, 1888–1895* (London: Marshall Bros., 1899), 84, 86.

10. Cable and French, *Something Happened,* 39.

11. Audrey Salters, *Bound with Love: Letters Home from China 1935–1945* (St. Andrews: Agequod, 2007), 3, 7, 10.

12. Stephenson, *Diary.*

13. Letter from J.A. Lloyd, *Our Sisters in Other Lands* 156 (January 1920): 5–6.

14. Brown, *Brockway,* 33.

15. Gladys M. Bevan, *Twenty Five Years in India* (Great Britain: Church in the Market Place Publications, 1993), 2.

16. Stephenson, *Diary.*

17. Brown, *Brockway,* 35–37.

18. Johnson, *Hilda Johnson,* 21.

19. Davies, *Among Hills,* 24.

20. Letter from Myfanwy Wood, December 31, 1908, Wood Letters.

21. Stephenson, *Diary.*

22. Dixon Hoste was the general director of the China Inland Mission.

23. Letter from Myra Carpenter, November 11, 1928, Carpenter Papers.

24. Stephenson, *Diary.*

25. Salters, *Bound with Love,* 20.

26. Davies, *Among Hills,* 33.

27. Johnson, *Hilda Johnson*, 22–25.

28. Extract of letter from Miss Scorgie, *News of Female Missions in Connection with the Church of Scotland* (April 1893): 73.

29. Jeffrey Cox, "Independent English Women in Delhi and Lahore," in *Religion and Irreligion in Victorian Society: Essays in Honor of R. K. Webb,* eds. R. W. Davis and R. J. Helmstadter (London: Routledge, 1992), 175.

30. Letter from E. R. Hughes, March 7, 1918, CWM/LMS, Fukien Incoming Letters, Box 12.

31. Bevan, *Twenty Five Years,* 3.

32. Davies, *Among Hills,* 34.

33. Extract of letter from Dr Isabel Mitchell, *Woman's Work. Zenana Mission Quarterly. Irish Presbyterian Church,* New Series 58 (April 1906): 219.

34. Quoted by Eugene Stock at an Anglican Missionary Conference in London in 1894. See Eugene Stock, *Beginnings in India* (London: Central Board of Missions and SPCK, 1917), Chapter 10, 1.

35. Mary Weitbrecht, *Female Missionaries in India: Letters from a Missionary Wife Abroad to a Friend in England* (London: James Nisbet & Co., 1843), 60.

36. Timothy Richard, *Forty-five Years in China: Reminiscences* (London: T. Fisher Unwin, 1916), 141.

37. Letter (trans) from Timothy Richard to his mother, July 3, 1879, Richard Papers.

38. Weitbrecht, *Female Missionaries,* 61.

39. James Johnston, ed., *Report of the Centenary Conference on the Protestant Missions of the World; Held in Exeter Hall, London, 1888* (London: J. Nisbet, 1888), 409.

40. C. F. Andrews, "Missions in India Today," *International Review of Missions* 22 (1933): 198.

41. Letter from Timothy Richard, July 26, 1895, BMS Archive, CH/4a.

42. A school for the sons of missionaries, Eltham College, was founded in 1842; the equivalent school for girls, Walthamstow Hall, a few years earlier in 1838.

43. Letter from Mary Richard, October 4, 1886, BMS Archive, CH/4a.

44. Bevan, *Twenty Five Years,* 17.

45. O'Neill, *Mitchell,* 61.

46. Bevan, *Twenty Five Years,* 2–3.

47. Jane Hunter, *The Gospel of Gentility, American Women Missionaries in Turn-of-the Century China* (New Haven, CT and London: Yale University Press, c. 1984), 211.

48. Kenneth Ballhatchet, *Race, Sex and Class under the Raj* (London: Weidenfeld and Nicolson, 1980), 5.

49. Quoted in Deborah Kirkwood, "Protestant Missionary Women: Wives and Spinsters," in *Women and Missions: Past and Present, Anthropological and Historical Perceptions*, ed. Fiona Bowie et al. (Providence, RI: Berg, 1993), 33–34.

50. World Missionary Conference (WMC), *Report of Commission V* (Edinburgh and London: Oliphant, Anderson & Ferrier, 1910), 149.

51. O'Neill, *Mitchell*, 40.

52. Extract of letter from Dr Isabel Mitchell, *Woman's Work. Zenana Mission Quarterly of the Irish Presbyterian Church* (April 1906): 283–284.

53. O'Neill, *Mitchell*, 91.

54. O'Neill, *Mitchell*, 91, 94.

55. O'Neill, *Mitchell*, 107–109.

56. Hunter, *Gospel of Gentility*, 75–77.

57. Dame Mary Scharlieb, *The Bachelor Woman and Her Problems* (London: Williams & Norgate, 1929), 53.

58. Annie Gray Buchan, *Adventure in Faith* (Peterhead: P. Scrogie, 1973), 31–35.

59. *Quarterly News of Woman's Work* (April 1894): 69–74.

60. Letters from Myfanwy Wood, January 12 and March 5, 1909, Wood Collection.

61. O'Neill, *Mitchell*, 97.

62. Over 1300 letters have survived and have been kept by the family.

63. Johnson, *Hilda Johnson*, 92–93.

64. Vanessa Wood, "Uninvited Guest, Myfanwy Wood, Welsh Missionary in China 1908–1951," *Symposium on Welsh Women in Christian Mission* (London: Institute of Commonwealth Studies, June 3, 1999).

65. Bevan, *Twenty Five Years*, 8.

66. Wood, "Uninvited Guest."

67. Letter from Amy Foster, December 17, 1887, CWM/LMS CP 1796–1899, Euphemia Barclay.

68. Lillie S. Ashburner, "An Old Friend with a New Name and in a New Sphere," *Quarterly News of Woman's Work* (1894–1895): 88–92.

69. Bevan, *Twenty Five Years*, 9.

70. *Mrs Mish: The Confessions of a Missionary's Wife* (London: Wyvern Books, 1963), 15.

71. *What Are the Qualifications for a Lady Missionary?* (1895), 5.

72. See also Georgina H. Endfield and David J. Nash, " 'Happy is the Bride the Rain Falls on': Climate, Health and 'the Woman Question' in Nineteenth-century Missionary Documentation," *Transactions Institute of British Geographers* 30 (2005): 368–386.

73. WMC, *Report of Commission V,* 149.

74. E. Aldersey White, comp., *A Woman Pioneer in China, the Life of Mary Ann Aldersey* (London: The Livingstone Press, 1932), 33–34.

75. Association of Medical Officers of Missionary Societies, *Health Instructions for Missionaries in the Tropics,* 3rd edition (London, 1923), 32.

76. Salters, *Bound with Love,* 67.

77. Letter from Myfanwy Wood, July 13, 1909, Wood Collection.

78. Salters, *Bound with Love,* 67–70.

79. Quoted in Nora Mitchell, *The Indian Hill-station: Kodaikanal* (Chicago: University of Chicago, 1972), 107.

80. E.M.M.L., *Guide to Kodaikanal and Its History* (Kodaikanal: Lillingstone, 1909), 9–22.

81. Book 1, Hunt Papers, Mss Eur F 241, 69.

82. Padma Anagol, "Indian Christian Women and Indigenous Feminism, c.1850–c.1920," in *Gender and Imperialism,* ed. Clare Midgley (Manchester and New York: Manchester University Press, 1998), 96.

83. Preface to Irene H. Barnes, *Behind the Pardah: The Story of CEZMS Work in India* (London: Marshall Bros., 1897), v.

84. S. Joseph, *Zenana Work, Its Importance, Defects and Hinderances. A Paper … with Criticisms, Replies and Additions* (Benares: Medical Hall Press, 1887).

85. Dana L. Robert, "Cross-Cultural Friendship in the Creation of Twentieth-Century World Christianity," *International Bulletin of Missionary Research* 35, no. 2 (2011): 100–107. See also Ruth Compton Brouwer, *Modern Women Modernizing Men* (Vancouver and Toronto: UBC Press, 2002), 23–26.

86. Geoffrey Carnall, "Marjorie Sykes 1905–1995," in *Oxford Dictionary of National Biography* (Oxford: OUP, 2004), 556–557.

87. Hunt, Book 1, 68. Nora Brockway was the founding principal of St. Christopher's Training College, attached to the WCC.

88. "In Remembrance: Eva Marjorie Rainey," *The Chinese Recorder* 62 (June 1931): 379.

89. Bevan, *Twenty Five Years,* 11–13.

90. Miriam Young, *Among the Women of the Punjab: A Camping Record* (London: Carey Press, 1916), 8–10.

91. Miriam Young, *Seen and Heard in a Punjab Village* (London: SCM Press, 1931), vii, 193–195.

92. Extract letter from Samuel Dyer, June 26, 1831, CWM/LMS, Malacca Incoming Correspondence, Box 3.

93. Letter from Rev. I. Tracy, February 27, 1835, CWM/LMS, Singapore Incoming Correspondence, Box 2.

94. Jeffrey Cox, *Imperial Fault Lines: Christianity and Colonial Power in India, 1818–1940* (Stanford, CA: Stanford University Press, 2002), 227–228.

95. John Gittings, "Lost Souls," *The Guardian*, August 2000. Earlier, the CIM had permitted George Parker, who married Shao Mianzi (known as Minnie) in 1880, to remain within the mission.

96. Hunter, *Gospel of Gentility*, 192–194.

97. Jane Wright, *She Left Her Heart in China: The Story of Dr Sally Wolfe Medical Missionary 1915–1951* (Groomsport: Cloverhill, 1999), 48, 50, 54, 70.

98. Bryan Papers, correspondence of Liao Hong Ying.

99. Maureen Clarke, "Postscript," in *Voice of a Stranger*, ed. Ruth Dibble (London: Ludhiana British Fellowship, 1968).

100. White, *A Woman Pioneer in China*, 73–74.

4

The Structure and Organization of Women's Missionary Work

The history of every religious and benevolent society in the civilised world shows the
female sex pre-eminent in numbers, zeal and helpfulness.[1]

A LADIES' MISSIONARY SOCIETY

"What female superintendents of schools have those societies sent out?" demanded the Hon. and Rev. Baptist Wriothesley Noel, a prominent evangelical
clergyman and an early supporter of women's missionary work: "Miss Newell is a solitary instance."[2] He had a point. Since male missionaries, and the
male boards that appointed them, conceived mission essentially as a task for
ordained men, any work carried out by women was necessarily separate, subsidiary, and unpaid, the proper territory of wives or other female relatives. By
the 1830s missionary societies such as the Church Missionary Society (CMS)
and the London Missionary Society (LMS) had been receiving and rejecting
applications from single women for a number of years. One of the earliest was
Miss J. J. Boogeard, from Holland, in 1799.[3] The LMS declined her application
on the grounds that it was "not within their plan to send out unmarried women
in their mission."[4] That society sent the "solitary instance," Maria Newell, as its

agent to Malacca in 1827, with the utmost reluctance. The first single woman missionary to go out to India, Mary Ann Cooke, went not as the agent of a missionary society but under the auspices of the British and Foreign School Society.[5] The case for "a ladies' society devoted to the object" seemed to be an absolute necessity.[6] So it was that on July 25, 1834 and in response to the timely appeal from David Abeel, the Society for Promoting Female Education in the East came into being. Although founded in an Anglican church, the new society was not tied to any particular denomination. It was to work in collaboration with all existing Protestant missions. Victorian Britain was to see a proliferation of ladies' associations, societies, and committees running charities directed to the welfare of women and children.[7] Few, however, had the global reach of the society created in Bedford Row.

Throughout the 65 years of its existence, the activities of the society were directed by women officers and committee members, with the support of women's local associations. By the mid 1890s they could claim that their area of operations "comprised not only India in its length and breadth, but China, Japan, the Straits, Mauritius, South and West Africa, the Levant and Persia."[8] But if its geographic range was great, the achievements of the society were modest. It did not set up schools of its own, but placed its agents in existing schools, usually belonging to one or other of the missionary societies. It also contributed to the founding and support of such schools, provided equipment and supplies, and supported the training of indigenous female teachers. In later years it expanded its work to include zenana visitation and medical work. But great numbers were not sent. At no time does the society seem to have had more than 40 agents in the field.

While a strong sense of vocation and self-sacrifice motivated most of its agents, they can also be regarded as early exemplars of professionally trained, salaried women.[9] The London Committee, on the other hand, consisted almost entirely of middle- and upper-class women of evangelical persuasion, blessed with sufficient leisure and dedication to conduct the society's business. The committee—comprising 24 members, the president and vice presidents, a treasurer, and two secretaries—met monthly. By today's standards, there were a surprising number of titled ladies in the upper echelons of the society. These conferred the necessary aristocratic patronage and establishment respectability, especially useful since the society's work was viewed askance in some quarters. In 1835, for example, the president was the Duchess of Gordon, and the vice presidents were the Marchioness of Cholmondeley, Lady Louisa Finch, Lady Georgiana Baillie, the Countess of Denbigh, Lady Barham, Lady Raffles, and Mrs. Sophia Vansittart. Less aristocratic members included Mary Ann Aldersey and the widow of Robert Morrison, as well as the Hon. Mrs. B. W. Noel and Mrs. Edward Suter, wives of the society's two leading male patrons.[10] The officeholders were envisaged as being honorary, but such was the volume of work that in 1841 a paid secretary, Rosamund Anne Webb, was appointed. The society's first treasurer was Mrs. John Bridges, but from 1838 onward, a male treasurer acted as custodian and investor of the society's funds, with a female subtreasurer sitting on the committee.[11] As was to be the case with other women's societies until late in the century, its public face was largely male. The platform party at annual meetings was dominated by male patrons and supporters. Publications promoting the work of the society in the early days were also chiefly the work of men, in particular Baptist W. Noel and the printer and publisher Edward Suter.

This situation changed in 1854 when the society's magazine the *Female Missionary Intelligencer* appeared. It was the chief responsibility of Secretary Rosamund Webb. Through the *Intelligencer,* published monthly, the London-based committee connected with its network of local associations, keeping them informed about committee activities and the progress of Female Education Society (FES) workers on the mission field. Webb also traveled the country recruiting agents and encouraging local fundraising. After a tour in 1856 by Webb and the ever-helpful Mary Weitbrecht, the society's income doubled. By 1872 it had reached 6,397 pounds sterling and 7,652 pounds in 1882, its highest recorded annual income.[12] Webb also marshaled what was in effect a domestic workforce through the activities of working parties of association members who met and worked at each other's houses. Garments produced by these working groups were astonishingly varied, including babies' and children's clothes, collars, cuffs, slippers, and household accessories, which were boxed and sent overseas to be sold to European families in Calcutta, Madras, Singapore, and elsewhere, to raise funds to spend on new schools, books, and equipment. The sums were not insignificant. Between 1834 and 1854 it was estimated that nearly a third of the society's income was raised by such means. In the pages of the *Intelligencer* and other society publications there appeared regularly precise and detailed instructions as to what goods would sell best and where, as well as the best means of packing and dispatching them.

Articles suitable for sale in Amoy (Xiamen), China, for example, were "Anti-Macassars and d'Oyleys, and Gentlemen's worked slippers; and for Ladies, Ribbons, pieces for dresses, straw bonnets, mittens and gloves,... Common Baby Linen; pinafores and aprons; large frocks and pinafores of strong, dark print, cotton handkerchiefs, coloured, Calico; needles, scissors, thimbles, thread and cotton."[13] A popular article for European homes in India were "ornamental bags, about the size of a finger, about half to three quarters of a yard in length, filled with shot, as weights for papers under a *punkah,* sometimes made to imitate snakes."[14]

THE IMPORTANCE OF LOCAL ASSOCIATIONS

The combination of a central committee with its officers, based in the metropolis, and an extensive network of supporting local associations throughout the country, as developed by the FES, was to be the pattern for most of the women's missionary organizations that followed. Throughout the 19th and into the 20th centuries, groups of women continued to meet regularly in working parties to make garments or accessories to be sold in support of missionary work, or given as prizes, and to hear news of the missions and missionaries they supported. Missionary publications were regularly distributed and sold. Personal gift boxes were given out and offerings collected. Associations would often have particular links with a mission station or missionary whose work they sponsored. The missionary so supported would be expected to write letters, which would be read at working parties or at local meetings, and published in missionary magazines and newsletters. Links with auxiliary groups would be strengthened during furloughs when missionaries were expected to undertake an extensive program of visits and meetings. Isabella Plumb's papers at the National Library of Scotland contain manuscripts of 26 talks given to home audiences during her lengthy period of missionary service. During one of her furloughs, she spoke at around 100 meetings.[15]

Goods produced by the working parties were not always acceptable, as an article in one of the missionary magazines made clear. What was required was "a supply of pretty, well-made and well-finished garments in the newest style and good material, which people will buy because they want," not "2 or 3 tea cosies of antiquated design."[16] Both adult and juvenile sewing parties were involved in another great task—the dressing of dolls—intended as prizes for attendance at mission girls' schools. The dolls, together with lengths of cloth, smart jackets, or work bags for older pupils, were presented at the annual prize day—the great show day of the year. Instructions were precise. They should not have flaxen hair, thought to depict old age but "dark hair," and they should be "dressed in bright-coloured clothes." They "should never be wax, for that melts in the hot climate."[17] The better-quality dolls would be set aside to be given to the upper-class pupils in the *zenanas*. A Poona (Pune) missionary visiting Calcutta wrote of being taken to a "great native house where ... I saw a number of dolls in a glass case. A merry set of women and children ... pointed them out ... as 'this you gave us two years ago; that before.' "[18] Such inducements to study and attendance were thought essential to the success of the work since, as one teacher admitted, "it is only the doll, or box, or workbag that keeps them steady and hopeful for any continued time."[19]

THE BIRTH OF THE CHURCH OF ENGLAND
ZENANA MISSIONARY SOCIETY

In the early 1850s a female missionary society more focused in scope than the FES—but bearing a considerable resemblance to it, indeed sharing some of the same members and supporters—was set up, initially as the London committee of a Calcutta-based group dedicated to the training of suitable Christian girls, mainly of mixed blood, to be teachers at the Calcutta Female Normal School. One of its founder members in London was Mary Jane, Lady Kinnaird. Mary Jane Hoare, the youngest daughter of a prominent banking family, was born in 1816. She early in life became part of the earnest, high-minded world of London evangelicals, choosing in 1837 to make her home with her maternal uncle, Baptist W. Noel. In 1843 she married the Hon. Arthur Kinnaird M.P. (later 10th Baron Kinnaird), a Scottish Presbyterian banker who shared her views. In the words of her biographer, "their manner of life from the outset indicated a sacred passion for doing good."[20] Their London home became a meeting place for similarly inclined Christian philanthropists and reformers, among them Lord Shaftesbury and Ellen Ranyard, founder of the Bible and Domestic Female Mission. When the London-based committee formally instituted itself as the Indian Female Normal School and Instruction Society (IFNS) in 1861, and began sending out zenana missionaries, its interdenominational nature was enshrined in a Statement of Fundamental Principle, drafted by Henry Venn, the revered secretary of the CMS.

The society's work in India would be "in co-operation with the Church Mission-ary and other orthodox Protestant Missions for the establishment and support of Normal and other schools."[21] Over the decades, however, and as nonconformist missionary societies set up their own women's auxiliaries, Anglican influence on the committee grew stronger while an overwhelming number of supporters in the country were drawn from the Church of England. In fact, according to Mary Weitbrecht, a committee member, most supporters were under the impression that IFNS was "a Church of England Society."[22]

Toward the end of the 1870s, the unity of the society was severely tested over the question of the continuance of its fundamental principle. Mary Kinnaird was determined to protect the society's interdenominational character, and for a num-ber of years had campaigned against growing Anglican dominance. In 1877 she attempted to reverse Anglican control of the society's local committees in India, a proposal she was forced to withdraw because of the threat of the mass resignation of Anglican members from the London Committee.[23] In December 1879 she pro-posed that Dr. J. Murray Mitchell of the Free Church of Scotland, a distinguished former missionary in India, become an officer of the society. She again found her-self opposed by Anglican committee members. Despite her efforts to maintain unity, an Anglican faction consisting of nine committee members and three of-ficeholders, a substantial number of supporters in the country, and many of its workers in India seceded in April 1880 to become the Church of England Zenana Missionary Society (CEZMS).[24] Despite this body blow, the IFNS continued, maintaining in the October issue of its magazine, the *Indian Female Evangelist,* that though it had "given up Madras and Lower Bengal" to the new society, it had kept "the whole of Bombay and Upper India," apart from Amritsar, as territory for its own agents that amounted to "nearly half the work." Later that year, there was a change of name to the Zenana Bible and Medical Mission (ZBMM), better reflect-ing, it was thought, both the society's changed circumstances and the nature of its work. Despite this brave stance, the society had suffered severely, losing practically overnight 287 of its local associations and three quarters of its income.[25] Out of this division the CEZMS emerged as Britain's largest and best-funded female missionary society. CEZMS income in 1882 was more than 23,000 pounds, far more than any other society spent on female missionary work.[26] By 1899 it was supported by 800 local associations and had 234 missionaries, to ZBMM's 89, working not only in India but also in China, Japan, and Ceylon (Sri Lanka).[27]

THE DEMISE OF THE FEMALE EDUCATION SOCIETY

In the last quarter of the 19th century, with so many other associations engaged in the work that it had pioneered, the FES found its support waning. While its dedicated secretary remained alive and active, the work continued; but following Webb's death in May 1899 the society dissolved itself with almost indecent haste. In July of that year the *Female Missionary Intelligencer* announced the decision to merge the society's work with other societies, the greater number of its agents transferring to the CMS, with which it had worked ever more closely. The demise of the FES, and the schism in the ranks of its sister society the IFNS, marked the end of an era when evangelical women were able to work harmoniously across denominational boundaries. In the late 19th century, the principle of interdenominationalism as an engine of female missionary enterprise was replaced by a spirit of competition, as one after the other the main denominational societies felt compelled to develop women's missionary work. Nor was the almost entirely female composition of FES governance followed by the female societies created in the second half of the century. These retained female-run committees but appointed a number of male-establishment figures to powerful executive positions. In the CEZMS, males supplied the roles of the clerical (general) secretary and financial secretary throughout its existence. The clerical secretary, an ordained clergyman, was considered *primus inter pares* conducting all correspondence concerning policy and principles, supervising the editorial department, and interviewing all missionaries and headquarters staff.[28] Enumerating several examples of men involved in the running of women's charities in late Victorian England, Frank Prochaska detects "a growing improvement in the business relations between men and women and the willingness on behalf of both sexes to work together in a benevolent cause."[29] This was not always the case in the missionary movement.

THE FORMATION OF LADIES' AUXILIARIES

Among Baptists, Congregationalists, Methodists, Presbyterians, and also the high-church Society for the Propagation of the Gospel (SPG), women's missionary work was developed through women's auxiliaries and committees, which mushroomed between 1858 and 1878. Women committee members and officers found themselves having to negotiate spheres of autonomy in a varied set of bureaucratic frameworks created by male clerics and mission officers with widely differing gender attitudes. Nevertheless, most women leaders were well able to cope, succeeding in establishing an authority and autonomy for women's work that male mission heads were content, for a while at least, to respect.

Calls for the founding of women's auxiliaries within the Methodist and Baptist missionary societies came not from the home base, but from missionary wives working in South Asia. Mary Twiddy at the age of 27 had gone out as an FES agent in 1841 to run a school at Jaffna in Ceylon (Sri Lanka). Asked to care for the son of a recently widowed Methodist missionary, she did so, marrying his father a year later. Moving to his station at Negapatam (Nagappattinam) in present-day Tamil Nadu, she opened a girls' school. From here she wrote in 1858 requesting support for a projected boarding school for Christian girls, and urging the need for a Methodist committee to be set up to send out young women teachers.[30] Her plea was approved by the General Committee, leading in December 1858 to the formation of "The Ladies' Committee for the Amelioration of the Condition of Women in Heathen Countries, Female Education, etc.," an auxiliary committee within the Wesleyan Methodist Missionary Society (WMMS). In the BMS, the start of zenana mission work among Hindu and Muslim women in North Eastern India, particularly Bengal, provided the impetus for the founding of a ladies' committee. Elizabeth Sale, the wife of a Baptist missionary, was among the first to visit and teach zenana women from the mid 1850s. Her example was followed by among others Marianne Lewis, also a missionary wife. When Lewis came with her husband to Britain on furlough in 1866, she campaigned effectively for Baptist women to sustain and develop the work. She gained both local support and central approval. As a result the "Ladies Association for the Support of Zenana Work and Bible Women in India, in Connection with the Baptist Missionary Society," later known as the Baptist Zenana Mission (BZM), was founded in 1867. In 1875, a ladies' committee was set up by the largely Congregationalist LMS, while the Women's Missionary Association (WMA) of the Presbyterian Church of England was formed in 1878.

Three of these four auxiliaries—Methodists, Baptists, and English Presbyterians—acquired a fair degree of autonomy within their parent organizations. The Wesleyan Methodist Ladies' Committee had several name changes. From 1877 it was known as the Ladies' Auxiliary for Female Education, becoming in 1900 the Women's Auxiliary.[31] In its early years the society was merely an agency responding to calls for women teachers from various parts of the Wesleyan Methodist mission field. Its organization at home "consisted almost entirely of sewing meetings" and "came in for a good deal of mild pleasantry."[32] All that changed with the arrival of Caroline Wiseman as its secretary in 1874. From a well-to-do Methodist family in Bath, Wiseman believed that she was "born to be Secretary of the Women's Auxiliary."[33] Capable, autocratic, energetic, and an effective organizer and speaker, she transformed the ladies' committee and its operations. Work overseas was developed to encompass first zenana and later medical work, and placed on a coordinated and planned footing. In its first 20 years, the ladies' committee had sent out only 34 missionaries. By her death in 1912, more than 200 women had been sent to Methodist mission fields. She carried out extensive tours of overseas stations and vigorously publicized the work at home, driving the annual income from around 2,000 to 22,000 pounds. During her time as secretary, the Women's Auxiliary was largely independent of the General Committee of the WMMS, and in 1916 it became a separate society.

Figure 4.1. Caroline Meta Wiseman, secretary of the Women's Auxiliary of the Wesleyan Methodist Missionary Society 1876–1912, in her *dhoolie* (covered litter) at Medak, Hyderabad State, with missionaries and *dhoolie* bearers, during an inspection tour, c. 1902–1903. (MMS Collection at SOAS © Trustees for Methodist Church Purposes. Used with permission.)

Despite close family ties with the parent society (the first secretary was Mrs. Amelia Angus, wife of a former secretary of the BMS), the BZM developed a considerable degree of independence. At its jubilee in 1917, it could claim to have been "from the first directed and controlled by a committee of women, and has collected and distributed its own funds." By 1920 it had sent out around 250 women to India and China.[34] When the WMA was formed by English Presbyterians in 1878, the wife of the convenor of the Foreign Missions Committee (FMC), Mrs. Hugh Matheson, was made the first president. As with Baptists and Methodists, the association developed no small degree of independence. However, friction between its agents and those of the FMC led to a plea in 1910 for "harmonious and fruitful co-operation both at home and abroad" and a proposal for "unification of the missionary work of the Church." This proposed unification provoked "deep-seated uneasiness in the ranks of the WMA," but the outbreak of World War I in any case brought a halt to all such plans.[35]

A different model for work by women emerged in the LMS. The ladies' committee, founded in 1875, was not allowed much independence. It did not appoint agents: it recommended them to the board. Committee members had little to do with the work of women in the field, who came under the direction of the district councils, and while members and supporters were allowed to raise funds for women's work, they had no control over expenditure. Despite these limitations the work flourished, and there were some signs in the 1880s that LMS women's work might achieve a degree of autonomy. Any such development was firmly nipped in the bud in 1891 "when the Board of Directors took the revolutionary step of inviting women to sit on the Board."[36] Despite the fact that they were heavily outnumbered—there were 33 out of a total membership of 295—this was a significant development, not emulated in other missionary societies for several decades. Thus the LMS led the way, among British missionary societies, in amalgamating women's work into the main work of the society, and in permitting at least some women a direct share in mission administration.

One of the earliest denominational societies to formally initiate female missionary work was the high-church SPG. The "Ladies' Association for the Promotion of Female Education among the Heathen in connection with the Missions of the Society for the Propagation of the Gospel" (SPG) was established in 1866, although it was not taken particularly seriously, or regarded sympathetically, in its early years. Changes came in 1902 with the arrival of Bishop H. H. Montgomery as SPG secretary, with the self-imposed task of modernizing the SPG and making it a worthy rival to the burgeoning CMS.[37] He wanted a more unified role for women's work within the SPG and obtained the important support of Louise Creighton, the widow of Bishop Mandell Creighton. Creighton, described as "the leading woman in the Church of England during the first two decades of the twentieth century," found her way onto many committees and commissions during her very active widowhood.[38] When at first she had "been put on the Women's Committee . . . [she] had regarded it in a somewhat perfunctory way . . . by degrees . . . [she] grew really interested." She now took a lead in discussions about the amalgamation of the association with the society, later acknowledging that she "was one of those who did much to get the work of men & women at SPG amalgamated, so that we should no longer work in separate compartments."[39] While the amalgamation agreement of 1903 ended the separate funding of the association, which now became the Committee for Women's Work, it provided a block grant for that work, the personnel and machinery of the association was retained, and local cooperation throughout the country was assured.[40] All told it was a significant advance for SPG women, since they had succeeded in keeping a degree of autonomy with secure funding while becoming an accepted part of the SPG. They were now far in advance of their sisters in Britain's largest and most successful missionary society, the CMS.

WALKING THE CORRIDORS WITH "EYES CAST DOWN"

The early 1880s found continuing reluctance within the leadership of the CMS to accept female applicants. Women desirous of going out to the field were still being referred to women's societies such as the FES and, from 1880, the CEZMS. Indeed Henry Wright, CMS secretary from 1872 to 1880, with other CMS committee members, had encouraged Anglicans on the IFNS committee to make the break and set up the new society. All the more reason then for CEZMS dismay when, in 1887, the CMS began to admit large numbers of single women missionaries. Nor was the CEZMS committee happy when the CMS suggested on a number of occasions that the two societies merge.[41] Members saw the danger of being swamped by the larger and more bureaucratic society, and of losing their identity as a women's mission for women. The strongest opposition to a merger came from CEZMS supporters in the country and from agents in the field who had grown used to running their own affairs. Despite frequent proposals for amalgamation, the two societies retained their separate identities, cooperating closely and fairly amicably until their final amalgamation in 1957.

By 1899 326 single women had been appointed to the CMS, more than to any other British missionary society.[42] As Peter Williams points out, female recruits outnumbered males in the last decade of the 19th century.[43] Yet for many decades women in the CMS had a lowlier place in the administration than in any other denominational society.[44] An attempt to give women seats on the General Committee in 1892 failed. The Women's Department, set up in 1895, had little influence and no authority. A handful of low-paid women held positions within the organization— including Georgina Gollock, editor of the CMS magazine, the *Gleaner*, and later secretary of the Women's Department; her sister Minna Gollock; and Edith Baring-Gould, who served the CMS for 54 years. The last describes how women working at CMS headquarters "would don their hats and gloves if they left their rooms [and] walk the corridors with their eyes cast down."[45] Steven Maughan attributes the great subordination of women in the CMS to a bureaucracy unwilling to offend conservative evangelicals.[46] As in the LMS after 1891, "CMS women ... [were] enjoined to support the whole of mission work, not just women's work."[47] Unlike LMS women, however, they had no share in executive authority. When they did meet, they could only do so in consultative committees obliged to send "advisory recommendations across to an executive body of men sitting in the next room."[48] Minna Gollock found the experience both stultifying and frustrating. "Few will ever know," she wrote, "what it has cost them to see ... their own best hopes and plans pass on to a sheet of paper into a men's board-room, to return altered and excised by those who have not first-hand knowledge, and who frequently do not call first-hand evidence to guide them in their adjudication."[49] In 1917 women, in modest numbers, were admitted to the General Committee, the decision-making body of the CMS—a move considered at the time bold and revolutionary.[50]

GENDERED CONFLICT ON THE MISSION FIELD

Single women initially received a warm welcome from their fellow missionaries on arrival in the field. They relieved many a wife of the almost impossible task of combining both a domestic and vocational role. Their arrival meant it was possible to implement long-cherished plans for opening purpose-built schools for girls, or developing women's evangelistic or medical work. With the arrival of large numbers of professionally and semi-professionally trained single women, however, difficulties began to arise. Many married women missionaries began to feel redundant to the missionary enterprise. There was displacement and consequent resentment.[51] When differences arose between their husbands and single women, wives invariably took their husbands' side rather than that of the newcomers, often to the surprise of the latter who had expected gender loyalty.

Men and women in the late 19th and early 20th centuries were simply unused to working alongside each other as colleagues. The problem was exacerbated by the sometimes isolated conditions in which they found themselves. Many men and not a few women agreed with the view urged at the 1888 Missionary Conference that "women's work in the foreign field must be careful to recognise the headship of man in ordering the affairs of the kingdom of God even though some women have displayed exceptional faculty for leadership and organisation."[52] The greatest cause of friction was the perceived independence of women's work. Men, dominant on overseas mission councils despite being outnumbered by women, were in no doubt as to their right to control all work in the field including that done by women. This was frequently disputed by single women missionaries, who looked to their home committees for direction rather than to the local councils. While the principle of women's work seems to have been readily accepted, the reality of how this would be organized and fitted into the work of the mission as a whole had not always been thought through. And where it had, as in the CMS with women missionaries always subject to the authority of male councils, it "led to resentment and heart-burning" and, at the very least, "did not make for harmonious working."[53] In other cases, women had been sent out by a women's auxiliary with very clear ideas, and instructions, on how they would develop evangelistic, educational, and medical projects among women and girls. On the ground, they found themselves having to deal with all-male district councils or boards, unsympathetic to or unfamiliar with this vision. It is not surprising that there were clashes.

In 1898 a crisis blew up among missionaries of the English Presbyterian Church in Tainan, Formosa (Taiwan). The FMC of the church had sent its first missionaries there more than 30 years earlier. The work had become sufficiently extensive by 1877 for missionaries to constitute themselves into the Tainan Mission Council, and meet monthly and keep minutes, copies of which were sent home to the FMC.

Eight years later, the English Presbyterian WMA sent two of its agents to develop the work, begun by the resident wives, among local women and girls. They were Joan Stuart and Annie Butler, who were to work hand in glove in a partnership that lasted for 33 years. The society's historian Edward Band attributed the "strong hand" in their partnership to Stuart with her "most virile personality," and the "velvet glove" to Butler, who "possessed a gentle and more winsome nature."[54] In 1888 they were joined by Margaret Barnett. Work settled down to a comfortable rhythm, the three taking it in turns to supervise a school for girls, the first to be built in southern Formosa, to itinerate among local women and to teach hospital patients. They trained as midwives, and in 1895 opened a training home for Bible women.

Figure 4.2. Tainan Girls' School, Old Girls' Association Reunion, April 1919. An inset photograph of Joan Stuart hovers over the group; she had retired the year before. Her former colleagues Annie Butler and Margaret Barnett are in the center of the front row. (By permission of the United Reformed Church.)

Rule III of the English Presbyterian Mission laid down how women missionaries were to relate to local missionary structures. "WMA agents," it stated, "should be under the supervision of the Mission Councils" of the various stations. They were "to meet separately for discussing and maturing plans which were afterwards to be submitted to the Council for approval." By the second half of the 1890s, there had been some modification of this rule, interpreted by WMA agents to mean that they could pursue their customary work without reference to the local mission council, but would bring to their attention "any extraordinary and special matter."[55] An 11-page letter written in September 1898 to the three single ladies of the mission by Rev. William Campbell, on behalf of the Tainan Mission Council, made clear that the council could no longer acquiesce in this interpretation.

The letter set out what amounted to charges of misdoings over a six-year period by the three single women. The council had been particularly vexed by "Misses Stuart and Butler" having left the mission compound for a period, moving out of "the bungalow we put up . . . at such an expense of money . . . to live among the Chinese in the City, and doing so without any consultation with their colleagues." Another grievance was that some local preachers had complained that their daughters had been refused admission to the girls' school because there were no places, despite some of the pupils having been there "for seven or eight years, thus preventing the benefits of the school from circulating throughout the church." There were further objections to Stuart and Butler, both of whom had midwifery certificates, carrying out maternity work and, also, to the construction of a Bible women's school without notifying the council. It was for them and not the women to undertake "the oftentimes troublesome task of acquiring mission property, of superintending external building operations or of carrying on prolonged negotiations with native officials." In conclusion they rebutted the looser interpretation that had been placed on Rule III, and asserted that they alone exercised authority in the mission field. They could not "regard any work done in this field as lying outside our cognisance; and, therefore, while not asking that every detail of every department be necessarily brought before us for approval, we feel that it is competent for us and incumbent upon us, to look into any matter, ordinary or extraordinary, which is having an influence, detrimental or otherwise, upon our general work."[56]

The women's reply was brief but firm. They reiterated their view that they had been merely carrying on their "ordinary" work, that is, "the teaching of women and girls and ways by which we can bring them under the power of the Gospel." They saw no reason why such work should be referred to the council. Their supervisory authority was the WMA committee in London and not the mission council on which, in any case, they were unrepresented. On receipt of this reply, the council decided to refer the whole matter to their home committee, the FMC and its secretary, Rev. William Dale.

Dale took time to respond. He asked advice from the secretary of the LMS, who admitted that "the difficulties of which you speak are familiar to us also. Such friction is I fear much too common." He waited to hear from Rev. Alex Connell, the convener of the FMC, who visited the missionaries in Formosa in January 1899 and discussed the matter with members of his committee and that of the WMA. A possible solution, which the LMS had already adopted, was to invite the single women missionaries to sit on the mission council, at least when discussions of their work were involved. This was the advice proffered by George Cousins of the LMS, but it seems to have been a step too far for the council in Formosa. As Elizabeth Mathew, WMA secretary, commented, "Not every Disciple has taken in the New Testament teaching that 'male and female are all one in Christ Jesus.'" She feared that he would have "great trouble" with the "gentlemen missionaries" if he went ahead with his proposal "to give the ladies a seat on the Mission Council."[57] He took her advice. English Presbyterian male and female missionaries were to meet regularly, but separately, and send each other copies of their respective meetings. It was to be several decades before they sat together as equal members in joint mission councils.

"PART OF A WHOLE" OR "WHOLE OF A PART"—THE DILEMMA FOR WOMEN MISSIONARIES IN THE 20TH CENTURY

Despite skepticism in some quarters, the concept of women's work for women with its supporting structures of women's societies and auxiliaries, had by the early years of the 20th century been an accepted part of mission strategy and practice for more than 50 years. Notions of offering sisterly aid to the benighted women of the East had propelled many to volunteer for missionary service overseas, and it continued to be a powerful and unifying cause for the prayers and money-raising efforts of women at home. The significance of the work had been lauded in mission literature and acknowledged at assemblies and conferences, notably at the international conferences held at London in 1888 and New York in 1900. Both these gatherings were well attended by women, and due emphasis given to the importance of their work: "this great feature of modern Christianity; the noble mission of women to women."[58] Male speakers predominated in the formal sessions at the earlier London conference, but a separate women's meeting—attended by North American and British women missionaries—initiated a World's Missionary Committee of Christian Women as a channel of communication between the women of the different societies. The lead in this development was taken by the Americans, the confident products of their independent women's missionary movement, and their vigor and boldness startled and impressed British delegates. One observer was "struck with their energy, and inclined to think they excelled us in systematic methods of work, as they certainly did in the freshness and point of their illustrations."[59] Women, almost entirely from North America, were even more in evidence at the Ecumenical Missionary Conference held in New York in 1900, when "they took part in the discussions, and read papers, besides holding ten sectional meetings on the various phases of woman's work. The crowds that thronged the churches where these meetings were held were so great that at some of them it was found necessary to lock the doors, while an immense number were turned away.... The enthusiasm was contagious, and as one delegate observed: 'If any man had had lurking in his heart any objections to woman's work, they must melt away before the impressive demonstration of these woman's meetings.' "[60]

However, when in 1908 plans were drawn up at Oxford for a third international missionary conference to meet at Edinburgh two years later, the all-male planning committee decided against including separate sessions on women's work. The 1910 conference was not to be "an inspirational jamboree for enthusiasts," but a serious gathering where experts would "subject the plans and methods of the whole missionary enterprise to searching investigation."[61] No line would be drawn "between work for men and work for women." Women were to be invited to join the eight preparatory commissions that would each examine and report on an area of concern. Their representation on the eight commissions was far from generous. They sat on six out of the eight and, of those, only two had more than two women as members.[62] Commission VI, charged with investigating the home structures of missions, was asked specifically to identify the difficulties arising from the existence of separate women's boards.[63] Yet of its 21 members, only 2 were women: Caroline Whyte, who had been secretary of the short-lived LMS Ladies' Committee, was one and Helen Barrett Montgomery, a leading figure in the American women's missionary movement, was the other. In its report the commission paid somewhat patronizing credit to women's organizations for zealous activity in their "systematic collection of small sums of money," for their conferences, prayer meetings, and working meetings. It also frankly acknowledged that in some churches "the only missionary interest discernible is that engendered and kept alive by devout women." Nevertheless, the commission found the relationship between women's boards and general church societies to be problematic. Their solution was that women's work should be integrated with that of "the general or parent or denominational society."[64] It is unlikely in the extreme that Montgomery, that great champion of women's missionary work, agreed to this recommendation, but, as Brian Stanley points out, her many commitments meant that she attended few if any of the commission's North American meetings.[65] The recommendation stood in the final version of the report without featuring in the main list of its conclusions and recommendations. Tactfully too, the commission left to each denomination the responsibility of deciding when the time was ripe for amalgamation.

While the conference proceedings maintained what Minna Gollock referred to as a "prudent silence" on the topic, a number of missionary organizations in both Britain and America moved toward the unification of missionary work in the years that followed, despite the opposition of members and supporters of women's societies and auxiliaries.[66] Women administrators saw only too clearly the loss of independence and of opportunities for leadership, as well as the likely falling off of funds that would ensue. It is hard not to see, underlying this change of direction, disquiet at the extent and success of women's efforts. In the words of John R. Mott, one of the most influential contemporary figures in the mission movement, there was "an impression in the minds of many that the missionary movement is largely a women's undertaking."[67] Envy of the extremely successful financial management of women's auxiliaries and societies was another factor. The healthy state of women's mission finances had been brought about through an effective combination of generous funding from committed supporters together with low running costs. Female missionaries were cheaper to employ and a sizable number were honorary. All this provoked resentment and concern that general missionary work was being financially jeopardized through the diversion of funds to less important goals. Many mission administrators and not a few male missionaries believed women's efforts in education, medicine, and evangelistic and welfare work among indigenous women to be ancillary to the major task of creating and nurturing new church structures in the mission field—tasks from which women were to a large measure excluded because of the ecclesiastical restrictions on their role within the church.[68]

But the shift toward unity came also and perhaps more decisively from progressive elements in the movement who wanted to believe that the work had passed beyond its old divisions. Individuals such as Minna Gollock, who with her sister Georgina had graced the platform of the Keswick Conventions in the 1880s and 1890s and ingested its universalism, accused separate women's organizations of operating in "unsuspected isolation at a time when fresh light from God is streaming on the essential unity of humanity." There were disadvantages, she thought, "in being the whole of a part" and not "part of the whole."[69] Within the ecumenical youth movements of the late 19th and early 20th centuries, which held sway in modernizing missionary circles, men and women could work alongside each other without, it was claimed, the antagonism of earlier generations.[70] The American Student Volunteer Movement had been founded in 1888, and its British equivalent, the Student Volunteer Missionary Union, followed in 1892.[71] The volunteer movements were closely linked to the Student Christian Movement in colleges and universities, founded in 1889, and its international arm the World Student Christian Federation, founded in 1895. This student involvement in mission has been seen as "the chief source of fresh ideas and enthusiasm" and enormously significant for both the British and the international missionary movements.[72] Products of the student movement, such as John R. Mott and J. H. Oldham, played a decisive role in the planning, proceedings, and aftermath of the World Missionary Conference of 1910.[73]

The turn of the century also saw the birth of the new woman, in rebellion against the restraints of the traditional social order, as well as the rise of the women's suffrage movement. Although their impact might have been less among British missionary women who saw Christianity as promoting rather than retarding women's advancement, there was nonetheless a realization that much of the

organizational structure of Christianity, including that of the missionary movement, was inherently patriarchal.[74] Commenting at the Pan Anglican Congress in
1908 on the lowly status of women in Anglican mission administration, Louise
Creighton asked, "Are the women not fitted or are the men unwilling to admit
them to an equal share in the government?"[75] An article in the *International Review
of Missions*, summing up a Conference of British Missionary Societies' report on
the role of women in mission administration, was critical of those women who
preferred to be the whole of a part rather than part of a whole, but censured societies that, while claiming to be doing "a general work for men and women," did not
promote the working of men and women "side by side in administration at home
and abroad." Missionary societies engaged in building Christian churches and
communities overseas needed to display "the Christian ideal of mutual helpfulness and mutual dependence" between the sexes:

> It seems only good that the natives should see the Christian women mis-
> sionaries not segregated, not treated as if they must by reason of sex be
> kept out of authority and responsibility, always subordinate, even the
> wisest and ablest, to the most callow and tactless young man; but treated
> by fellow-missionaries as honoured and trusted fellow-workers, fellow-
> thinkers.... The women cannot give their best, either in example or pre-
> cept, till this opportunity is afforded them.[76]

"A SOMEWHAT UNCERTAIN PLACE
IN JOINT ADMINISTRATION"

During the course of the 20th century the women's independent societies and
auxiliaries either merged with their parent societies or ceased to exist. Among the
last to disappear was the CEZMS, which finally merged with the CMS in 1957. Its
sister society, the ZBMM, began in 1952—its centenary year—to send out male as
well as female agents. Little has been written about the roles and responsibilities
of women missionaries during the 1920s, 1930s, and beyond. Even so it is clear
that with the demise of the women's societies and auxiliaries, women occupied
for a number of years the "somewhat uncertain place in joint administration" predicted by Minna Gollock in 1912. There continued to be a sizable gap between the
rhetoric of full and equal cooperation between the sexes and the degree of balance

achieved. As one female administrator observed, the "way of co-operation is a more difficult road to tread for many, perhaps most, men and women than the ways of separation." Some men, she thought, were simply unable to work on "a basis of equality with women," while women for their part could be guilty of "sex-antagonism."[77] The general missionary societies were slow to involve women in the top levels of administration. One of the first to do so was the LMS, which in 1920 appointed Mrs. I. Parker Crane as Joint Home Secretary of the entire society. It was not until more than 20 years later that the CMS included its woman secretary in its "group of Secretaries that were in effect the Society's equivalent of a board of directors."[78] Several women succeeded in carving out a role for themselves in the various structures set up in the wake of the Edinburgh Conference. Betty Gibson joined the office staff of the Conference Continuation Committee in 1916, becoming assistant secretary of the International Missionary Council (IMC) in 1925. Georgina Gollock became associate editor of the *International Review of Missions* in 1920 and its coeditor in 1921, as well as taking on the role of secretary of the Board of Study for the Preparation of Missionaries. Both women served very much at first as assistants to J. H.Oldham, who had founded the journal in 1912 and was the first secretary of the IMC. It was said of Oldham that he sometimes found it difficult to remember that "half the people in the world are women." Nonetheless, as Ruth Compton Brouwer remarks, he and others worked with female colleagues in collegial if not egalitarian fashion.[79]

Not all societies were happy with the ecumenical and liberalizing developments of the international missionary movement in the interwar period, and persisted in giving women little role in mission administration. Within the conservatively evangelical China Inland Mission (CIM), it looked for a time in the early 1920s as if women missionaries would gain a place on the China Council. But when the home councils in London, the United States, and Australia were consulted, only London approved and it was decided not to "proceed in this matter at the present time." A wider consultation in 1928 found that a majority of "lady workers, both in the homeland and in China" did not favor the representation of women on the China committee, a verdict that meant that the issue could safely be laid to rest.[80] It was not until 2001 that the Overseas Missionary Fellowship, the successor body to the CIM, opened its boardroom to women. Even that decision was not unanimous, dissenters adhering to the view that "the biblical teaching on male headship implies that leadership should be limited to men."[81]

CONCLUSION

From the start, women were a life-giving source of home support and funding not just for women's work, but for the entire overseas missionary enterprise. The concept of women's work for women was the chief driving force for women missionaries in the field, members of central committees at home, and members of local associations and auxiliaries who funded and supported so much of the work. It was a strategy derived from the prevailing notions of separate spheres, which governed gender relations both at home and overseas until, in the early 20th century, a new generation of ecumenically minded modernizers moved to breach the gender divide. While the movement threw up some strong individual women such as Louise Creighton, the Gollock sisters, Mary Jane Kinnaird, and Caroline Wiseman, British women leaders did not display such strong feminist convictions as did North American leaders such as Lucy W. Peabody and Helen Barrett Montgomery. Nor did they embrace the principle of women's work for women so tenaciously. Kinnaird operated inside a mixed-gender executive and committee, and Creighton and the Gollock sisters welcomed the unifying ideas of the modernizers and the move toward shared mission administration. Rank and file supporters were by and large unmoved by arguments in favor of gender equality. At a 1912 conference on the issue, Jane Craig, secretary of the English Presbyterian WMA, pointed out the difficulties of bringing "the women in the Churches to see that this closer co-operation would be a good thing," while forces of conservatism within the CMS could claim that there was no grassroots support for giving women greater authority.[82] In the interwar period, there was a marked waning of support and interest for the cause of overseas missionary work. Some saw this as directly resulting from the ending of separate spheres and of women's efforts specifically directed toward the spiritual and material advancement of women in the non-Western world.[83]

NOTES

1. Temperance campaigner Clara Lucas Balfour quoted in Susan Thorne, *Congregational Missions and the Making of an Imperial Culture in Nineteenth-century England* (Stanford, CA: Stanford University Press, 1999), 89.

2. "Appeal of the Hon. and Rev. B. W. Noel," Appendix B, *History of the Society for Promoting Female Education in the East* (London: Edward Suter, 1847), 272.

3. From 1819, the CMS exceptionally employed a few single women school teachers in its Sierra Leone Mission. Eugene Stock, *The History of the Church Missionary Society: Its Environment, its Men and its Work* (London: Church Missionary Society, 1899–1916), 3, 367.

4. Minutes of the LMS Examination Committee quoted in "A Women's Number," *Chronicle of the London Missionary Society* (January 1931): 6.

5. Letter from M.A. Aldersey to Rev. H. Townley, January 25, 1831, CWM/LMS, Malacca Incoming Correspondence, Box 3.

6. The Hon. and Rev. B.W. Noel, "Appeal," 272.

7. Frank Prochaska, *Women and Philanthropy in Nineteenth-century England* (Oxford: Clarendon Press, 1980), 32.

8. Society for Promoting Female Education in China, India and the East, *60th Report for the Year Ending January 1st 1895*, 2.

9. Clare Midgley, "Can Women Be Missionaries? Imperial Philanthropy, Female Agency and Feminism," in *Feminism and Empire*, ed. Clare Midgley (London and New York: Routledge, 2007), 97–98.

10. Society for Promoting Female Education in China, India and the East, December 1835.

11. Margaret Donaldson, "'The Cultivation of the Heart and the Moulding of the Will...' the Missionary Contribution of the Society for Promoting Female Education in China, India and the East," *Studies in Church History, Vol. 27, Women in the Church*, eds. W.J. Shiels and Diana Wood (Oxford: Basil Blackwell, 1990), 431.

12. Donaldson, "The Cultivation of the Heart," 432.

13. *Female Missionary Intelligencer* 1 (1854): 13.

14. The Hon. and Rev. B.W. Noel, "Appeal," 287–88.

15. Hannah Adcock, "The Indomitable Miss Plumb," *Edinburgh Review: Calcutta Connects* 119 (2007): 66.

16. *India's Women* 13 (October 1893): 465.

17. Hilda M. Johnson, *The Dolls who Travelled* (London: London Missionary Society, 1908), 8.

18. "Notes of Miss Bernard's Visit to Calcutta," *News of Female Missions in Connection with the Church of Scotland*, New Series, no. 6 (April 1877): 67.

19. "Miss Pigot's Report," *News of Female Missions in Connection with the Church of Scotland*, New Series, no 7 (July 1877): 89.

20. Donald Fraser, *Mary Jane Kinnaird [A Biography]* (London: Nisbet & Co., 1890), 29.

21. Fraser, *Mary Jane Kinnaird*, 114.

22. Quoted in Church of England Zenana Missionary Society, *Jubilee Souvenir 1880–1930* (London: Church of England Zenana Missionary Society, 1930), 9.

23. Steven Maughan, "Regions Beyond and the National Church: The Foreign Missions of the Church of England in the High Imperial Era, 1870–1914" (Ph.D. diss., Harvard University, Cambridge, MA, 1995), 291–292.

24. "Narrative of Events Connected with the Recent Secession" *The Indian Female Evangelist* V no. 36 (1880): 289–290.

25. J.C. Pollock, *Shadows Fall Apart. The Story of the Zenana Bible and Medical Mission* (London: Hodder and Stoughton, 1858), 54 and Rosemary Keen, "Introduction to the Catalogue of the Papers of the Church of England Zenana Missionary Society," *Adam Matthew Publications* (1987), http://www.ampltd.co.uk/digital_guides/cms.

26. Harriet Warner Ellis, *Our Eastern Sisters and Their Missionary Helpers* (London: Religious Tract Society, 1883), xv.

27. Maughan, "Regions Beyond," 364.

28. Keen, "Introduction."

29. Prochaska, *Women*, 31–32.

30. See John Pritchard, "Women's Work: Mary Batchelor to Muriel Stennett," in *Angels and Impudent Women: Women in Methodism*, ed. Norma Virgoe (Loughborough: Teamprint, 2007), 147–166.

31. The 1890s saw a trend to drop Ladies' from the names of associations and auxiliaries in favor of the more inclusive Women'.

32. Anna Hellier, *Workers Together: The Story of the Women's Auxiliary of the Wesleyan Methodist Missionary Society* (London: Cargate Press, 1931), 52.

33. Lena Tyack, *Caroline Meta Wiseman* (London: C. H. Kelly, 1915), 13.

34. Laura Lauer, "Opportunities for Baptist Women and the 'Problem' of the Baptist Zenana Mission, 1867–1913," in *Women, Religion, and Feminism in Britain, 1750–1900*, ed. Sue Morgan (Basingstoke: Palgrave Macmillan, 2002), 217.

35. Presbyterian Church of England Women's Missionary Association, *Jubilee History of the Women's Missionary Association, 1878–1928* (London, [1928]), 17–18.

36. Rosemary Seton, " 'Open Doors for Female Labourers': Women Candidates of the London Missionary Society, 1875–1914," in *Missionary Encounters: Sources and Issues*, eds. Robert A. Bickers and Rosemary Seton (Richmond, Surrey: Curzon Press, 1996), 55.

37. Maughan, "Regions Beyond," 335.

38. Brian Heeney, *The Women's Movement in the Church of England 1850–1930* (Oxford: Clarendon, 1988), 92–93.

39. Louise Creighton, *Memoir of a Victorian Woman: Reflections of Louise Creighton* (Bloomington, IN: Indiana University Press, c. 1994), 144.

40. Maughan, "Regions Beyond," 341.

41. Proposals to amalgamate CEZMS and CMS were made in 1888, 1895, 1919, 1926, 1939, 1940, 1944, 1951, and 1957. See Keen, "Introduction."

42. Maughan, "Regions Beyond," Table 3.1, 364.

43. C. P. Williams, " 'The Missing Link': The Recruitment of Women Missionaries in Some English Evangelical Missionary Societies in the Nineteenth Century," in *Women and Missions: Past and Present, Anthropological and Historical Perceptions,* eds. Fiona Bowie et al. (Providence, RI and Oxford: Berg, 1993), 55.

44. Maughan, "Regions Beyond," 278, 295.

45. Quoted in Maughan, "Regions Beyond," 317.

46. Maughan, "Regions Beyond," 352–353.

47. Maughan, "Regions Beyond," 315.

48. Georgina Gollock, *Eugene Stock: A Biographical Study 1836–1928* (London: Church Missionary Society, 1929), 172.

49. Minna C. Gollock, "The Share of Women in the Administration of Missions," *International Review of Missions* 1, no. 4 (1912): 683.

50. Gordon Hewitt, *The Problems of Success: A History of the Church Missionary Society, 1910–1942,* Vol. 1 (London, SCM Press, 1971–1977), 435.

51. See Jane Hunter, *The Gospel of Gentility, American Women Missionaries in Turn-of-the-Century China* (New Haven, CT and London: Yale University Press, c. 1984), 97 on the displacement of married women missionaries.

52. Speech of Rev. J. N. Murdoch, *Report of the Centenary Conference on the Protestant Missions of the World Held in Exeter Hall, London, 1888,* ed. James Johnston (London: J. Nisbet, 1888), 167.

53. Hewitt, *The Problems of Success,* Vol. 2, 316–317.

54. Edward Band, *Working His Purpose Out, the History of the English Presbyterian Mission 1847–1947* (London: Presbyterian Church of England, 1948), 116–117.

55. Band, *Working His Purpose,* 109.

56. PCE/FMC Series V, Box 16, File 4.

57. PCE/FMC Series V, Box 16, File 4.

58. Right Rev. Bishop Baldwin opening a session held on June 14, 1888, *Report of the Centenary Conference,* ed. Johnston, 1: 397.

59. Letter from the Editor, *Quarterly News of Woman's Work* (October 1888): 4.

60. *Report of the Ecumenical Conference on Foreign Missions, Held in Carnegie Hall and Neighboring Churches, April 21 to May 1* (New York: American Tract Society, 1900), 1, 46.

61. Brian Stanley, *The World Missionary Conference, Edinburgh 1910* (Grand Rapids, MI: William B. Eerdmans Publishing Co., 2009), 26 and Keith Clements, *Faith on the Frontier: A Life of J. H. Oldham* (Edinburgh: T&T Clark, 1999), 77.

62. Stanley, *Edinburgh 1910*, 313.

63. World Missionary Conference, "Problems of Administration," in *Report of Commission VI: The Home Base*, Chapter 13, 222–234.

64. World Missionary Conference, *Report of Commission VI*, 201.

65. Stanley, *Edinburgh 1910*, 313.

66. Gollock, "Share of Women," 674 and Stanley, *Edinburgh 1910*, 314–315.

67. John R. Mott, *The Home Ministry and Modern Missions* (London: Hodder & Stoughton, 1905), 73.

68. Some argued, however, that these secondary aims had come to be considered as primary. See Jeffrey Cox, *The British Missionary Enterprise since 1700* (New York and London: Routledge, 2010), 255–256.

69. Gollock, "Share of Women," 682.

70. Tissington Tatlow, *The Story of the Student Christian Movement of Great Britain and Ireland* (London: SCM Press, 1933), 596.

71. See Andrew Porter, *Religion versus Empire? British Protestant Missionaries and Overseas Expansion* (Manchester and New York: Manchester University Press, 2004), 301–306.

72. Porter, *Religion*, 305.

73. Mott, secretary of the World's Student Christian Federation, chaired the WMC and its Continuation Committee and Oldham was the organizing secretary of WMC and secretary of the Continuation Committee and founded the *International Review of Missions* in 1912. Both were instrumental in founding, in 1921, the International Missionary Council.

74. See Jacqueline de Vries, "More than Paradoxes to Offer, Feminism, History and Religious Cultures," in *Women, Gender and Religious Cultures*, eds. Sue Morgan and Jacqueline de Vries (London and New York: Routledge, 2010), 188–210.

75. Quoted in Maughan, "Regions Beyond," 345.

76. Gollock, "Share of Women," 684.

77. M. M. Underhill, "Women's Work for Missions, Great Britain and Ireland," *International Review of Missions* 15, no. 2 (April 1926): 260.

78. Keen, "Introduction."

79. Ruth Compton Brouwer, *Modern Women Modernizing Men* (Vancouver, BC and Toronto, ON: UBC Press, 2002), 31.

80. Valerie Griffiths, "The Ministry of Women in the China Inland Mission and the Overseas Missionary Fellowship 1920–1990" (M.A. diss., Oxford University, Oxford, 1958), 67, 69.

81. *Fellowship News* (Internal Organ for Members from Overseas Missionary Fellowship Council), September 2001, 14.

82. *Report of the First Annual Conference of the Conference of Missionary Societies in Great Britain and Ireland* (London: 1912), 65–66, and Maughan, "Regions Beyond," 356–357.

83. For discussion of this issue, see Dana Robert, *American Women in Mission: A Social History of Their Thought and Practice* (Macon, GA: Mercer University Press, 1996), 306–307.

5

Missionary Women and Education

Before 1820, it seems that no native female could write, read or sew.[1]

This morning the village school opened. I had twenty scholars. But three of the number can read: none write or cipher. Several knit, and a few sew a little.[2]

THE INTRODUCTION OF SCHOOLING IN BENGAL

Wives, sisters, and daughters were busy teaching basic reading, writing and numeracy skills, needlework, and the tenets of Christianity almost from the start of the Protestant missionary enterprise. Their pupils were Eurasian girls, the wives and daughters of converts, orphans, and as many as they could reach of the wider female population. The region where this work commenced was India, particularly Bengal, where during the second decade of the 19th century the cause of native female education brought together, at least for a time, the exertions of missionaries, Indian reformers, and secular philanthropists.[3] Strong arguments were conventionally advanced against girls' education in India. They did not require education for purposes of employment, since they were destined to carry out domestic duties at home. The customary age of marriage for girls was between

8 and 10 years, so schooling above that age was ruled out. In addition there was a widespread superstition "that a girl taught to read and write will soon after marriage become a widow, an event which is regarded as nearly the worst misfortune that can befall the sex."[4] William Adams, who surveyed education on behalf of the Bengal government in the 1830s, reported that in general "there is no instruction" of girls. He had found isolated examples, such as two women belonging to landowning families who were "alleged to possess a competent knowledge of Bengali writing and accounts." Literate women were also to be found among the followers of Vishnu known as the *Vaishnava* sect, although, according to Adams, they were considered "the lowest in point of general morality, and especially in respect of the virtue of their women."[5]

Carey and his fellow missionaries at Serampore had early become involved in education, first teaching local Eurasian children as a means of financing their mission, and subsequently opening schools for Indian boys. By 1816 they began admitting girls to their schools, using mat partitions as screens. In Calcutta progressive elements in the Calcutta School Society, formed in 1818 to improve and extend the provision of schooling in the city and surrounding area, began campaigning for girls' schools despite the opposition of orthodox Hindus. An obvious methodology for the mass extension of education was the recently devised monitorial, or Bell-Lancasterian, system, promoted in England through the British and Foreign School Society (BFSS) and its Anglican equivalent, the National Society for Promoting the Education of the Poor in the Principles of the Established Church. Bengal missionaries like Robert May of the London Missionary Society (LMS) and the Marshman family at Serampore had been early pioneers of the system in Bengal, seeing it as "the most prudent and peaceable means of instruction which may be exercised on the multitudes of orphans who have no religion ... and Christians who scarcely know why they are called by that name." Dramatic results were predicted: the "schools might be conducted in many instances by native teachers and after twenty or thirty years ... idolatry would be cut up by the roots."[6]

An appeal from William Ward, one of Marshman's colleagues, at the Annual Meeting of the BFSS in 1821 led to Mary Ann Cooke being sent out to Calcutta to train native teachers under the aegis of the Calcutta School Society. She had to begin at the beginning. It was difficult to get her young pupils "either to sit or stand still, much more so, to keep them reading or writing, for more than a quarter of an hour at a time." By 1823, and now the wife of CMS missionary Isaac

Wilson, she had set up 22 schools with around 400 pupils. In 182 the newly formed Ladies' Society for Native Female Education in Calcutta and its Vicinity took over financial responsibility. The society's president was Lady Amherst, wife of the Governor General. This connection marked the start of a lengthy period of private patronage of female education at a time when government felt unable to provide official support. The lady patronesses made a point of visiting the schools, especially on examination day.

> The first classes were able to read with ease "The Tract on Female Education" by a learned pundit, rather a difficult book from the number of Sanskrit phrases. Others read in books of fables and in Watt's Catechism, translated into Bengali; their needlework was then shewn and the composure and seeming delight with which the little creatures went through the task, seated at the feet of their kind patronesses, much exceeded what had been anticipated.[7]

Both Mrs. Wilson, who remained as head of the schools, and the ladies' committee ensured the prominence of Christian content in the curriculum or, at the least, the learning by rote of key Biblical texts. At one examination, a "little girl about three years old was observed, when brought to Lady Amherst, to repeat correctly the Lord's Prayer in her own native language." Despite the strong Christian element, the schools continued to receive Indian support during the 1820s, Rajah Boidonath Roy Bahadur donating nearly half the money required for a new Central School. It opened in 1828 with 58 pupils, rising to between 200 and 300 by 1835. But there were problems. Miss Wakefield, writing from Calcutta on December 23, 1835, explained that

> The time we have them is so short, that it is of importance to secure it all for making them acquainted with the Scriptures; the first three classes read the testament; the next four Bible History; the next six Watt's Catechism and the rest compose the spelling and ABC class. The average number is 300. . . . February and March are the great marrying months. . . . This takes place every year, so that probably 100 children are thus exchanged, or rather 100 are married away, and 100 new ones are brought in.[8]

By the late 1830s it was clear that attempts to tackle the education of Indian girls through the medium of mission schools were failing. Very few girls from respectable families were now attending. The schools drew for the most part pupils from low-caste families who were attracted by the small sums paid out as inducements. The Christian convert, Rev. Behari Lal Singh, wrote of the feeling "that little or nothing is to be hoped for in the way of ameliorating the wretched condition of Bengalee females by way of Day-schools ... the low caste of the children, ... their early marriage, the difficulty of counteracting the influence of evil example at home, the necessity of some temporal inducement to secure their attendance, and the scanty fruits that have resulted in the shape of direct conversions."[9] Missionary efforts therefore began to be directed toward establishing boarding schools for the children of native converts, and also to setting up orphanages to accommodate children found destitute, or who had been orphaned in the many famines that afflicted the region.

EDUCATION IN THE INDIAN HOME

However, from the beginning of the 1840s, fresh ideas on how to educate Indian girls and women began to be voiced both by the missionary community and by progressive Hindus. In an article published in the *Calcutta Christian Observer* of March 1840, Rev. Thomas Smith of the Free Church of Scotland urged that the only way to make" female education a respectable thing" was to send "European ladies to teach the females in their own apartments."[10] The prominent Christian convert Krishna Mohan Banerjea thought that "a goodly number (of native gentlemen) would gladly accept the services" of lady teachers "if they could get them free of charge within their doors." He added that "the European community is indebted to this country, whence they are drawing so much of gold and silver, and where they exercise as it were a lordly supremacy ... they owe it to the natives ... to instruct and enlighten their sons and daughters."[11]

Education in the home and particularly in the secluded area of the house set aside for women, the *zenana*, became an important feature of women's missionary work during the second half of the 19th century. The development met a need increasingly felt by upper- and middle-class Indian families, particularly those of the urbanized élite. Progressive husbands and fathers desired both education and an introduction to European cultural influences for their wives and daughters, but in the secluded surroundings of their homes. Malvika Karlekar points out that the "success of home tuition, was, in large part, based on the fact that it preserved the ideal of feminine seclusion and at the same time prepared women to become better housewives and mothers."[12] One Calcutta missionary reported that "the only difficulty has been how to take up the homes that have been opened to us. The ladies in the Zenanas nearly all wish to learn English ... and many ask to be taught to play some instrument, especially the harmonium."[13] One big obstacle was the religious element of the teaching, which missionaries felt compelled to introduce. Some families were happy to tolerate an element of Christian teaching as part of an educational package, or felt able to accept Bible stories simply as story books.[14] Many more orthodox homes, however, kept their doors firmly shut, as did most Muslim ones. One missionary reported from Madras (Chennai) that many houses "would gladly receive her" if she would limit herself to teaching "English and needlework." Even in more tolerant homes, some delicacy was required as to how the Gospel message was introduced:

> We sit down, generally on a mat on the ground, with an idol or two over our heads, and begin to help our pupils with their work. We teach them plain and fancy sewing, reading or music, all the time talking to them and watching for every opportunity of sowing the seed. Before leaving we read and explain a few verse[s] from the Gospel, and sing some hymns which they dearly love.[15]

"PLAIN" AND "FANCY" NEEDLEWORK

Western forms of needlework were assiduously introduced by women missionaries into India, and later China. There was a civilizing and feminizing purpose to inculcate desirable moral traits such as cleanliness, discipline, and application. While needlework formed part of the curriculum at most mission girls' schools, it was also taught to two very different classes of women: poor, low-caste women converts to whom it might be the means of earning an income, and girls and women of the leisured classes found in the *zenanas* who were thought to need rescuing both from idolatrous practices and from the evil of having nothing to do.[16]

Martha Mault is generally credited with being the first to introduce lace-making into southern India. With her husband she had come out to join the LMS mission in Travancore in 1819. By 1821 she had set up a boarding school for Christian girls and in 1823 started a lace-making class for her girls and local

Christian women. She taught the pillow or cushion variety, which she had evidently learnt in Malta. Her pupils would sit in neat lines on the ground, their pillows or cushions in front of them. On each pillow lay their lace, which they worked at using bobbins and pins. Lace-making was considered "so light that even delicate women and girls can work at it."[17] More importantly, it could be done at home and was thus a means of introducing desirable domestic habits to women who might otherwise have worked in the fields. In some cases it afforded the possibility of buying freedom: slavery was not abolished in Travancore until 1855. While lace-making enabled such women to earn a living, funds were also ploughed back in support of female missionary work, proving a fruitful source of funding. Lace-making was adopted by other missionary societies and introduced into other parts of southern India. During the course of the 19th and into the 20th centuries, it became something of an industry. Handmade collars and cuffs, stoles and scarves, berthas and boleros, flounces, chemise tops, table centers, bedspreads, baby caps, and wedding veils were exported to all parts of the Empire, Europe, and North America.

Figure 5.1. Lace workers at Ikkadu, Tiruvallur. Methodist missionary Mollie Scott instructing a group of Indian women in the pillow method of lace making, c. 1900. (MMS Collection at SOAS © Trustees for Methodist Church Purposes. Used with permission.)

The fancy work—embroidery, wool work, felt slippers, and so on—taught in mission schools and *zenanas* proved a popular attraction. As time went by, however, it attracted critics. Those concerned with educational standards thought the preoccupation with fancy work a frivolous waste of time, a view shared, for other reasons, by the more zealously minded missionary of the 1880s and 1890s, such as Amy Carmichael, who was repelled by a suggestion from a Bible woman that she should start teaching needlework as a way of attracting converts.[18] Others attacked its banality. "In no branch of Indian art has British influence been so mischievously detrimental," pronounced Mary Billington, a journalist visiting India in the 1890s. "Western wool-work, in all the worst hideousness of Berlin cross-stitch and crewels ... have been adopted and perpetrated in the vilest form." She went on to sneer at those responsible. "Drawn as so large a percentage of their teachers are, from the lower middle classes, and imbued with the worst philistinism of their order, these instructors from outside were equally unable to appreciate the wondrous beauties of form and colouring of indigenous embroidery, or to impart a knowledge of anything better than the decadent tastes of the back parlour."[19] While India had its own traditional embroidery (e.g., *chikan,* white on white embroidery, and *shisha* or mirror work), most embroiders, at least those working commercially, were men. Western missionaries, not surprisingly, taught Indian girls and women the forms of needlework, which they themselves had learnt. It seems highly likely that many Indian women found Western forms exotic, or at least novel. Requests to be taught fancy work or to play the harmonium were frequently the first indications that a *zenana* might be open to Christian agency.

GOVERNMENT FUNDING AND MISSION SCHOOLS

Government, while generally approving of missionary efforts in India in the early part of the 19th century, was slow to take active steps in support of female education. The first official pronouncement in its favor was not until 1854. For a number of years thereafter, the government contented itself with rewarding local initiatives with grants-in-aid rather than in taking any direct steps to set up schools for girls. Mission schools and missionary efforts in the *zenanas* were eligible for the government funding. This, while greatly welcomed as a means of supporting and extending their educational work, resulted in some modification of the missionary syllabus to meet qualifying requirements. After 1859 the government had to observe strict religious neutrality, and could only support the teaching of secular subjects. In 1876 the first inspectors of female education were appointed. The Church of England Zenana Missionary Society magazine *India's Women* reported from Bengal in 1881 that

> Within the last two or three years a lady has been appointed as Govern-
> ment Inspectress of Zenana and Girls' Schools and as the different Mis-
> sionary Societies receive grants-in-aid from Government, it is quite right
> and fair that it should be so. A short time ago however we received a list of
> "standards" in accordance with which our Zenana and school pupils are to
> be taught; and after a time the grants will probably be given according to
> results rather than the present plan. This will naturally have the effect of
> making us more systematic and careful in giving secular instruction, but
> there may also be the danger of our being tempted to pay less attention to
> the teaching of Scripture and its life-giving truths.[20]

Zenana instruction in Bengal did not greatly impress the government's education department, although half of its grant had in 1876–1877 been given in support of Calcutta zenana agencies. The author of a report observed in 1878 that

> It is mainly through the reports of Mrs Wheeler, the Government Inspec-
> tress of Schools, that the very meagre character of the instruction given to
> the bulk of the zenana pupils has become accurately known to the depart-
> ment.... The time devoted by a mistress to each house visited is on aver-
> age only two hours a week.... The contraction rather than the extension
> of zenana work is, I am convinced, the object at which Missions should
> now aim.[21]

Despite departmental reservations, zenana education through mission agency continued to be supported by the government. The Hunter Commission of 1882 recommended that grants to support the teaching of secular subjects in the *zenana* should be "recognised as a proper charge on public funds."[22]

TRAINING INDIAN TEACHERS,
CALCUTTA, 1870s–1880s

The scarcity of suitable trained teachers to meet the sudden expansion in girls' education in India in the second half of the 19th century was a problem confronting all educational undertakings, secular or religious. Mary Carpenter, who had undertaken a six-month high-profile tour of India in 1866, drew attention to the importance of teacher training, noting that in this respect, Bengal lagged far behind Madras, Bombay, and Ahmedabad.[23] Missionary societies engaged in zenana education found it difficult to obtain the services of suitably trained lady governesses—for ladies were distinctly preferred—to enter private houses of upper-class Indians and instruct girls and women in the *zenanas* before the 1880s, when unmarried women missionaries from Britain began to arrive in some numbers. The Church of Scotland's Ladies' Association for the Advancement of Female Education in India, which had been in existence since 1837, was eager to embark on this branch of work in the 1860s, but only found a suitable agent in 1870 when Mary Pigot, who had been educated at the Calcutta Female Normal School, was invited by the church's senior chaplain in Calcutta to establish this endeavor on their behalf. What particularly recommended her were her enviable contacts with élite Bengali families. Most of these were with members of the Brahmo Samaj, the Hindu reform movement that saw female education as one of its key social aims.[24] As head of the Church of Scotland's Female Mission, Mary Pigot made excellent progress. By 1882 with 75 boarders, 890 day-school pupils, and 453 zenana students, making a total of 1418 pupils, the Church of Scotland's Female Mission had more students than any other mission in Calcutta.[25]

In 1876 Pigot set up a boarding school for her more advanced pupils, and developed teacher training. Promising girls, often originally famine victims from rural areas, became first pupil teachers, then day-school teachers or assistant teachers, and interpreters in the *zenanas*. She remarked how pupils who "often negligent of lessons, untidy and unpromising … as soon as they obtain charge of a class, or of zenanas, their diligence knows no bounds."[26] She had difficulty in holding on to her best pupils, since these were much in demand as marriage partners of native men attached to the various Christian missions. At the end of 1878 she wrote of her reluctance to part with Isabel, one of the best orphanage-trained pupil teachers. Isabel's suitor was a scripture reader at the General Assembly's Institution, and Pigot had come under pressure from male colleagues there to let the girl marry him.[27] The following year two of her four lady teachers were lost to her through marriage. The training and placing of older indigenous Christian women as teachers became, in consequence, even more important.

An important feature of the expansion of female education was the necessity of training women educators who were not bound by the rules of caste or religion of the upper castes, including purdah. Inevitably, these were lower-caste women, "often widows, orphans or mendicants"; more mobile than those with family ties but also viewed as lacking social status and respectability.[28] In her letters, Pigot referred frequently to her "anxious cares" in the supervision of her trainee teachers. She wrote home that she had set aside Wednesdays for zenana training work: "I have all our zenana native teachers to come to me. They get a Bible lesson, and then prepare all the lessons they have to teach their pupils in the intervening days."[29] She was also concerned to cut down on the amount of walking her staff had to do, an activity that brought them under suspicion. In 1877 the mission acquired an "omnibus ... the largest in Calcutta—almost the length of a tramway car" to convey her native teachers.[30] At the end of that same year, large new premises at Bow Bazar were acquired for the Female Mission, one of its advantages being that Pigot could bring more of her teachers within its walls. Previously they had been "morally exposed, living in cheap lodgings among the lower class of heathens." They themselves did not feel that any scandal about them was possible since they were "kept like *bows* [young married girls]. We go and return in the omnibus, and are kept shut up in this house". What risk, they asked "do we run for any scandal against this Mission?"[31]

However, Pigot could not be too careful. In the early 1880s, she and her assistant staff came under increasing censure from a new generation of Church of Scotland personnel in Calcutta, some of whom considered it improper for a Eurasian to be in charge. She faced a number of allegations, among them that her trainee teachers had "immodest ways," and that some went out at night for immoral purposes. In 1883, as a result of these and other charges, she was dismissed. An investigatory commission sent out by the General Assembly of the Church of Scotland in 1884 concluded that the mission "was no worse off in respect of its native agents than all Missions of a similar character."[32] The novel spectacle of single women, not drawn from respectable classes, living together was almost bound to attract unwelcome attention. A government female teacher-training school set up in Nagpur had been closed in 1874, when a number of women were discovered to be suffering from venereal disease; and women at the Dhaka Normal School were found in 1873 to be leading lives of gross immorality and the school was closed.[33] The Bengal government concluded it was safer to support teacher-training enterprises within the moral safety of a mission establishment.[34] Pigot's successor, Emily Bernard, was impressed by the teachers she inherited.

She found them "a better trained body of teachers than any others whom I have met in the course of my experience, especially in method, in the power of imparting knowledge, in the maintenance of discipline and interest in their work in the children committed to their charge."[35] For years after Pigot's departure, teachers trained by her continued faithfully to serve the Church of Scotland's mission in Calcutta. She seems to have succeeded in her training methods at a time when few others did. It was to be several decades before a satisfactory system for teacher training in India was put in place.

THE DEVELOPMENT OF SECONDARY EDUCATION

There was a wider acceptance in India toward the end of the 19th century that girls could and should attend school. In Bengal, for example, the number of day schools for girls trebled between 1900 and 1910.[36] Mission schools were among the first to offer girls a secondary syllabus, a survey finding in 1907 that "the bulk of female Secondary education is provided by missionaries." Such schools catered to a small élite, since the same survey recorded the existence of only 43 girls' high schools in the entire country.[37] Notable among those in North India were the Kinnaird High School, later Kinnaird College, founded by the Zenana Bible and Medical Mission in Lahore; and the school for girls founded at Lucknow by the American missionary Isabella Thoburn, educational institutions that became "the backbone of women's higher education in the early twentieth century."[38] There was also a network of successful Catholic convent schools. The first of these was set up by a group of Loreto nuns from Ireland in Calcutta in 1841, with the aim of providing schooling for European and Anglo-Indian Catholic girls. The prospectus offered instruction in "writing, arithmetic, grammar, geography, with the use of the globes, chronology, history, French and plain and fancy needlework."[39] By the late 1840s, several schools had been opened in and around Calcutta and, in 1846, at Darjeeling. Indian girls began attending the Loreto schools in significant numbers from the 1890s. By 1962 the schools' historian was able to claim that everyone knew "the five big Calcutta Day-Schools managed by the Irish Branch of the Institute of the Blessed Virgin Mary and its Boarding and Day-Schools strung across the plains … and across the hills in Darjeeling, Shillong and Simla."[40] The success of the Loreto brand was acknowledged by an Anglican woman missionary: "the school which is most successful as a missionary agency is a Roman Catholic convent school, where no Bible or Christian teaching is given, but where the atmosphere of peacefulness and prayerfulness greatly attracts these Indian girls."[41]

PIONEERING EDUCATIONAL WORK IN CHINA

While on furlough in Hackney, London during 1824–1825, Robert Morrison, the first Protestant missionary to China, began giving Chinese lessons to women interested in going to the East as teachers. One of his keenest students was Mary Ann Aldersey, the daughter of a local and prosperous wholesale stationer. Aldersey does not at this point seem to have been interested in going to the East herself, but attended his lessons in order to show support. In any case she had to take care, for a number of years, of her brother's children. However by 1837 she found herself free to go, establishing for the time being a school at Batavia (Jakarta). With the opening up of treaty ports at the conclusion of the First Opium War in 1842, the intrepid Aldersey decided to move to the Chinese mainland. The city she selected, Ningpo (Ningbo) in Chekiang (Zhejiang) Province, was never to possess a large Western community. In 1854, when Aldersey had been there for 11 years, there were still only 22 foreign residents, mainly Protestant missionaries.[42] She rented a large building in the center of the town and began to acquire her pupils who lived in the school as boarders. Her chief method of doing so was to enter into an agreement with the parents who handed over their daughters in return for a financial inducement. A few of her pupils were orphans. Despite protestations, allegations, and hostile demonstrations, her school was so successful that she appealed to the Female Education Society for support. The society sent out an assistant, Miss Selmer, who reported on her superior's single-mindedness in the following terms:

> Imagine thirty-five children screaming at the very top of their voices, all repeating different words. The discordance and the shrillness of these sounds are beyond description, and no human beings but Chinese could produce them. Dear Miss Aldersey does not perceive the unpleasant disturbance ... her whole soul, and all her thoughts, are entirely wrapped up in the one great aim, that of making known to these poor heathens the way of salvation.[43]

By 1854, when the youthful Robert Hart arrived in Ningpo to take up his duties in the consular service, Aldersey was a senior figure in the missionary community.

He thought her merely "a very nice old lady; rather old-maidish in dress," his attention being rather more drawn to one of her assistants, Maria Dyer, later to marry James Hudson Taylor, founder of the China Inland Mission.[44] Other observers were more impressed. The American missionary Dr. W.A.P. Martin wrote of Aldersey that "the impression she made on the Chinese, whether Christian or pagan, was profound.... As England was ruled by a woman, so Miss Aldersey had been delegated to be the ruler of our foreign community."[45] Aldersey continued to work until 1857 when, at the age of 64, she handed her work over to the American Presbyterian mission, and retired to live with her nieces in Australia.

GIRLS' SCHOOLING IN CHINA, 1880s–1920s

Prior to 1898, the only schools for girls in China were those founded by missionaries. This is not to say that there was no tradition at all of education for girls. Those in élite homes might well have been tutored privately. But it was generally held to be unseemly for Chinese women of good class to leave their homes, and it is significant that girls initially attending mission schools were either the daughters of Chinese Christians or those "whose parents had to be bribed by promises of food and clothing... homeless foundlings... and despised little slave girls."[46] Some, like Aldersey, used financial inducements. It was not always enough. A missionary reported in 1870 the closure of a school she had opened with great difficulty the year before, since many of her pupils "had become large enough to pick over tea and thus make from fifty to one hundred *cash* [low denomination coin] a day, whereas I give but seven *cash*. Their parents really did not value the instruction given... they have not the slightest interest in the education of their girls and would not give a *cash* toward supporting a girls' school."[47] The widespread custom of foot-binding also posed a problem. If schools insisted on only admitting girls with unbound feet, this might act as a deterrent to attendance. Some schools actually participated in or oversaw the binding process. As time went by, women missionary teachers took a firmer stand on the matter, refusing to admit girls with bound feet. In this they were encouraged by the various anti-foot-binding campaigns, most notably that of Alicia Little, who founded the Natural Foot Society in 1895. There was also a shift of opinion on this subject among more progressive Chinese.[48]

The aim of the first mission schools was comparatively simple: to instruct the girls in the truths of the Gospel and in the knowledge of the scriptures, and to teach such other subjects as would fit them to be good wives and mothers. These might include arithmetic, as well as needlework. However, by the late 19th century, syllabuses had broadened to include the Chinese classics and characters, English, history, geography, and music—in some measure a response to an increasing take-up, by Chinese of the entrepreneurial classes, of places for girls in the treaty-port mission schools. However, girls from "good families" did not attend mission schools, as one agent was told as late as 1904.[49] In the interior of China where traditional Confucian values held sway well into the 20th century, attitudes to mission schools continued to be both dismissive and hostile. But when a non-missionary school for girls was founded by a reformist group in Shanghai in 1898, missionaries and other western women were looked to for advice and assistance. Mary Richard, wife of Baptist missionary Timothy Richard, was invited to the formal opening of the school and assisted for some time after. She recorded that

> at the request of the directresses I, for some time, visited the school once a week, examined them in their progress in English, gave a lesson in geography and other subjects which the then native staff could not give. Taking with me Betel's Portable Globe, which shuts up like an umbrella, it was easy to explain the different motions of the earth, and the cause of seasons and eclipses. That such explanations were necessary not only for the girls but for the Chinese ladies always present on these occasions, will be plain from the fact that at the second lesson one of the otherwise intelligent Chinese ladies, who reads and writes Chinese well, gravely asked if in England we had the same sun and moon that they have in China.[50]

Despite the educational reforms, introduced in the first decade of the 20th century and developed further by the new Republican government after the fall of the Qing dynasty, progress on the ground in respect of girls' schooling was slow indeed. By 1921 the enrolment of girls at primary level was an estimated six percent of the whole.[51] Missionary schools could claim that they provided more places for girls than did government schools until well into the 1920s.[52] By this time, Protestant mission schools were united under the Chinese Christian Educational Association and offered education at kindergarten, lower and higher primary levels for pupils up to 14, and middle school for senior pupils. Scripture was still taught, and daily attendance at service was expected of all pupils. The syllabus had however broadened to include Chinese classics and language, history, geography, elementary science, and optional English at lower primary level. All pupils at higher primary level were taught mathematics and English; those in middle schools were additionally taught zoology, botany, physics, and chemistry. Physical education formed part of the syllabus, taking the form, in many girls' schools, of drills or country dancing.[53] Missionary schooling was thus making no small contribution to the raising of a generation of Chinese youth familiar with Western-style learning, particularly in the sciences. Not all missionaries were happy with the stress placed on education: "Western education, especially the vast middle-school curricula are futile ways of winning China for Christ," commented a disgruntled male missionary.[54]

By 1920, missions from North America amounted to nearly 60 percent of the total missionary presence in China, a dominance they retained throughout this period. American missions now took the lead in the founding and development of Christian schools, colleges, and universities, although some were part-funded by British missionary societies. For women, there were the North China Women's College at Peking, founded by Luella Miner in 1905, and Ginling at Nanking (Nanjing), founded by a number of missions in 1915. The influential British missionary Myfanwy Wood of the LMS distrusted some aspects of higher education for women, preferring that efforts should instead be directed to producing "women who in homes as wives and mothers live out their membership of Christ." At the 1916 Meeting of the Society in London, she expressed her concern that the effects of an overhasty emancipation of Chinese girls in cities and ports was leading to "unbridled licence because they had been thrust so violently into the glare of noonday-light of Western civilization." She contrasted this with LMS efforts in a rural mission "where a small group of girls ... were being tenderly and lovingly led into the light."[55]

EDUCATION IN TIME OF REVOLUTION

At a remote mission station at Tingchow (Chanting) in Fujian Province, another LMS missionary, Marjorie Rainey, also considered that her main aim as a teacher was "to help the ordinary girl to live a more intelligent and useful life in her own home and better fulfil her duties as a wife and mother, and a member of Christ's Church." She recognized, however, the importance of training "a few special girls" as teachers.[56] One such special girl was Liao Hongying, the daughter of a local Confucian scholar, who began attending the LMS girls' school at Tingchow at the age of five or six. Hongying, who eventually settled in England, wrote a number of draft sketches of her life on which a published biography has been based.[57] These include an account of her education at her mission schools so that we have her commentary and perspective on her school days to set alongside correspondence and reports in the LMS archive.

Tingchow was in a rural and backward region, a 10-day journey from Amoy (Xiamen), the center of LMS work in the province. Its setting was amid magnificent mountain scenery; this made access difficult, and the people chiefly spoke Hakka, a language often unintelligible to those coming from outside the area. The first LMS missionary had in fact been a Chinese pastor, who had come up from Amoy in 1890. Despite initial hostility, he had succeeded in founding a church, while a special fund established by the will of the Leeds philanthropist Robert Arthington enabled the LMS to start educational and medical work. One of their agents arriving in 1907 was Edith Benham, who set up the first girls' school in the area. In 1915 arrived Marjorie Rainey, a university graduate who had signed the Student Volunteer Declaration, and, at the time of her application to the LMS, had specified that she wished to serve in China.

After several months of intensive language learning she began to teach games and drawing. Before the end of her first year, she had assumed charge of the school, which had some 30 pupils and around 20 in the kindergarten. She also taught singing in the boys' school and noted quite a contrast with her girls. While the boys were "immensely self-assured," the girls were shy and "heavy." She wrote later that it was "an endless battle to excite spontaneity in thought and work among school girls here. Mental laziness and lack of courage are the chief defects." The parents were at fault, since they "send girls too late and take them away too early." The school was visited, from time to time, by local civil and educational officials, but they "make no comment. They are pleased and content that a girls' school exists and are relieved that someone else will run it for them." Nor did Rainey find the Christian community in Tingchow supportive—"the preachers and men-teachers employed by the Church refuse to give more than a passing thought to the problem of girls' education."[58] There were staffing difficulties too. In 1921 she was trying to figure out how "four people can teach seven classes."[59] Nevertheless by 1922 fair progress had been made: with 54 kindergarten pupils,

56 girls at the lower primary level, and 23 in the higher primary level.[60] On the eve of her 1923 furlough Rainey felt optimistic enough to consider the possibility of establishing higher educational facilities for girls in Tingchow. The local Chinese district superintendent had assured her "that any such education will be a joint effort of the city and of the mission." That happy prospect was to be the high watermark of mission–city cooperation.[61] On her return from furlough in 1924, she was to find a dramatically changed situation.

The fact that a girls' school run by missionaries existed in her hometown had come to the attention of the young Liao Hongying about two or three years after it opened. She seems to have heard of it through attending the mission's Sunday school, where she particularly enjoyed the tea and biscuits given out to all who attended. At or about the age of five, she had begun attending a private coeducational school run by a friend of her father. There was, however, only one other girl pupil and she begged to be sent instead to the mission school. Her father was very much opposed to her going to a school run by foreigners and Christians, but finally consented. He had in fact been teaching her himself. At the age of three he had taught her to recite extracts from Tang dynasty poetry, while her elder brother, a teacher at the local boys' school, later taught her both to know and to understand the core Chinese classics—the Confucian Analects, the Great Learning, the Doctrine of the Mean, and the works of Mencius (Meng Zi). On arrival at the mission school she found that most of the pupils, other than those in the kindergarten, were much older than her. Indeed some of them were married women, the wives of local Christians or of husbands studying abroad.

A bright child and benefiting from her earlier tuition, Hongying soon emerged top in her exams. This meant that her family no longer had to pay school fees. On one occasion, she was presented with a doll as a prize, with eyes that opened and shut, much admired by her family, including her older brothers. A New Testament, given to Hongying by a Chinese teacher at the school, was not so well received. On two occasions her brother Er-Ge tore up the copies presented and threw them away.[62] In 1919 14-year-old Hongying, with three other pupils, graduated from the higher primary class. Rainey, intending the graduation ceremony to be an important event in the locality, invited all the prefectural and county officials. As the top pupil, Hongying was called on to respond to the speech made by the County Magistrate and evidently did so with poise and panache—her words were greeted with cries of astonishment.[63] Since there was no high school for her to attend, she remained in the capacity of pupil teacher, showing no qualms in teaching adult pupils who were being trained as Bible women. In 1923 she departed for the neighboring province to attend the prestigious Baldwin School for Girls run by the American Methodist Episcopal Mission, her expenses being met by Rainey and a network of home supporters. Hongying found the facilities "magnificent in comparison with our Changting Primary School."[64]

When Rainey returned from her furlough in 1924, she discovered that even remote Tingchow was affected by the patriotic movement pulsating through the country. The movement intensified after the infamous May 30th Incident in 1925, when officers of the Shanghai Municipal Police shot at a Chinese student demonstration, killing 11. There was much that Rainey saw as positive in the wave of patriotism. She approved of the formation of societies among the young, dedicated to "advance China's good—our own little school has three or four," and was delighted that her girl pupils were taking a full part. "Some of us almost gasped to see maidens of sixteen and seventeen setting out, unaccompanied, to attend a Committee meeting in the Government Boys' School." During the months of demonstrations and agitation, much of which was directed against the British, who were blamed for the Shanghai Incident, her pupils had shown "great loyalty" and she felt she had friends "among the leaders of the patriotic societies."[65]

During 1926, Tingchow fell under the control of forces of the Northern Expedition, commanded by Chiang Kai-shek. The girls' school's 20th anniversary celebrations of the following year were disrupted by the opponents of Christian education. However, Rainey received apologies and, emboldened by this and the support of Chinese friends, resolved to stay at her post together with two other LMS missionaries, one of them the senior missionary E. R. Hughes.[66] Their decision was reached against consular instructions that all missionaries in the interior should seek the safety of the treaty ports. Hughes and Rainey seem to have held similar views on how to handle the anti-British and anti-Christian sentiment enflaming the young. Hughes had stood bareheaded outside the LMS buildings as the students marched by in protest against the Shanghai Incident. Both posted notices announcing their willingness to register their schools, as was now demanded. The situation was less critical in respect of the girls' school and in any case, as Hughes told LMS headquarters, Rainey had "won the confidence of the people to so remarkable a degree." Both of them, he assured LMS Foreign Secretary Hawkins, had received specific and highly placed assurances that they as "people who in their life here had cut themselves off from any concern with British state matters" would be safe if they remained.[67] The girls' school continued, even increasing its roll to 200. The boys' school was however declared redundant and closed, so that the girls inherited the boys' "hideous but palatial" building. But Rainey had to stand down as principal, and "every scrap of worship and Bible teaching" in the school was in future to be voluntary. From this point on, Rainey was on dubious ground as a missionary. The school in which she still taught, and retained a great deal of unofficial influence, had become a largely secular day school with very few pupils attending the out-of-hours Christian activities. Rainey insisted it was possible to "work for Christ even in a purely secular school, and . . . we are a standing witness to there being something in religion which inspires people to come here and stay here."[68] But "one is definitely and unmistakeably both British and Christian, and Principal, staff and pupils all have hearts which are torn by conflicting loyalties." What somehow kept it all together was "an amazing loyalty to the school."[69]

Figure 5.2. Group photograph of all the teachers of Leyu (Joy of Learning) Primary School, Christmas Day, 1928. Marjorie Rainey, seated second from right, with other members of the staff of Tingchow Girls' Primary School. (Bryan Papers, by permission of the SOAS Library.)

At Nanchang, Hongying had been radicalized and was the first student at her school to appear with short hair, thus making public her revolutionary credentials. Concerned at what was happening to her friends at Tingchow, she returned in the summer of 1927 and, as "the best educated girl in town," was asked to speak at one of the mass rallies. In a show of solidarity with her teachers, she condemned attacks on foreign residents.[70] Left-wing students were being targeted by anticommunist forces and Rainey, concerned for Hongying's safety, arranged for her to travel to London to prepare for entry to a British university. This she did, obtaining a place to study agricultural chemistry at Oxford. Once again it was Rainey who ensured she had sufficient funds to spend four years at Oxford rather than the usual three, a stipulation on which Margery Fry, principal of Somerville College, had insisted. Hongying's subject of study held no personal appeal. She had simply chosen it in order to contribute to China's development. She wrote simply of this decision: "China is a vast country and there are natural calamities almost every year. The people need food so I must help to improve the agriculture."[71]

The end for Rainey and her LMS colleagues came in February 1929. In that year Communist forces from Kiangsi Province occupied Tingchow and a Chinese Soviet was established. The girls' school along with the rest of the LMS mission was almost obliterated. The attack was thoroughgoing; equipment and books as well as buildings were destroyed, "even the trees" were "cut down and flowers pulled up." Rainey, who lived in the school and who with other missionaries managed to escape before the attack, lost all of her possessions. She detected a personal note in the scale and intensity of the destruction. The attack was led, she wrote, "by a young man whose fiancée, a pupil of mine, refused to marry him."[72] Somehow or other, the school under its Chinese teachers contrived to reopen a couple of months later and continued to function under Communist rule. In 1935 the area was recaptured by Kuomintang forces and a reduced LMS mission presence was renewed. But Rainey was unable to return.

Tingchow was a particularly remote station, yet nevertheless found itself caught up in the political turbulence of the 1920s and particularly in the changing fortunes of the contending forces that passed through the region. Rainey and Hughes were among the very few missionaries who remained at their posts during the mid-1920s, setting aside personal safety, because they felt so strong a need to express their loyalty and commitment to their friends who were building a new China. Rainey's commitment to Tingchow was total and she expected to

return there. On reaching the United Kingdom, she had to undergo surgery for an old complaint, but wrote from her hospital bed of her determination to return "if the doctors and mission policy make it feasible." From Tingchow came a letter, urging her return to help build up the school after the destruction, for "you know very well that there are too few girls' schools in China."[73] It was not to be. Rainey was suffering from terminal cancer and died in 1931 at the age of 40. While she had undoubtedly worked hard for all her pupils, it was nonetheless the few special girls, especially Hongying, who received her devotion. Benefiting from her will, Hongying continued her education in England before returning to China in 1936 to take up a post at the newly established Department of Agriculture at Wuhan University. Rather as a missionary might, Hongying saw herself as going out to this post as a bride. "I really regard my going to Wuhan as to my husband! A feeling of security and happiness attaches to this coming event."[74] Like Rainey, she consciously eschewed conventional notions of womanhood in order to follow a higher cause. Although both were committed Christians, it seems the more immediate cause for them was the reform of China.[75]

THE FOUNDING OF WOMEN'S CHRISTIAN COLLEGE, MADRAS

While American missions led the way in establishing colleges of higher education for women in China, the Women's Christian College (WCC) at Madras (Chennai) came about largely as the result of efforts by British missionary societies. Even here, however, American financial support proved crucial. At the start of the 20th century, missionary circles in Madras saw the need for a higher educational institute for girls. But little progress was made toward making the idea a reality, since such a goal was beyond the funding capability of any one society. In 1913, one of the keenest advocates of the college, Rev. George Pittendrigh, of the United Free Church of Scotland's Foreign Mission in Madras, contacted members of the Educational Committee[76] in London. He obtained for the college not only the support of the committee, which had both American and European members, but also the personal commitment of Joseph (J. H.) Oldham, its influential secretary. Six British societies agreed to fund the new venture with the possibility of additional help from American missions. The college opened its doors to students in 1915. But its early years were dogged by difficulties that at times seemed all but insuperable.

Most of the problems were financial. The outbreak of war in August 1914 meant that some of the supporting British societies found it difficult to keep to their agreed annual contributions. The proposed new college was also faced with uncertain financial support from the Government of Madras, which unexpectedly proved hostile to the plan. The Governor, Lord Pentland, while he agreed that the need for higher education of women in Madras was great, wrote that he had to bear in mind "a strong orthodox caste Hindu opinion which, growing sensitive of the influence of Christianity in public education, is peculiarly distrustful of its influence upon Hindu women and girls."[77] He thought that the local committee should reconsider, pointing to the improbability that his "Government will be able to respond favourably to any . . . request" for financial aid.[78] The Government of Madras was at that time making plans to set up a government college for women. Madras College for Women, later Queen Mary's College for Women, opened its doors to students in 1914. Taken aback by this unhelpful stance, the committee nevertheless resolved to press on.

Oldham and other British mission administrators were initially skeptical about possible American support for a women's college in India, since their hands were so full with "schemes for China and Japan." But Oldham, as his biographer remarked, had "not given due attention to the independent line often taken by the women's missionary committees" in the United States.[79] His misapprehension was pointed out to him in a letter from Lucy W. Peabody of the Woman's American Baptist Foreign Missionary Society. It was no use, she wrote, approaching the General Missionary Boards of America to support the college scheme.

> Our Women's Boards are the responsible bodies in America. They are in charge of the educational work for women and girls on the foreign fields.... In matters of support and administration and appointment of representatives the Women's Boards are directly responsible. They will, of course, be glad to consult with such men as you mention, but having specialized success for forty years or more in the department of women's education in the East, it is rather expected that the men of our General Boards will come to the Women's Boards for light in this department.[80]

George Pittendrigh, back in Madras in January 1914, also benefited from bracing discussions with "two Baptist ladies from America" who "are most zealous and have large ideas." One of these was the redoubtable Mrs Peabody, and the other

Helen Barrett Montgomery. These two prominent figures in the American women's missionary movement were visiting India as part of a tour to explore the possibility of establishing Christian colleges for women in India, China, and Japan. Proposals for a women's Christian college in Madras thus fell within their remit, and they informed Pittendrigh that they would write "a joint letter to the various Home American Boards" urging financial support. It was a "great thing," Pittendrigh added, "to have such forceful personalities moving among these missions."[81] Much of the capital funding for the new college was to come from America, either channeled personally through Lucy Peabody or through funds collected by the Women's Union Christian Colleges in the Orient appeal. A sum of 25,000 dollars from a Rockefeller legacy made it possible, in 1916, to secure the handsome property of Doveton House, built in the late 18th century and set in spacious grounds. The building required some repairs and modernizing:

> An interesting group of fine old buildings which had stood more than 100 years and lodged many a British judge or high official, and occasionally a rajah or other Indian potentate. There was stabling for twenty horses, a

Figure 5.3. Women's Christian College Madras. The WCC opened in Madras (Chennai) in 1915. Formerly known as Doveton House, it boasted the tallest porch in Madras. Lantern slide, c. 1925. (MMS Collection at SOAS © Trustees for Methodist Church Purposes. Used with permission.)

band stand, a little tower for monkeys to live in, a small bungalow, a wilder-
ness of servants' houses, a zenana and a very large and stately mansion ...
sheltered by wide verandahs on both sides, and ... by the tallest porch in
Madras.[82]

With funding from England and the Government of Madras, the main building was refurbished and repaired, and a hostel for students built in 1919. Further
American funding made possible a chapel and, in 1925, an impressive new science
block. The "beauty and dignity" of the WCC campus was in part the achievement of Eleanor McDougall, the first principal.[83] Appointed in 1915, she steered
the college through its first two decades. With the united support of British mission partners, McDougall, an English classics lecturer from Westfield College,
London, managed to gain and retain the all-important North American connection. During a visit to the United States prior to taking up her post, she met and
was approved of by the American Women's Boards. Lucy Peabody reported that
her "admirable" address at the Triennial Conference of Women's Boards of Missions had delighted the audience with its "spiritual tone."[84] McDougall also managed to win over Lord Pentland, thus ensuring the crucial grant-in-aid from the
government.

A woman of deep spiritual convictions, McDougall took a pragmatic yet distinctly Christian view of what constituted higher education.[85] As she explained
to the college supporters, her students had to follow the university-prescribed
courses, including the study of Indian history and philosophy, since that was
what parents and university authorities required. But, she insisted, Christianity
had "everything to gain and nothing to lose by the widest diffusion of knowledge," since "ignorance, prejudice and apathy are its greatest enemies."[86] Her aim
was to educate a cadre of young women, intellectually equipped to become the
wives of educated men as well as qualified to enter appropriate professions such
as teaching, medicine, law, or social work. She recognized that many, if not most,
of her students would marry shortly after leaving college, but pointed out that
a number of these would need to teach in order to supplement family incomes.
She was not wrong. The majority of college leavers going into professions became teachers, and a teacher-training college affiliated to WCC was set up in 1923.
McDougall took a keen interest in the material and, even more, the spiritual welfare of the students, her task being made easier by the relatively small size of the

college. At no time before independence in 1947 did numbers exceed 200, about 120 being residential. Not all were Christian; about one-fifth, chiefly day students, were Hindu and there were a handful of Muslim students. All were, however, obliged to attend college services, and also to take part in a weekly scripture class. McDougall's published journal displays at times an old-fashioned missionary zeal, perhaps calculated to reassure supporters both in Britain and the United States. In one entry, she mentioned her great regret "that so very few of our Hindu and Moslem students have definitely become Christians."[87] She does not seem to have shared the view of a contemporary, Alice Varley, principal of Bentinck High School for Girls, a feeder school to the college, who "saw her task as befriending and appreciating rather than converting" her students.[88]

McDougall retired from WCC in 1938, so that challenges during what was to be the last decade of British rule fell to the lot of her successor, Eleanor Rivett. The year 1942 proved exceptionally difficult. Early in the year, there was the threat of Japanese air raids. The great challenge came in August with Gandhi's call for a campaign of nonviolent civil disobedience in support of Indian independence. Respected, not to say idolized, by some of the more liberal missionaries in the interwar period, Mahatma Gandhi was a revered figure to many of the college's staff and students. McDougall, wanting her students to experience the best in Indian culture and society, had invited both Gandhi and, on another occasion, Rabindranath Tagore to address them. During his visit in March 1925 Gandhi had met the assembled students, seated Indian style on mats, a number wearing saris of *khadi* (hand-spun and handwoven cloth), and had spoken in his customary blunt and direct manner. While acknowledging the great strides made in female education in Indian towns and cities, he pointed out the great need for education of "our illiterate sisters" among the rural poor. He dwelt on the gulf between middle-class students, particularly those of the Christian community, and the great majority of impoverished Indians living in the countryside, advocating the introduction of spinning into the college's activities as an aid to bridge the gap.[89] In fact, social work of one sort and another had always formed part of the extracurricular activity of the college. Again this was seen as a form of service, testifying to its Christian ethos. Throughout the 1920s and 1930s, students and members of staff had participated in welfare work at baby clinics, had taught hygiene to village girls, helped run Sunday schools, and had taught adult literacy classes. A regular Friday evening commitment was a visit to a slum area in Madras known as the

Mohammedan Gardens. In the difficult months following the launch of the Quit India Movement, a broad program of social activities, with a distinctly Gandhian flavor, was taken up with zest and vigor.

In August 1942, it looked as though the college would be brought to a halt by a student strike. But this proved divisive, with about half the students continuing to attend classes. Instrumental in finding a harmonious way forward was a temporary staff member, Marjorie Sykes, who had responded to a plea to help out with teaching at WCC. Sykes had taught for 10 years at Bentinck High School for Girls, but had then accepted an invitation from Rabindranath Tagore to teach at his educational center at Santineketan.[90] Gandhi's educational ideas had informed much of her work at Bentinck, where she had abolished prizes and competition, introduced one kitchen for all, and insisted that her pupils help with the cleaning of the school premises.[91] Gandhi's program of positive action was now to be implemented as far as was practical at WCC. Classes in Hindi were started; students took up spinning and, led by Sykes, a "Grow More Food Campaign" was begun in the college grounds. A more sustained college presence in Mohammedan Gardens was achieved when Sykes moved into a small house nearby and, with the aid of a trained kindergarten teacher, opened a nursery school for children there. At the college, enthusiasm for spinning and the study of Hindi lapsed after a while, but the nursery school, sustained by contributions from WCC staff and students, flourished.[92] Thus, a seemingly harmonious blend of Christian and Gandhian principles, forged through political necessity, enabled the college community to emerge in 1947 united and largely unscathed into the dawn of Indian freedom.

NOTES

1. Reginald Heber, Bishop of Calcutta, quoted in *Society for Promoting Female Education in China, India and the East* (London: Edward Suter, [1840]), 10.

2. Jane Eyre describing her pupils at Morton in North England, Quoted in Charlotte Bronte, *Jane Eyre* (London and Glasgow: Library of Classics, n.d.), 439.

3. There were similar developments at Madras where a school for Eurasian girls opened in 1819 and at Bombay where Margaret Wilson opened a school for Indian girls in 1829.

4. William Adams, *Reports on Vernacular Education in Bengal and Bihar Submitted to Government in 1835, 1836 and 1838 with a Brief View of Its Past and Present Condition* (Calcutta: Home Sec Press, 1838), 131–133.

5. Nevertheless, Vaishnavi women were employed as governesses to the womenfolk of the Tagore family.

6. J. C. Marshman quoted in George F. Bartle, "The Role of the British and Foreign School Society in Elementary Education in India and the East Indies 1813–75," *History of Education* 23, no. 1 (1994): 18.

7. Priscilla Chapman, *Hindoo Female Education* (London: R. B. Seeley & W. Burnside, 1839), 83.

8. Society for Promoting Female Education in China, India and the East, *Female Agency among the Heathen. As Recorded in the Correspondence of the SPFEE* (London: Suter, 1850), 54.

9. Behari Lal Singh, *The History of Native Female Education in Calcutta* (Calcutta: Baptist Mission Press, 1858), 27.

10. Rev Thomas Smith, "Hindu Female Education," *Calcutta Christian Observer*, (March 1840): 124.

11. Smith, "Hindu Female Education," 130.

12. Malavika Karlekar, *Voices from Within: Early Personal Narratives of Bengali Women* (Delhi and Oxford: Oxford University Press, 1991), 85.

13. Quoted in *India's Women and China's Daughters* 16, no. 115 (1896): 12.

14. Geraldine H. Forbes, "In Search of the 'Pure Heathen': Missionary Women in Nineteenth Century India," *Economic &Political Weekly* 21, no. 17 (1986): WS6.

15. Quoted in Benoy Bhusan Roy and Pranati Ray, *Zenana Mission, the Role of Christian Missionaries for the Education of Women in 19th Century Bengal* (Delhi: ISPCK, 1998), 127.

16. See Jane Haggis, "Ironies of Emancipation: Changing Configurations of 'Women's Work' in the 'Mission of Sisterhood' to Indian Women," *Feminist Review* 65 (2000), 108–126 and Eliza Kent, *Converting Women: Gender and Protestant Christianity in Colonial South India* (Oxford: Oxford University Press, 2004), 143–144. Lace-making, embroidery, as well as carpentry, printing, etc. were part of what became known as industrial missions, developed, particularly in southern India, for the maintenance of low caste Christians.

17. A. E. Henderson, *A Paper on Wool-work, Needle-work and Lace-work* (Madras: Dowden & Co., [1907]), 14.

18. Kent, *Converting Women*, 144.

19. Mary Frances Billington, *Woman in India* (London: Chapman & Hall, 1895), 189–190.

20. "Report of Miss Condon," *India's Women* (April 1881): 68.

21. Bengal (India) Education Department, *General Report on Public Instruction in Bengal for 1876–77* (Calcutta: Bengal Secretariat Book Depot), Paragraphs 268–269.

22. *Report of the Indian Education Commission* (Calcutta: Printed by the Superintendent of Government Printing, India, 1883), Paragraph 618.

23. Mary Carpenter, *Six Months in India* (London: Longmans & Co, 1868), 185.

24. Meredith Borthwick, *The Changing Role of Women in Bengal 1849–1905* (Guildford: Princeton University Press, c. 1984), 85.

25. Reported in *The Chronicle of the London Missionary Society* (1882): 355.

26. "Miss Pigot's Report," *News of Female Missions in Connection with the Church of Scotland,* New Series, no. 7 (July, 1877): 83.

27. "Letter from Miss Pigot," *News of Female Missions,* New Series, no. 13 (January 1879): 5–6.

28. Parna Sengupta, "Teaching Gender in the Colony: The Education of Outsider Teachers in Late Nineteenth Century Bengal," *The Journal of Women's History* 17, no. 4 (2005), 33.

29. "Letter from Miss Pigot," *News of Female Missions,* New Series, no. 6, (April, 1877): 50.

30. "Miss Pigot's Report," *News of Female Missions* (April 1877): 90.

31. "Annual Report," *News of Female Missions,* New Series, no. 15 (July 1879): 82.

32. "The Commissioners' Report on our Female Missions," *News of Female Missions,* New Series, no. 3 (July 1885): 113.

33. See Tim Allender, "Instructing the Women: Changing State Agendas in Colonial India, 1854–1924," in *Asia Reconstructed: Proceedings of the 16th Biennial Conference of the ASAA* (Wollongong, 2006), http://coombs.anu.edu.au/SpecialProj/ASAA/biennial-conference/2006/Allender-Tim-ASAA2006.pdf, 5–6 and Sengupta, "Teaching Gender," 34.

34. Allender, "Instructing the Women," 6–7.

35. Extract from Emily Bernard's evidence to the commissioners, *News of Female Missions* (July 1885): 115–116.

36. Dagmar Engels, *Beyond Purdah?: Women in Bengal, 1890–1939* (Delhi and Oxford: Oxford University Press, 1996), 172.

37. Quinquennial Survey 1907, quoted in Minna Cowan, *The Education of the Women of India Illustrated* (Edinburgh and London: Oliphant, Anderson & Ferrier, 1912), 50.

38. Gail Minault, *Secluded Scholars: Women's Education and Muslim Social Reform in Colonial India* (Delhi and Oxford: Oxford University Press, 1998), 172.

39. Mother Mary Colmcille, *First the Blade, History of the IBVM (Loreto) in India 1841–1962* (Calcutta: Firma K. L. Mukhopadhyay, 1968), 23.

40. Colmcille, *First the Blade,* iii.

41. "Pilot Letters" describing the work of women missionaries of SPG, reprinted from *The Home Workers' Gazette* III (1915): 19.

42. Frances Wood, *No Dogs and Not Many Chinese. Treaty Port Life in China 1843–1943* (London: John Murray, 1998), 36.

43. A.F.S., *Missions to the Women of China*, ed. Miss Whately (London, Edinburgh, 1866), 100.

44. Katherine F. Bruner, John K. Fairbank, and Richard J. Smith (eds.), *Entering China's Service: Robert Hart's Journals, 1854–1863* (Cambridge, MA: Harvard University Press, 1986), 61–62.

45. E. Aldersey White, comp., *A Woman Pioneer in China, the Life of Mary Ann Aldersey* (London: The Livingstone Press, 1932), 33–34.

46. M. Burton, *Education of Women in China* (New York: F. H. Revell Co., [1911]), 51.

47. Burton, *Education*, 46.

48. For a fuller discussion of the topic, see Alison R. Drucker, "The Influence of Western Women on the Anti-footbinding Movement 1840–1911," *Women in China: Current Directions in Historical Scholarship*, eds. Richard W. L. Guisso and Stanley Johannesen (Youngstown, NY: Philo Press, 1981).

49. This was the American mission educator Luella Miner. See Jane Hunter, The *Gospel of Gentility, American Women Missionaries in Turn-of-the Century China* (New Haven, CT and London: Yale University Press, c. 1984), 233.

50. Burton, *Education*, 108.

51. Paul J. Bailey, *Gender and Education in China: Gender Discourses and Women's Schooling in the Early Twentieth Century* (London: Routledge, c. 2007), 6–7.

52. *Christian Education in China: A Study Made by an Educational Commission Representing the Mission Boards and Societies Conducting Work in China* (New York, Committee of Reference and Counsel of the Foreign Missions Conference of North America, 1922), 259.

53. Ida Belle Lewis, *The Education of Girls in China* (New York: Teacher's College, Columbia University, 1919), 21–23.

54. Letter from Harold Marsden, July 19, 1925, CWM/LMS, South China (Fukien) Incoming Correspondence, Box 14.

55. *The Chronicle of the London Missionary Society* (July 1916): 132.

56. CWM/LMS, South China (Fukien) Reports, Rainey, 1920.

57. Innes Herdman, *Liao Hongying—Fragments of a Life: From Changting to Norwich* (Dereham: Larks Press, c. 1996).

58. CWM/LMS, South China (Fukien) Reports, Rainey, Five Year Report 1920.

59. CWM/LMS, South China (Fukien) Reports, Rainey, 1921.

60. "Survey of Work at Tingchow," CWM/LMS, South China (Fukien) Incoming Correspondence, 1924.

61. CWM/LMS, South China (Fukien) Reports, Rainey, 1922.

62. Herdman, *Fragments of a Life*, 28–29.

63. Bryan Papers, biographical file.

64. Bryan Papers, autobiographical jottings.

65. CWM/LMS, South China (Fukien) Reports, Rainey, 1925.

66. Ernest Richard Hughes (1883–1956), later reader in Chinese Philosophy and Religion at Oxford University.

67. Letter from E.R.Hughes, July 2, 1925, CWM/LMS, South China (Fukien) Incoming Correspondence, Box 14.

68. Letter from E.M. Rainey, January 26, 1926, CWM/LMS, South China (Fukien) Incoming Correspondence, Box 14.

69. CWM/LMS, South China (Fukien) Reports, Rainey, 1926 and 1927.

70. Herdman, *Fragments of a Life*, 42.

71. Herdman, *Fragments of a Life*, 72.

72. Letter from E.M. Rainey, May 28, 1929, CWM/LMS, South China (Fukien) Incoming Correspondence, Box 15.

73. Letter from Lo-you Girls School, Tingchow, November 12, 1929 CWM/LMS, South China (Fukien) Incoming Correspondence, Box 16.

74. Herdman, *Fragments of a Life*, 77.

75. On the importance of national survival and girls making "decisions for China rather than for God," see Jane Hunter, *Gospel of Gentility*, 249.

76. Set up by the Continuation Committee of the World Missionary Conference of 1910.

77. Letter from Lord Pentland, governor of Madras, to Sir Andrew Fraser, chairman of European Section of the Educational Committee, May 9, 1914, MSS Eur F220/1.

78. Letter from Lord Pentland, August 19, 1914, MSS Eur F220/1.

79. Keith Clements, *Faith on the Frontier: A Life of J.H. Oldham* (Edinburgh: T&T Clark, 1999), 118.

80. Letter from Lucy W. Peabody to John [*sic*] Oldham, January 5, 1915, MSS Eur F220/2.

81. Letter from Pittendrigh to Lunt, secretary of the British Board of the Madras Christian College, January 13, 1914, MSS Eur F220/4.

82. Eleanor McDougall, *Women's Christian College, Madras, 1915–1925* (Madras: Women's Christian College, 1926), 9.

83. Letter from K. N. Brockway to E. J. Bingle, August 12, 1956, MSS Eur F220/87.

84. Letter from Peabody to Lunt, February 12, 1915, MSS Eur F220/2.

85. Brockway letter, MSS Eur F220/87.

86. Eleanor McDougall, *Women's Christian College, Madras, 1915–1935* (Madras: [1936]), 6.

87. *Principal's Journal,* Women's Christian College, Madras, 39, October 1936, 8.

88. Geoffrey Carnall, "Marjorie Sykes 1905–1995," in *Oxford Dictionary of National Biography* (Oxford: Oxford University Press, 2004), 556.

89. *Sunflower,* Women's Christian College, Madras, April 1925, 18–20.

90. Norman Goodall, *A History of the London Missionary Society, 1895–1945* (London: Oxford University Press, 1954), 74.

91. Martha Dart, *Marjorie Sykes: Quaker-Gandhian* ([York]: Sessions Book Trust in association with Woodbrooke College, c. 1993), 25.

92. *Sunflower,* Women's Christian College, Madras, September 1943, 12–13 and Dart, *Marjorie Sykes Quaker Gandhian,* 40–42.

6

Missionary Women
and Medical Aid

A single medical missionary might do more than twenty evangelistic missionaries.[1]

The attempts by Sophia Jex-Blake and other women to train and qualify as doctors were greeted with hostility and derision in many circles in the Britain of the 1860s and 1870s. However, at roughly the same period, powerful calls for women to undertake medical training in order to assist the missionary enterprise overseas began to appear in print. One of the earliest came in January 1873 from Dr. William Elmslie, a pioneering Church Missionary Society medical missionary in Kashmir. While some *zenanas* in cities like Calcutta had been opened up to Christian influences by female educators, he urged that a different strategy be adopted where Indian homes, particularly Muslim ones, remained obdurately shut.

> The agency of English education alone is quite insufficient to gain for the Zenana worker an entrance into Mahommedan homes, and that politically it is of the utmost importance to find some agency which ... will open up a way into those dark and dangerous dwellings for the Christian philanthropist and evangelist. Female Medical Missions, we believe, are calculated to be that agency.[2]

The evangelical and political argument was closely followed by the humanitarian one. Like most Westerners in India, Elmslie was dismissive of India's existing medical practitioners: the "native *hakims*" who were "totally ignorant of western medicine and surgery" and, for that matter, of women's "ailments," and the *dais*, or midwives, who were "generally very ignorant, meddlesome and immoral." Since the traditional secluded lifestyle and innate modesty of Indian women rendered medical treatment at centers, or by trained medical men, inappropriate, Elmslie and others argued that the only answer was to bring to them the skilled attentions of trained medical women. Such women could only come, in Elmslie's view, from the West since "Western medical and surgical skill" was "esteemed everywhere."[3] Indeed, a couple of fully trained Western medical women had already arrived in India at the time he was writing. Dr. Clara Swain, who had graduated from the Woman's Medical College, Philadelphia, in 1869, began a practice at Bareilly in 1870, while another, Sara C. Seward, opened a dispensary in Allahabad in 1872. Both had come out under the auspices of American missionary societies.

A great obstacle stood in the way of sending medically trained women missionaries from Britain. There was not as yet a women's medical school, nor was it possible for a woman to qualify in Britain as a doctor. Elmslie himself did not see the need for medical qualifications: "no diploma is needed to enable a Christian lady to practise medicine and to cure diseases in the Zenanas of India." She should follow a course of study "including obstetrics, diseases peculiar to women and children, diseases of the skin, and diseases of the eye" perhaps at the hands of a "refined Christian medical man." Attendance at a "mixed class" in an existing medical school, he added, could not "be condemned in too severe language."[4] The practicality of training numbers of women in this manner was not put to very great test. The year after the publication of his article, the London School of Medicine for Women (LSMW) opened its doors to its first 12 students.[5] One of these, Fanny Butler, became Britain's first fully trained female medical missionary and the first British woman to practice in India as a fully qualified doctor. A "volunteer for God's service from childhood," she was no militant advocate of woman's rights. Her first reaction to reading Elmslie's "Plea for Female Medical Missions for India" was to say "I could not do it: I do not care for the medical women's movement." Eventually persuaded by herself and her sisters that she could, she was among the first to enroll at the new medical school.[6] In the 30 years following her qualification as a doctor in 1880, 94 graduates of the LSMW went on to serve as medical missionaries, 59 in India and 16 in China.[7]

Fanny Butler was not however the first British woman missionary in India to engage in medical work. Zenana women missionaries such as Priscilla Winter, the daughter and wife of a missionary, became aware of the medical needs of the Indian women and children they visited during the 1850s and 1860s. With her husband, Winter had arrived in post-Mutiny Delhi in 1863. In addition to zenana visiting, she established an outdoor dispensary on the banks of the River Jumna (Yamuna), where she distributed basic remedies to "all classes of Hindu women, the majority of whom, if they go no where else, yet go down every morning to the river both to make their vows and dip in the sacred stream."[8] Later, the Winters extended and developed their work as the Delhi Female Medical Mission. For this they needed a dedicated worker with medical training. In 1875 they appointed Miss Engelmann, who had acquired her medical knowledge in much the way William Elmslie had advocated: "while on furlough she had taken a training … in midwifery and 'by sitting beside a doctor in his consulting room learned to use a stethoscope and something about eyes.' "[9] Thus equipped, Engelmann continued in this post until 1891 when the mission appointed its first fully qualified female medical practitioner.

The question of full or partial medical training was one that greatly exercised the supporters and critics of female medical missions. Was it necessary, many asked, for women whose main business was to win souls to subject themselves to lengthy, costly medical training for which they might not, in any case, possess the necessary mental, physical, and emotional stamina? Counterarguments, however, became increasingly vigorous. The influential John Lowe, secretary of the Edinburgh Medical Missionary Society, argued that since female medical missionaries represented "the professional skill of the West," it would not do for them to fail in tackling the critical medical cases with which they would have to deal.[10] Elizabeth Beilby's early experiences with difficult maternity cases certainly bore out this view. In 1875, after a year at the LSMW, she went out to Lucknow as an agent of the Indian Female Normal School and Instruction Society, where she opened first a dispensary and then a small hospital. She found that while she was able to help many, other cases were simply beyond her.

People … know nothing of the hours of anxious reading … and of, one time, broken health because the task was too much for me. . . . Whatever I may

have done, I should have done better had I been qualified.... I could tell of
many cases where, from prolonged suffering, the poor woman has been in
such a serious state, that many medical men would have hesitated to undertake such a case alone.[11]

She became convinced of the absolute necessity of undertaking full medical
training and in 1881 left India for Britain; returning in 1885, as a fully qualified and trained physician, though no longer a missionary.[12] A warning that the
reputation of missionary societies would suffer if they continued to send out
inadequately prepared female medical workers was forcefully enunciated by
Dr. Elizabeth Garrett Anderson, who acidly pointed out in a letter to *The Times*,
of October 31, 1881, that it would hardly "recommend Christianity to Hindoo
ladies to send them missionaries in the disguise of indifferent doctors."[13] The
issue was also taken up by Jex-Blake, who was particularly critical of the Church
of England Zenana Missionary Society, which she called a "notorious offender"
in disregarding "professional skill."[14] Concern was expressed at the LSMW that
their graduates who became medical missionaries should maintain the highest possible professional standards. Dr. Edith Pechey, speaking at the school in
1881, urged women students intending to become missionaries to go out "with
the best credentials possible and as you belong to two professions, see that you
serve both faithfully."[15] Another pioneer, Dr. Frances Hoggan, while advocating
the need for medical women to go out to India, strongly argued that they be "dis-
connected from any proselytizing or sectarian agencies."[16] Missionary societies
were slow to respond to the criticism of their medical and nursing policies, but
by the early 1900s, most required fully trained and qualified medical practitioners and nurses to run their dispensaries and hospitals. The World Missionary
Conference of 1910 strongly urged that all medical missions "should be under
the charge of fully qualified Medical Missionaries with properly staffed and
equipped Hospitals."[17]

Even when fully trained, medical missionaries both female and male frequently
found the sheer scale and range of the work overwhelming. Breakdowns in health
were far from uncommon.[18] Balfour and Young's 1929 study recalled how the pioneer female medical missionary worked "alone, usually without an assistant....
On occasion, she was her own anaesthetist and her own compounder."[19] Much
of the medical and surgical work initially took place in dispensaries, which literally thousands of women would visit. After an initial period of service in Central

India, and later Bihar, Fanny Butler moved to Kashmir, where she opened a dispensary and a small hospital in Srinagar. According to the traveler and writer Isabella Bird Bishop, visiting in 1889,

> It was a terrible sight to see the way in which the women pressed upon her at the dispensary door. . . . The crush was so great as sometimes to overpower the men [guarding the door] and precipitated the women bodily into the consulting room. The evil odour, the heat, the insanitary condition in which Miss Butler did her noble work of healing and telling of the Healer of souls were, I believe, the cause of the sacrifice of her life.[20]

According to her niece, Fanny Butler frequently worked a 12-hour day, often seeing several hundred women during that time. She died of dysentery and complications in October 1889 at the early age of 39.[21]

A PIONEER WOMAN DOCTOR IN MANCHURIA

China had proved notoriously difficult terrain for the first generation of Protestant missionaries. Not only did the population exhibit strong resistance to the Gospel message, they were openly, and sometimes violently, hostile toward the Gospel bearers. Yet medical missionaries like the American Peter Parker and William Lockhart of the London Missionary Society (LMS) found that successful treatment of diseases and medical conditions beyond the skill of local practitioners gradually overcame suspicion and antagonism. Lockhart expressed his certainty that "medical missions in China have been successful in winning an entrance for the Gospel to the hearts and consciences of the people which no other agency could have so well effected."[22] By 1887, it was estimated that more than 70 Western medical missionaries were working in various parts of China; in 1911, that figure had grown to more than 350, 128 coming from Britain.[23] China's women never exerted quite the pull on British consciences, from the Queen-Empress down, of the constantly portrayed wretched condition of Indian *zenana* women. Nevertheless, many British missionary women were to serve in China in a medical or nursing capacity.

Isabel Mitchell's experiences were typical of the pioneering female medical missionary. Born in Belfast in 1879, the daughter of an Irish Presbyterian minister, she had responded in 1895 to a call for women doctors in China.

With financial support from friends at home, she undertook training at Glasgow. Appointed by the Irish Presbyterian Mission to the remote town of Fakumen (Faku) in Manchuria, she was prevented by the Russo-Japanese War from sailing until 1905. Initially, she left her drugs "at the railway that I might not be tempted to begin medical work before I had a grasp of the language," but by June 1906, she had set up a dispensary "in two little native rooms in the Girls' school compound." By October of that year, she was driving out "in the little blue covered cart" with Mrs. Fo, the Bible woman, to treat villagers.[24] She wrote home that she did not "at all astonish them with what I can do but by what I can't!" During her first year or so, she was able to call on the advice of another mission doctor, Emma Crooks, at Kirin (Jilin), but from 1907, she was, and felt, very alone. "Do you realize," she wrote her family, "that I am quite alone medically, I mean. Every day I think the Mission could not have left a more inexperienced doctor anywhere ... to tackle this big work alone in Fakumen. I would be ashamed to tell you how frightened I have been." She found her first operation, which was carried out in the dispensary, particularly nerve-racking. Her patient was a young woman, unable to walk, brought in by cart. The foot was "the size of a football and wrapped in layer after layer of Chinese paper.... Before long my little dispenser had to open all the windows as we all felt ill." It was quite clear the foot would have to be amputated. "I knew it should be done and done at once, in spite of shaking knees."[25] The operation was performed successfully and soon Dr. Mitchell had trained a small band of young Chinese women assistants who could help in operations, and with compounding and dispensing medicines. The women's hospital, which she had long planned, was opened by the wife of the Fakumen magistrate in September 1909. She enthused about the new building in letters home to family and friends:

> The Hospital is built in two blocks of one storey. The front block is the out-patient department. The second block stands behind this with garden spaces between, and is for in-patients. There are two large wards here with accommodation for forty, a good operating-room with bright windows, at present shining in all its bravery of new white-enamelled furniture.[26]

Its cost, 600 pounds sterling, was paid for mainly by supporters in Ireland, though just over 10 percent had been raised locally. Mitchell was very pleased that the hospital was debt free and by taking in some wealthy patients, particularly for opium cures, ensured it remained so. In October 1910, after five years' service, she returned to Ireland on furlough, the hospital being forced to close as there was no substitute doctor. It was three years before Mitchell was able to return. During this time she suffered a complete breakdown in health, apparently both physical and nervous. Returning to Fakumen in October 1913, she was reassured to find that she was no longer the sole Western-trained doctor in town. She enjoyed meeting and consulting with Dr. Hsu, a graduate of Peking Union Medical College, now in charge of Fakumen's government hospital. Mitchell wrote home, "I had nice Dr Hsu over for a consultation yesterday. I like him better each time." She was delighted to discover that he was "a real Chinese gentleman, an earnest Christian and a keen doctor." He chaired her open day when the elders and pastor of the church came to look round her domain; they were fascinated by the operating theater with chloroform, lancets, and sterilizers. Hsu brought his male assistants with him on that occasion, causing consternation to her own female dispensers. The latter proved too bashful to give the visitors tea as had been planned, but rallied in confidence, and hospitality, on the arrival of members of the Dorcas Society, older Chinese women who made quilts and bedding for the hospital.[27] In the course of her work, Mitchell greatly relied on her six young dispensers, giving each of them individual responsibilities, though she regretted the lack of a nurse. In January 1917 the hospital closed for a fortnight; it was simply too cold to continue. This enabled Mitchell, who saw herself very much a physician evangelist, to play a full role in the women's meetings held at the Chinese New Year. She also submitted what would be her last hospital report (for 1916) during which treatment had been given to 7,865 patients. In March 1917 Dr. Hsu was called in again, this time to diagnose Mitchell herself. He found her to be dangerously ill with diphtheria. Despite responding to treatment, the strain was too much for her heart. She died on March 23 aged 38. Much of the town turned out for her funeral:

> First came a large cross covered with flowers and the Chinese inscription, "Chi Tai Fu (Dr Mitchell) walks with God," then ten white banners telling of her love and devotion for their people, for whom she had laid down her life. Then the white bier carried by eight men. The missionaries followed, then came her six Hospital dispensers and about one hundred of her little

Sabbath School scholars. Next, the Elders and Chinese Pastor, then the school girls and boys, followed by the long procession of Church members and old patients—five hundred in all, I am sure. As we passed through crowded streets, we caught the words, "Good Doctor," so often. Everyone who knew her loved her.[28]

Mitchell had had great ambitions for her second term of service, but in the months before her death she experienced considerable disappointment. She had hoped that her partnership with Dr. Hsu could improve sanitation and encourage the townsfolk to take preventive measures against such prevalent diseases as tuberculosis. They had, in fact, made some progress along these lines. She also had hopes that Hsu might look after her hospital when she took her next furlough. But in 1916 the Prefect of Fakumen appeared to turn against the influence of Western medicine in the town. Mitchell was furious. "He (the Prefect) has gone and extended his patronage to an old Chinese quack, and they are starting a school of

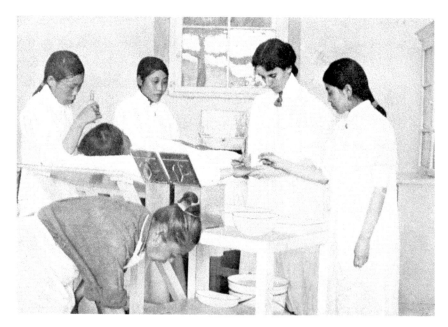

Figure 6.1. In the operating room. Dr. Isabel Mitchell, her three dispensers, patient, and hospital worker in the Women's Hospital, Fakumen, Manchuria, c. 1913–1916. F.W.S. O'Neill, ed., *Dr. Isabel Mitchell of Manchuria [Letters]* (London: J. Clarke & Co., 1917), 140. (Courtesy of the Council for World Mission.)

medicine, so-called. Only Chinese methods to be taught, no Anatomy, or Physiology, or any rubbish of that sort. They want eighty pupils, and these young men are to graduate in a year and a half." Hsu doubted whether he would now be able to remain in post.[29] Nor had her plans to find a trained medical colleague, and possible successor to herself, succeeded. Funding had been raised to train a female medical student at the Peking Union Medical College and, after a careful search, a suitable student was selected. However, the young woman in question fell ill with typhoid while studying in Peking and died. It had proved much harder to find qualified staff to run the hospital than to build it. Like many pioneer medical missionaries, Mitchell's strength had not been sufficient for the tasks she had diligently and single-handedly taken on. The women's hospital at Fakumen was closed following her death and remained so for several years.

THE FOUNDING OF THE FIRST MEDICAL SCHOOL
FOR WOMEN IN ASIA

Dr. Edith Brown was one of the two first women medical missionaries sent out to India by the Baptist Zenana Mission (BZM) in 1891.[30] She shortly afterward found herself like Mitchell in a remote and unsupported situation, this time in the town of Palwal, 60 kilometers south of Delhi, where the Baptist Missionary Society (BMS) had only recently established a mission. Brown had first studied natural sciences at Cambridge before going on to become a student at the LSMW. Steeped in her evangelical faith, ambitious, determined, and administratively gifted, she was to make a major contribution to the development of Christian medical education in India. The foundation of her life's work lay in her early experiences as a medical missionary, which she found frustrating and limiting. After a preparatory year acquiring Urdu and working at a small hospital for women at Ludhiana in the Punjab, it had been agreed with the BZM that she would begin medical missionary work at their new station at Palwal, south of Delhi. She was not favorably impressed by the journey there:

> I hardly know how to describe the journey to Palwal. I may say that I never imagined such shaking and jolting. The first eleven miles I came out in the Mission *tum-tum* which is a kind of low dog-cart with a hood. Then Mangalia (the Indian girl who is to help with the nursing and dispensary)

and I got into an *ekka*. This is a little cart without springs and with only room to sit on the floor with one's knees up to one's chin. The more comfortable position is to let one's legs hang over the side but they soon got very badly bruised against the edge of the cart and I had to return to the Indian woman's usual way of sitting.... After eleven hours of this we got out and rested for a couple of hours at a bungalow in Balangha, had tea and lay down to get straightened out, then we mounted to our seats again and had fifteen miles more, this time over very bad roads. I was indeed thankful to reach the end of my journey.[31]

Her destination was disappointingly small and insignificant. She wrote home "Palwal is a town of 14,000 inhabitants but there are no European residents here outside the mission compound. It has one main street or bazaar." She also discovered that the language spoken was Hindi rather than the Urdu she had learnt at Ludhiana.[32] The work too was discouraging. Prospective patients seemed frightened, with female patients preferring to consult the local *hakim* rather than submit to operations. Others threw away the medicines she prescribed. When she was able to carry out an operation, she found the facilities vastly inferior to those at Ludhiana, and the lack of trained assistants exasperating. She was also conscious, as she was at Ludhiana, of a profound cultural barrier between herself and her patients. Her biographer, Francesca French, who knew her well, explained the effect of contact with such patients on a young doctor, evangelically minded, socially reserved, and Western-trained: "every day each part of her being, her body, her mind and her spirit was wearied with the sustained conflict with wrong-doing, with wrong-thinking and with wrong-believing."[33]

She became convinced that a Western medical missionary working on her own in an isolated posting could never meet the overwhelming health needs of the women and children in the surrounding area. Trained indigenous doctors and nurses who could have closer intimacy with their patients than she ever could were required, and in large numbers. During her year at Palwal and at Simla (Shimla), where she had a short but welcome respite, she conceived the notion of a Christian medical school to train "suitable Indian girls" as medical assistants, nurses, dispensers, and midwives, all attached to an existing missionary hospital. Remote Palwal with its "sticky heat" could never house such a center, but Ludhiana, which already had a hospital and good communications, since it was on the Grand

Trunk Road, could.[34] She intended that the center should serve the needs not just of Ludhiana and the Punjab, but also of neighboring provinces. Such a bold plan needed supporters. She had made it her business, while in Simla, to meet the Surgeon General of India, and had obtained his encouragement for her plan. She now called together a conference of British and American women medical missionaries working in the Punjab, North-West Provinces, and Rajputana to meet in Ludhiana in December 1893.[35] Thirteen attended, of whom some six were fully qualified doctors, representing seven missionary societies. While all those who attended gave her scheme their backing, there were considerable doubts about its viability. Could the necessary clinical facilities be provided at the small Ludhiana hospital and who might be qualified and able to teach? Less than a year later, the North India School of Medicine for Christian Women opened its doors to four medical students, two trainee dispensers, and a small group of nurses. A class for *dais,* who were paid to attend, was started shortly afterward. The teaching staff consisted of the principal, Edith Brown, who had been temporarily released from

Figure 6.2. The staff of Ludhiana Christian Medical College, c. 1895. Back row, left to right: Miss Hoyd, Dr. Edith Brown, and Miss Thornett. Front row: Drs. Dodson and Gellatley. (Royal Free Archives Centre, Ludhiana Medical College Collection.)

her duties by the BMS and who was able to teach in both English and Urdu, while two American women medical missionaries in their first year of medical service in India taught part-time in English.

From the start, and for the next half-century, issues of funding and staffing, crises caused by outbreaks of plague and cholera, and civil and political unrest meant that the very survival of the institution itself was often in doubt. However, Brown's deep Christian faith, her grasp of finance—she had the "accounts of college and hospital at her finger tips"—and her business sense enabled her to grapple with and overcome problems that would have floored countless others.[36] Her negotiating skills with government led to the recognition of the school, and annual government grants from 1904. Donations made possible the building of a larger hospital, in memory of one of the Greenfield sisters, founders of the first hospital at Ludhiana, and further government grants enabled the completion of quarters for doctors, college staff, and students. Persuaded that single-sex medical education was the way forward for the Punjab, the government requested in 1909 that Ludhiana open its doors to non-Christian students on the grounds that this would enable such students to come under the "refining and elevating influence of Christian women during their years of training."[37] Following the transfer of women students from Lahore in 1915, students at the college numbered between 250 and 300, and the institution was renamed "The Women's Christian Medical College with which is incorporated the Punjab Medical School for Women." An additional stream of revenue came from the private patients attracted not only by Brown's reputation as a skilled doctor and surgeon, but also by the great trouble taken to meet their varied religious requirements. Brown, who loved nothing better than "poring over plans and blueprints with her Indian overseer," ingeniously contrived wards that had both public and private entrances.[38] Thus "every private ward patient was accessible to her husband at all hours through one entrance, yet, coming and going, he never sighted another patient," while all the wards were "open through the main courtyard to doctor and nurses."[39] Despite the extra sources of income, money was always tight and Brown zealously controlled expenditure on hospital equipment and supplies. One of her colleagues described how "stocks of rubber gloves were kept in an airtight tin hatbox, which must have come out with Dr Brown in 1891, and from here the gloves were given out and dates kept of issue."[40]

Brown's religious faith was both an inward and an outward component of her life and work. She rose every day at 4 A.M. for prayer and bible reading, and ensured that the day for her students began with a service and Bible exposition in the college chapel.[41] On doctrinal matters she felt strongly. Even her friends commented that her doctrinal rigidity caused problems for those who might have given her and Ludhiana greater support. Her insistence that all who came to work at Ludhiana should agree to a basis of faith including "belief in the whole of the Bible as the Inspired Words of God" was enshrined in the college's constitution. As late as 1923, she obtained a victory over those on her governing body who ventured to disagree with her.[42] Francesca French, who with her sister Evangeline and close colleague Mildred Cable had visited Ludhiana and were great admirers of Brown's work, considered that her mind "had not moved from its foundation principles," and that such an attitude was not practical in an institution reliant on the support and participation of a number of missionary societies of varied Christian persuasions. Eventually, Brown was outvoted, and this, according to French, resulted both in the appointment of staff members with higher professional qualifications and the additional advantage that they were supported financially by their own missionary societies.[43]

By 1941, the jubilee year of Brown's arrival in India, more than 400 doctors of the licentiate standard, 143 nurses, 168 dispensers, and over 1,000 midwives had graduated from Ludhiana.[44] Brown herself had received a number of honors, including the unique distinction for a British missionary of being made, in 1932, Dame Commander in the Order of the British Empire. There were disappointments. Her aim had always been to achieve M.B., B.S. status for her graduating students but throughout her time at Ludhiana, they were only considered eligible for the Licentiate Diploma of the Punjab State Medical Faculty, which meant that they could never attain anything beyond assistant doctor status. This was not the case with the prestigious Lady Hardinge Medical College for Women in Delhi, which opened in 1917 and whose students were eligible to study for the full medical degrees of M.B., B.S. Only in 1952, after Brown had retired, was the Christian Medical College at Ludhiana able to offer the upgraded course to its students who were, for the first time, to include men. Brown was a pioneer of medical training for women in India, but her "name and work ... never caught the popular imagination in this country and even in Christian circles" was "not as well known as it should be."[45] In writing these words, her obituarist, and former secretary, might have been thinking of the famous Dr. Ida Scudder, founder of the Christian Medical College and Hospital at Vellore in southern India. Opened in

1918, Vellore, backed by 11 missionary societies, grew rapidly in size and reputation to become the foremost Christian hospital in India. Vellore's many enviable "large and beautiful buildings" were largely the result of its being selected as one of seven women's institutions in Asia funded by the Women's Union Christian Colleges in the Orient appeal launched in America in 1920, a degree of financial support not vouchsafed to Ludhiana.[46]

THE RISE OF THE MISSIONARY NURSE

By the early 20th century, it had become clear that there was a crying need for nurses to run the many mission hospitals that had been established both in India and China. Statistics compiled at the time of the World Missionary Conference in 1910 show that there were 550 mission hospitals worldwide, the great majority of which were situated in China and India.[47] Attempts had been made by missionary doctors to train local nurses. But progress was slow. One of the problems on the ground was that the concept of a hospital nurse, particularly a female one, was alien to both countries. Edith Brown explained some of her early difficulties in attempting to train local nurses at Ludhiana:

> Nineteen years ago when I came out to India, there was nothing which could be called nursing in the Woman's Hospital, and it was exceedingly difficult to get any woman or girl of good family to enter a course of training. Sanitary work was objected to as a "sweeper's work" and personal care of the patients as "ayah's work," while there was no appreciation of the necessity for accuracy or method in the giving of medicines and food. Some of the orphan girls were sent from the orphanage to learn nursing, the reason for their coming being such as the following: "as she has only one eye and cannot be a teacher," or "as she is so disobedient, I can do nothing with her" or, "as has such a bad temper that she cannot be trusted in the school, because she beats the children."[48]

In China too nursing was regarded as menial work. Etiquette precluded women from waiting on men outside the family or working alongside men in a public place. In any case, the pool of educated women was so small it was almost impossible to find suitable female recruits. By 1921, however, Dr. Harold Balme could marvel that there "had been few events in China within recent years which have marked so fundamentally a change of mental attitude on the part of the people … it has now been found possible … to introduce into Chinese hospitals the practice of nursing on a modern basis."[49] In India too, it was claimed that "in the training of nurses and in the department of nursing generally Christian missions have made one of the most distinctive contributions to India."[50]

The new factor that brought about such a change, more rapid in China than in India, was the arrival in mission hospitals of the fully trained Western nurse. It was a move that was also to transform the efficiency of the mission hospital. Even though the new breed of nurses, in the Nightingale mould, were still in a minority in Britain and America at the end of the 19th century, they were an ever-growing force, both in numbers and influence.[51] In 1887 the British Nurses Association had been founded and, soon after, a register of nurses was established only admitting those who had had three years training in a recognized training school. By the early 20th century most of the main missionary societies in Britain were actively seeking fully qualified and experienced nurses capable both of running hospitals and of providing modern up-to-date training for indigenous staff. This development was assisted in 1903 by the founding of the Nurses' Missionary Union, later renamed the Nurses' Missionary League. To better inform prospective candidates, the league brought out *A Missionary Directory for Nurses,* which listed the requirements of the various societies. In addition to professional qualifications, some were expected to undergo a period of missionary training and to sit examinations. The LMS required all its candidates to be examined in scriptures, Christian evidences, the leading doctrines of Christianity, and the history of missions. The society was obliged to lower the pass level in order to make sure that a sufficient number of nurses passed.[52] Despite the challenges, there were by 1916 over 500 Western-trained nurses serving in Protestant overseas missions, most of whom had been sent to serve in hospitals in India and China.[53]

Through the *Missionary Directory for Nurses,* the Wesleyan Methodist Missionary Society cautioned nurses considering missionary service that those "who have had a regular training in first class hospitals only, are not likely to adapt themselves easily to the scanty equipment, and other drawbacks of the embryo mission hospital; those used to District, slum or mission nursing" would be better prepared.[54] The experiences of two British missionary nurses arriving in China in the second decade of the 20th century amply illustrated those warnings.

Elspeth Hope-Bell was appointed matron of the Men's Hospital run by the LMS at Hankow in 1911, the first matron appointed to a hospital for males. She was taken on a tour shortly after her arrival and wrote home "it is truly an awfully dirty place."[55] Circumstances, including the outbreak of the 1911 Revolution in October, contrived to keep her out of the hospital until the September of the following year, but then she started as she meant to go on. The hospital vocabulary she began compiling on her first day showed where her initial energies were directed. She began the list with the Chinese for "dust, to dust, duster, towel, mop, broom, rub, floor, cupboards, turn upside down." On the second day, "apron, rubbish, rubbish pail, clear away, put away" were added. "And so," she added, "I shall go from day to day."[56] Nor was she impressed with the building as a whole. Like the equivalent LMS hospital she saw in Tientsin in 1914 it was "a ramshackle old tumble-down building." She also had some grumbles about the LMS itself, which she saw as lacking in direction, vitality, and, above all, funding, especially when contrasted with the more ambitious American societies with plentiful funds. Despite her criticisms, she was to remain at the hospital until 1925.

Each summer Hope-Bell, like many other missionaries, would retreat from the unbearable heat of towns and cities and travel up to the resort of Kuling on the Lushan Mountain for rest and recreation. Here she had some stimulating and practical talks with other British and American nursing sisters and matrons, particularly in the summer of 1913 when a group of them put together a unified syllabus for the training of Chinese nurses. In this way the Nurses' Association of China (NAC), first inaugurated in 1909 largely through the efforts of an American missionary nurse, Cora Simpson, came more formally into being. Nina Gage, also American, was the NAC's first president and Hope-Bell its second. It thus fell to Hope-Bell to preside over the NAC's annual conference, which met in the summer of 1915 at the prestigious buildings of the Peking Union Medical College. Here she met distinguished figures such as Sir John Jordan, the British minister; Surgeon-General Ch'uan, head of the Government Army Medical College in Tientsin whom Hope-Bell greatly admired; and Roger Green, director of the China Medical Board of the Rockefeller Foundation, which now funded the Peking College. All of them were keen to demonstrate their support for the new association and turned up to make speeches on the opening day. The conference proceedings were almost entirely in English, but there were some sessions in Chinese for the 30–40 Chinese nurses in attendance.

Gladys Stephenson, a sister in the Wesleyan Deaconess Order, arrived in China in 1915 at the age of 26. She had wanted, she said, to become a nurse so that she could be a missionary. Her first posting was at the Hodge Memorial Hospital at Hankow. Here she spent a year, familiarizing herself with hospital work, learning Chinese and acquiring a Chinese name "Si Teh Fen," meaning "Be a Tower of Fragrance and Virtue." In 1917 she traveled to Anlu in Hubei Province, northern China to take up the position of matron at the Methodist Mission Hospital. Here she found much more primitive conditions. There were only four nurses, boys aged 15–16, all, she noted, rather small. There were 60 primitive beds made from planks of wood, and 20 sheets that the doctor returning from furlough had brought with him. The newly appointed matron's first act was to acquire a sewing machine and start making sheets, pillowcases, and mattress covers. A local carpenter made bedside tables and, eventually, iron bedsteads were brought in. She found time to recruit and train more nurses as the first patients began to fill up the hospital. Many of them needed eye operations, while others, the area abounding with bandits, had gunshot wounds. A bandit leader was an unpopular patient at one point. By 1919, and despite the small size of her hospital, Gladys Stephenson was running an NAC-approved training school for nurses. James Liu, one of the four original nurses at Anlu, took his examinations to become a registered nurse and passed in fourth place in the whole of China. Once Stephenson had got used to the idea, she thought there were considerable advantages in employing male nurses. It was easier to find educated youths than educated girls. They were not "hampered by small feet" and their services at marriage were not lost.[57] However, during the course of the 1920s, more and more of the students training to be nurses were female rather than male. In 1921 the China Medical Board decided to use only women nurses in its new hospital at Peking, a step that, as a contemporary noted, was "bound to exercise a considerable influence upon public opinion in China."[58]

Stephenson, a tall and imposing figure in her Deaconess uniform, which she wore "as though it were a battle-dress," greatly impressed other members of the NAC when she spoke at its annual conference in 1922.[59] She was appointed vice president and shortly afterward became acting president. The association's secretary, Cora Simpson, wrote of her admiringly that she "was one of the most splendid nurses ever trained in Britain. Under her leadership the Association is making wonderful forward progress this year." She especially approved of the motto Stephenson had chosen for the NAC—"With God nothing shall be impossible."[60] At that date, mission nurses made up one-third of the total number of around 140 NAC nurses, foreign nurses still predominating. Numbers were set to increase dramatically. By 1926 there was an estimated membership of 1,200, around 100 schools of nursing, and 2,000 student nurses.[61]

In 1925 Simpson was succeeded as secretary by Hope-Bell. A difficult period ensued, with antiforeign and anti-Christian movements affecting the hospitals and nursing schools, especially in the interior. NAC headquarters had to be moved from Hankow to Shanghai. There were demonstrations by student nurses and strikes among nursing staff, and Hope-Bell left her position earlier than had been expected to take up a post in Shanghai. Shortly afterwards she was summoned home to take care of her elderly parents. She was only one of many Western nurses who left China at this period, most departures taking place during the troubled years of 1926–1927. In the late 1920s, leadership in the NAC passed to a core of Chinese Christian nurses of some standing. This was particularly true of Mary Shih (Shih Hsi En), the sister-in-law of Dr. C. T. Wang, foreign minister in the Nationalist government, who became general secretary of the NAC from 1929.[62] By 1930 the years of numerical superiority by Western nurses were well over. In that year there were only 200 foreign nurses in the association out of a total membership of around 2,000, a dramatic turnaround, considered too speedy by one historian "for sound consolidation."[63]

Among those who stayed on was Gladys Stephenson. She was out of the country during the antiforeign and anti-Christian demonstrations of the mid-1920s, using her furlough to train for further work in nursing education. As was explained to readers of *The British Journal of Nursing,* such training was not yet available in the "Mother Country," so she had to journey to Cleveland, Ohio, in the United States, where her course included instruction in "the Principles of Teaching, Educational Psychology, History of Nursing, the Curriculum in Schools of Nursing, Teaching of Nursing Principles and Methods, Supervision in Hospitals and Schools of Nursing, Observation and Practice, Teaching and Sociology."[64] Because of the turbulent conditions in China, she remained in America, fearing "to open the morning newspapers" and trembling to read "letters and telegrams" from China. She eventually returned in June 1927, not to her former hospital at Anlu, which was still unsafe, but to Hankow where the Communist government had been overthrown. Later that year she was appointed principal of the School of Nursing, attached to the new Union Hospital, somehow erected during the disturbances, while also retaining a base at the Methodist General Hospital.[65]

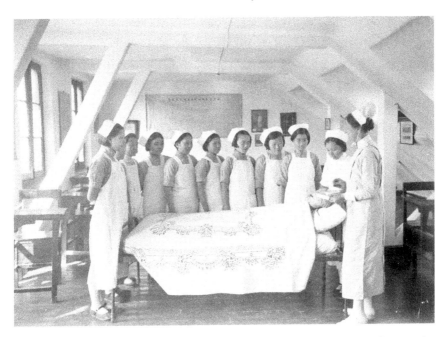

Figure 6.3. A bedside class. Sister Gladys Stephenson with nursing students and a dummy patient, School of Nursing, Hankow (Wuhan), China, c. 1937. (MMS Collection at SOAS © Trustees for Methodist Church Purposes. Used with permission.)

Here she remained apart from the interruptions of floods—including the great Yangtze flood of 1931, one of the worst natural disasters of the 20th century—furloughs and wartime internment, until finally forced to leave China in 1951. Her work as principal of Nursing and as matron of the Methodist General Hospital at Hankow was the center point of her life's work, as was also her continuing role in the NAC. Physically impressive, energetic, and enthusiastic about everything she undertook, she was very much in the mould of the first generation of new British nurses—Christian, patriotic, heroic, and, some would say, socially elitist—proud to carry the mantle of the great Florence Nightingale to all corners of the world. Those who came into direct contact with her were on the whole positive, but there were others who found her rather hard to take. Dr. Mary Cram, an obstetrician and gynecologist in the Hankow Methodist General Hospital, recorded on one occasion that she had "got in a raging temper with Sister Gladys and her high-handed ways," which had "spoilt the whole day," while her small sons found Stephenson "terrifying."[66] In the pages of the *British Journal of Nursing* (*BJN*), edited, until shortly before her death in 1947, by the founder of the British Nurses' Association, the formidable Ethel Bedford-Fenwick, there are a number of glowing tributes to Stephenson's work in China. Thus we read in the February 1934 issue that "our profession could not have a more valuable personality at work in China than Miss Gladys Stephenson, somehow so comprehensive and understanding with her courage and wide sympathy and love of life," while another commends her "adventurous and missionary spirit."[67] Unusually for a woman missionary, Stephenson was a great publicist on behalf of her own work and that of her nurses, frequently sending to be printed in the *BJN* accounts of achievements at the hospital, especially during testing times. These are often accompanied by photographs showing herself with groups of her nurses or, on one occasion at a nursing pageant, pictured in the regal robes of Queen Margaret of Scotland.[68] Domineering and difficult to work with she may have been, but no one could have been a keener apostle for the ideal of Western-style, Christian nursing in China than Stephenson.

In India, Western nurses more than kept pace with their counterparts in China, forming a Trained Nurses' Association of India in 1908. But Indian nurses were very sparsely represented in the association, and leadership of the nursing profession in India remained in Western hands until shortly before Independence in 1947. Nor was it even then a numerous and widely distributed profession. This contrast to the swift adoption of Western-style nursing in China is partly explained by the great reluctance of Hindu and Muslim communities to allow their daughters to enter into what was seen as degrading work. Most Indian nurses, therefore, came from the Eurasian and Indian Christian communities and not from the girls of good family for whom the training schools longed.[69] In examining the role of nurses in colonial India, Rosemary Fitzgerald reports the disappointment of the first Western educators in their nursing recruits, who seemed rarely to constitute "the right stuff from which to make a fleet of Indian Nightingales." Their eager desire to impose Western methodologies and expertise reveals, as Fitzgerald remarks, an inability "to transcend differences of class, race and nationality."[70] By contrast, there seems to have been no cultural barrier to Indian women coming forward to receive medical training as doctors. But few of those with the highest medical qualifications were employed in mission hospitals. Dr. Hilda Lazarus, the first Indian to be appointed to the Women's Medical Service, noted that women's hospitals in the missionary sector usually had a foreign medical missionary in charge and only employed Indian women as assistants and on a lower salary scale. Was this policy or lack of funding, she wondered?[71] Most likely it was both. British missionary societies were having to cope with falling revenues, and the Christian medical schools from which the mission hospitals recruited their staff could not award qualifications above that of licentiate.

THE CHANGING ROLE OF THE MEDICAL MISSIONARY, 1920s–1950s

While the opening up of unpromising areas to Christian evangelism was the initial rationale for much medical missionary work, humanitarian considerations had never been far from the minds of those who advocated this development. At the large assembly of missionaries meeting at the London Centenary Conference of 1888, many could agree that Christianity was a religion "which cared for the body as well as for the soul."[72] But the dual ministry to body and soul posed a considerable strain on medical missionaries who, in addition to heavy clinical and medical duties, were expected also to respond to the higher call to evangelize. Western-trained medical missionaries arriving in some numbers in India and China in the late 19th and early 20th centuries found the burden on them of their medical, surgical, and training duties frequently overwhelming, leaving them very little, if any, time or energy to spend on evangelical work. Some felt apologetic and self-reproachful that they were unable to devote sufficient time to the direct evangelism understood to be the justification for their work.[73]

But a later generation of medical missionaries, coming out to China and India in the years after World War I, no longer felt, as did the pioneer generation, the call to a dual ministry. As R. Fletcher Moorhead, medical secretary of the BMS, observed, "the pendulum has swung considerably."[74] The new view of medical missions as a ministry in itself was fully accepted at the Jerusalem meeting of the International Missionary Council (IMC) in 1928, as its *Messages and Recommendations* made clear. "In the missionary enterprise the medical work should be regarded as, in itself, an expression of the spirit of the Master, and should not be thought of only as a pioneer of evangelism or as merely a philanthropic agency."[75] While some missionaries, older or more conservative-minded, continued to view medical missions as an evangelistic agency, others felt freer to concentrate on their work confident that they were expressing their Christian beliefs through actions rather than words.[76]

The Jerusalem meeting of the IMC's *Messages and Recommendations* in 1928 reflected another concern of the interwar period, in part a criticism of the pioneer generation for their overwhelming concentration on hospital-based work. "In view of the waste of life, especially infant life, due to preventable diseases, there is urgent need of devoting far more attention to preventive medicine and welfare work. Hitherto medical missionaries have been almost wholly engaged in curative work."[77] A factor in the new emphasis on preventive medicine may well have been the realization that the existence by the 1920s of better-equipped and staffed government hospitals in many urban areas in both China and India made the previous concentration on hospital work less relevant. Preventive medicine and welfare work, especially in rural areas among village men, women, and children, were perhaps well suited to the humbler sort of woman missionary, not afraid to bury herself in an isolated part of rural India.

"THE WOMAN WITH THE WHITE HAIR WHO BICYCLES": DR. CLAIRE THOMSON AND PREVENTIVE MEDICINE IN INDIA

Dr. Claire Thomson was far from being a typical missionary, having had a checkered career before her arrival in India in December 1939 at the ripe age of 46. The daughter of an Anglican mother and a Scottish Presbyterian father, she had been orphaned young and brought up by an aunt. Educated in a somewhat desultory way, she eventually obtained an arts degree from St. Andrew's University. For a time a teacher and then a hospital almoner, and not feeling fulfilled in either, she began a medical degree in 1930. By 1939 she was in London at the Annie McCaul Maternity Hospital in Clapham. Unnerved by the outbreak of war on September 3, she prayed, "Oh God, if I am alive tomorrow, I'll try to serve you." Days later she offered her services to the Society for the Propagation of the Gospel (SPG) warning them that she "was not much good either medically or spiritually."[78] But she was prepared to go out on a year's trial at her own expense, and on that basis she was sent. She arrived in December, at the start of what proved to be an immensely fulfilling missionary career spanning the period before and after Indian Independence. She was to find in her "quiet backwater" that that event, when it came in August 1947, seemed to make "very little difference."[79]

At the outset of her service and on medical advice, she was posted to Chota Nagpur, 2,000 to 3,000 feet above sea level, where a mission had first been opened by German Lutherans in the mid-19th century. The center of SPG work was Ranchi, the summer capital of the Bihar government, now the capital of Jharkhand state. There were three missions in the district: Roman Catholic, German Lutheran, and the SPG. In her unpublished memoir, Thomson described the mission thus: "The Bishop and one or two priests looked after the cathedral and the boy's school and about ten women missionaries worked in schools, a book shop, a hospital and a needlework centre in which a number of Indian women could earn a living."[80] As was customary within the SPG, Thomson had not been appointed to any particular post. It was the responsibility of the bishop to deploy his staff. At first there did not appear to be anything "definite for her to do," so she had time to learn the language and become familiar with the prevalent diseases in the area—hookworm, dysentery, malaria, leprosy, and tuberculosis. She was horrified at the numbers of young teachers and nurses who died from the latter disease, "our worst scourge."[81] She spent some time based at a mud-brick hospital chiefly administering to some of the aboriginals—Oraons, Mundas, Hos, and Santals,—who inhabited the region and "who scratched a living by growing upland rice and keeping scrawny cows and goats." When the rains permitted, Thomson would cycle out to patients, usually difficult maternity cases. She was forced to realize that people consented to use the hospital only as "a place of last resort." Their preference was to rely on folk remedies such as "cowdung for wounds; a pounded frog for inflammation; dung beetles and the juices of many plants and leaves for sore eyes; and standing on the expectant mother's stomach to hasten delivery."[82]

Eventually she was placed at Itki, about 14 miles from Ranchi, where there was a small 18-bed hospital, run by the Anglican sisters of the Community of St. Denys. Here she spent some 14 years. She was away for a three-year period between 1943 and 1946, first on furlough, then on a missionary training course, and finally a period when she filled in for another medical missionary elsewhere. She returned to find many of the local population looking alarmingly thin. Examining 650 school children, she found over a third to be suffering from malnutrition and immediately instituted a regime of dietary supplements—shark-liver oil, marmite, iron, and powdered milk. Famine struck again some years later and once again Thomson arranged for food supplements to be distributed, as well as free school meals for those most badly affected.

The arrival of new drugs, like penicillin and sulfa, meant that Thomson was not so tied to the hospital as patients were now staying for shorter periods. On the other hand, it could cause problems since the better-off were charged when the expensive drugs were used. Thomson was told by one man that it was her "religion to take his wife's tooth out for two annas."[83] But she was now freer to concentrate on what she saw as underlying problems. There was need, she wrote home, to stop merely treating "the fringe of the misery caused by malnutrition and poverty by handing out vermifuges, anti-biotics, fish oil, vitamins and milk powder" and instead tackle the "root causes of this misery," which she saw as "sin, apathy and ignorance."[84] Together with Sister Lilian Tooke, a colleague "very keen on health teaching," she began to introduce simple illustrated leaflets, in English and Hindi, on hygiene, worms, flies, and head lice, for use by health workers. The key people to target she thought were "the educated people living in the village." She involved local church personnel in her campaigns, padres, catechists, and Bible women, instructing them and issuing them with tablets for malaria, eye drops, and powders for lice. In the 1950s, she brought out *Better Health: Illnesses We Need Never Have* and *Improving Village Health: A Handbook for Rural Workers.* She later wrote an illustrated booklet entitled *A Christian Approach to Family Planning* published in 1963.

Many of these health teaching materials had been distributed through the Christian Medical Association of India (CMAI), which greatly benefited from generous American funding. Thomson attended its meetings and conferences, often staying with colleagues whose salaries and standard of living she found to be "considerably higher than those of British missionaries."[85] She had now in the mid-1950s reached the normal retirement age. Instead, she was asked by the CMAI to take up a new post as health secretary with special responsibility for preventive medicine. Joyfully accepting, she prepared for her new duties by attending a course at the London School of Tropical Medicine and Hygiene. Returning to India, she based herself in Nagpur, the headquarters of the CMAI and a better center for a work that consisted of visiting Christian hospitals and health centers throughout India. For more local visits, her chief form of transport remained her bicycle. Thomson's chief concern remained the health problems of villagers, since it was in villages that the vast majority of Indians—85 percent she estimated—lived. She was convinced of the need for change, particularly as regards diet, hygienic practices, and sanitation. But did a Westerner's approach meet the "felt needs" of villagers? Of that she was not so certain, in the end concluding that "foreigners are not the people to try to change the pattern of village thinking."[86]

Thomson remained in her post for 6 years, retiring in 1964 at the age of 70. During a visit to the United States and Canada in 1956, she noticed the continuing enthusiasm there for overseas mission work. Her warm reception contrasted with the poorly attended meetings at which she had spoken about her work in Britain a few months earlier.[87] While she admired her North American colleagues in India for their efficiency and enthusiasm, Thomson was not uncritical. Their superior lifestyles, their modern, well-equipped hospitals, and highly professional staff tended, she thought, to place them at a considerable distance from the lives of ordinary Indian villagers.[88] She realized too that the newly independent Indian church, most of which did not see healing as part of its responsibilities, could never, in any case, assume the financial burden of maintaining Western-style hospitals. Toward the end of her service in the early 1960s, Thomson increasingly found herself the only white face in her immediate surroundings. But when the time came for her to go, she was extremely reluctant to leave, feeling that a door was about to be "slammed on one of the happiest times" of her life. In looking back over her career several years later, she was able to write that "in spite of old age, growing disability—and not too much cash—the afterglow of job satisfaction still persists."[89]

NOTES

1. Isabella Bird Bishop, quoted in Irene H. Barnes, *Between Life and Death: The Story of CEZMS Medical Missions in India, China and Ceylon* (London: Marshall Bros., 1901), 3.

2. W. J. Elmslie, "On Female Medical Missions for India," *Indian Female Evangelist* 1, no. 5 (January 1873): 195.

3. *Medical Missions: as Illustrated by Some Letters and Notices of the Late Dr Elmslie* ([Edinburgh]: Edinburgh Medical Missionary Society, 1874), 187–189.

4. *Medical Missions*, 194–196.

5. Antoinette Burton sees a direct link between the opening of LSMW and opportunities in India for trained women doctors. See "Contesting the Zenana: The Mission to Make 'Lady Doctors for India,' 1874–1885," *The Journal of British Studies* 35, no. 3 (1996): 369–373 and passim.

6. E. M. Tonge, *Fanny Jane Butler, Pioneer Medical Missionary* (London: Church of England Zenana Missionary Society, [1930]), 9.

7. LSMW graduates also served with the National Association for Supplying Female Medical Aid to the Women of India, supported by a fund established by the Countess of Dufferin, Vicereine of India, in 1885.

8. J. C. Muller, "Some Personal Reminiscences of Work in the Delhi Medical Mission, 1884–1910" quoted in Rosemary Fitzgerald, "A 'Peculiar and Exceptional Measure': The Call for Women Medical Missionaries for India in the Later Nineteenth Century," in *Missionary Encounters: Sources and Issues,* eds. Robert A. Bickers and Rosemary Seton (Richmond: Curzon Press, 1996), 188.

9. Fitzgerald, "Peculiar and Exceptional Measure," 190.

10. John Lowe, *Medical Missions, Their Place and Power* (London: T. Fisher Unwin, 1886), 195.

11. Quoted in Lowe, *Medical Missions,* 190–191.

12. She took charge of a new women's hospital in Lahore, the Lady Aitchison Hospital, opened in 1888.

13. Quoted in Burton, "Contesting the Zenana": 384.

14. Quoted in Burton, "Contesting the Zenana": 393.

15. Quoted in Burton, "Contesting the Zenana": 379.

16. Dr. Frances Hoggan, "Medical Work for Women in India," *The Englishwoman's Review* CXLIV (April 1885): 149.

17. World Missionary Conference, *Report of Commission 1,* 317.

18. Andrew Walls, " 'The Heavy Artillery of the Missionary Army': The Domestic Importance of the Nineteenth-Century Medical Missionary," in *Studies in Church History, Vol 27, The Church and Healing,* ed. William J. Sheils (Oxford: Blackwell, 1982), 291–292.

19. Margaret I. Balfour and Ruth Young, *The Work of Medical Women in India* (London: OUP, 1929), 16.

20. Quoted in E. C. Dawson, *Heroines of Missionary Adventure* (London: Seeley, Service & Co., 1925), 59–60.

21. Tonge, *Fanny Jane Butler,* 45.

22. Quoted in Lowe, *Medical Missions,* 123.

23. James S. Dennis, Harlan P. Beach, and Charles H. Fahs, *World Atlas of Christian Missions* (New York: Student Volunteer Movement for Foreign Missions, 1911), 83.

24. Isabel Mitchell, "Fakumen," *Woman's Work. Zenana Missionary Quarterly of the Irish Presbyterian Church* (July 1906): 263 and F.W.S. O'Neill, ed., *Dr Isabel Mitchell of Manchuria [Letters]* (London: J. Clarke & Co., [1917]), 69–70.

25. O'Neill, *Dr Isabel Mitchell*, 92–93.

26. O'Neill, *Dr Isabel Mitchell*, 116.

27. O'Neill, *Dr Isabel Mitchell*, 156.

28. "Isabel D. Mitchell, M.B.," *Woman's Work* (Summer 1917): 305.

29. O'Neill, *Dr Isabel Mitchell*, 168–169.

30. The other was Dr. Ellen Farrer.

31. Quoted in Francesca French, *Miss Brown's Hospital, The Story of the Ludhiana Medical College and Dame Edith Brown OBE Its Founder* (London: Hodder and Stoughton: 1954), 19.

32. French, *Miss Brown's Hospital*, 21–22.

33. French, *Miss Brown's Hospital*, 16.

34. French, *Miss Brown's Hospital*, 24.

35. Edith Brown, "Obituary," *British Medical Journal*, December 22, 1956, 1490.

36. Maureen Pritchard, "Dame Edith Brown Memorial Number," *Conquest by Healing* 33, no. 1 (1957): 6.

37. M. Edith Craske, *Sister India* (London: RTS, 1930), 43.

38. Pritchard, "Edith Brown," 6.

39. French, *Miss Brown's Hospital*, 52.

40. Pritchard, "Edith Brown," 7.

41. Craske, *Sister India*, 49.

42. Ludhiana Women's Christian Medical College, *Annual Report* (1924–1925): 10.

43. French, *Miss Brown's Hospital*, 76.

44. Susan L. Cohen, "Brown, Dame Edith Mary (1864–1956)," in *Dictionary of National Biography* (Oxford: OUP, 2004–2011), 20.

45. Pritchard, "Edith Brown," 5–6.

46. Christian Medical Association of India, *The Ministry of Healing in India, Handbook of the Christian Medical Association of India* (Mysore: Wesleyan Mission Press, 1932), 106.

47. Dennis et al., *World Atlas*, 115–120.

48. Quoted in Lavina L. Dock, *A History of Nursing from the Earliest Times to the Present Day with Special Reference to the Work of the Past Thirty Years* (New York and London: G. P. Putnam's Sons, 1912), 245.

49. Harold Balme, *China and Modern Medicine, a Study in Medical Missionary Development* (London: United Council for Missionary Education, 1921), 134.

50. C. B. Firth quoted in Rosemary Fitzgerald, " 'Making and Moulding the Nursing of the Indian Empire,' Recasting Nurses in Colonial India," in *Rhetoric and Reality: Gender and the Colonial Experience in South Asia*, eds. Avril A. Powell and Siobhan Lambert-Hurley (New Delhi: OUP, 2006), 193.

51. Fitzgerald, "Making and Moulding," 201.

52. Rosemary Seton, " 'Open Doors for Female Labourers': Women Candidates of the London Missionary Society, 1875–1914," in *Missionary Encounters: Sources and Issues,* eds. Robert A. Bickers and Rosemary Seton (Richmond, Surrey: Curzon Press, 1996), 65.

53. Fitzgerald, "Making and Moulding," 205.

54. E. Theodora Fox, *A Missionary Directory for Nurses* (Nottingham: H. B. Saxton, 1908), 56.

55. Letter from Elspeth Hope-Bell, June 18, 1911, Hope-Bell Papers, CWM/LMS, China Incoming Correspondence, Personal Box 12, File 1.

56. Letter from Elspeth Hope-Bell, September 16, 1912, Hope-Bell Papers.

57. Gladys Stephenson, "The Glory of the King in Central China: Some Personal Memories of the Twenty Wonderful Years in the Service of the King," MMS/MRP China Box 7a, Folder 2, Ch. 3.

58. Balme, *China and Modern Medicine,* 150.

59. Pauline Webb, *Women of Our Time* (London: Cargate Press, 1963), 117.

60. Cora E. Simpson, "Nursing Association of China," *The British Journal of Nursing* (September 1923): 139.

61. Kaiyi Chen, "Missionaries and the Early Development of Nursing in China," *Nursing History Review* 4 (1996): 137.

62. Gladys E. Stephenson, *A Short Outline of Nursing History* (Shanghai: The Nurses Association of China, 1936), 90.

63. Chen, "Early Development of Nursing," 144.

64. Extract of letter from Gladys Stephenson, *British Journal of Nursing,* (October 1926): 228–229.

65. Stephenson, "The Glory of the King," Ch.10.

66. Redhead Diary, November 17, 1938, Lincolnshire Archives, CRAM Papers 69, 25. I am indebted to Dr. Jocelyn Chatterton for this reference and information about the reaction of the Cram children to Sister Gladys.

67. Extracts, *British Journal of Nursing* (February 1934): 48 and (April 1940): 69.

68. Photograph, *British Journal of Nursing* (February 1934): 48.

69. It was estimated in the 1940s that 90 percent of Indian nurses came from the Christian community. Fitzgerald, "Making and Moulding," 212.

70. Fitzgerald, "Making and Moulding," 208, 212.

71. Hilda Lazarus, "The Sphere of Indian Women in Medical Work in India", in *Women in Modern India,* ed. Evelyn C. Gedge (Bombay: D. B. Taraporewala, 1929), 60.

72. Quoted in Andrew Porter, *Religion versus Empire? British Protestant Missionaries and Overseas Expansion* (Manchester and New York: Manchester University Press, 2004), 312.

73. Rosemary Fitzgerald, "Peculiar and Exceptional Measure," 194.

74. R. Fletcher Moorshead, *The Way of the Doctor, a Study in Medical Missions* (London, Carey Press, 1926), 102.

75. International Missionary Council, *The World Mission of Christianity, Messages and Recommendations of the Enlarged Meeting of the IMC Held at Jerusalem, March 24th to April 8th 1928* (London: [1928]), 71.

76. See Jocelyn Chatterton, "Protestant Medical Missionary Experience During the War in China 1937–1945: The Case of Hubei Province" (Ph.D. diss., University of London, London, 2010), 56–58.

77. *Messages and Recommendation*, 72.

78. Dr. Claire Thomson, "Memoir," Thomson Papers, (Mss Eur D1102), 1, 142–143.

79. Dr. Claire Thomson, "Memoir," 2, 184.

80. Thomson, "Memoir," 2, 144.

81. Thomson, "Memoir," 2, 149.

82. Dr. Claire Thomson, "Personal View," *British Medical Journal* (October 30, 1971): 295.

83. Dr. Claire Thomson, Circular Letter, March 23, 1952 (Mss Eur D1102), 3.

84. Dr. Claire Thomson, "Report" (Mss Eur D1102), 3.

85. Thomson, "Memoir," 2, 189.

86. Thomson, "Memoir," 2, 229.

87. Thomson, "Memoir," 2, 214, 224.

88. Thomson, "Memoir," 2, 199.

89. Thomson, "Personal View," 295.

7

⁓

Missionary Women
and Evangelism

Should a woman speak publicly in face of 1 Timothy ii 12 and 1 Corinthians xiv 34?[1]

Evangelism was at the very heart of the 19th-century Protestant missionary movement. Ordained men were appointed to the mission field to translate the Gospels, preach, convert, found new churches, and foster their growth and development. The role of women was subsidiary to, and supportive of, these male efforts. Even their connection was tangential. The wives, sisters, and daughters of ordained missionaries, together with a few single women agents, set up schools and orphanages and taught Christianized women to read and sew. In addition, they *instructed* their charges in the teachings of Christianity through Bible reading, singing hymns, and storytelling—but not through direct exhortation. Preaching was considered wholly inappropriate for a female. A correspondent in the pages of the *Christian Lady Magazine* of 1837 could not see "any ground for supposing that the work of an 'evangelist' ... is in any manner suited to a female."[2] In 1861, when a second society was formed to send single women agents to India, it was at first suggested that it be called "The Society for the Evangelization of the Women of India." This was dropped on advice from Henry Venn, secretary of the Church Missionary Society (CMS), since it was considered to extend the female role inappropriately. The far more limiting (and cumbersome) title of "The Indian Female Normal School and Instruction Society" was adopted instead.[3] Even in the China Inland Mission (CIM), a mission that appointed both men and women as evangelists, Geraldine Guinness, who later became the founder's daughter-in-law, emphasized the limitations of her sex. Women could never "fill the place of men-missionaries in the Church; ... they cannot preach or teach as men do," but had much to offer indigenous men and women "by their quiet, unobtrusive moral and spiritual influence."[4]

Beneath the official affirmation of woman's modest and self-effacing role— supporting, but not challenging, the primary role of the ordained male—lie definite traces of a subversive narrative. From the very start of the missionary movement, some appear to have had a much bolder conception of woman's contribution. Mary Ann Wilson, née Cooke, the first single woman missionary sent to India, pointed out that while women came out "in the first instance to teach children ... they would also endeavour to use every opportunity to give religious instruction to adults, whether male or female."[5] Wilson had been in India for 14 years when she made this statement. It is highly likely that during the course of her labors she had encountered male as well as female inquirers and did not see the need to withhold the Christian message on grounds of gender. Clare Midgley cites the case of Elizabeth Harvard, wife of Methodist missionary W. M. Harvard, who, as the couple itinerated in the island of Ceylon (Sri Lanka), felt compelled to speak to "benighted idolators" herself. Harvard, who published a memoir of his wife, was careful, however, to state that she never "conceived that the occupation of the pulpit fell within her line of duty."[6] This and other evidence reveals that, on the mission field, some women and men accepted a wider role for women than that conceived of in the mission houses, churches, and ministerial training colleges in Britain.[7] But by and large, women in the first half of the 19th century seem generally to have accepted that any evangelization on their part should be informal and chiefly, though not entirely, confined to indigenous women and girls.

In the second half of the 19th century missionary wives, and increasing numbers of single women, took their mission to the "secluded denizens of the *Zenanas*" in Hindu and Muslim houses in India's northern towns and cities.[8] The education they offered aimed to civilize as much as to Christianize the debased woman of the East: the one implying the other. Religious instruction formed only a part of the zenana syllabus, which might include reading, writing, and instruction in general subjects such as geography and astronomy, and an introduction to the womanly arts of needlework and the playing of musical instruments. Some missionaries offered advice on hygiene and health and medical intervention when necessary. There were few conversions to the Christian faith. Zenana teachers expected that "much of the fruit of their instructions [would] remain hidden." They would watch and nourish "the work of grace in their pupils' hearts, and . . . let their quiet life at home tell, as a holy life ever will, on the husbands and unbelieving circles around them."[9] The importance of zenana mission as a strategy outlived its usefulness. By the end of the century, it was becoming increasingly acceptable for middle-class Indian girls to attend school, and the need for zenana visits in India's towns and cities began to diminish.

Providentially, as it seemed, reports began to filter back to Britain in the early 1880s of opportunities for missionary women outside urban confines. Robert Clark, CMS missionary in the Punjab, advocated the deployment of women agents in rural India:

> The evangelization of the heathen village women is equally important, if not more important, than the zananas of the towns. The minds of the industrious village women, who breathe open and purer air, and are in a position to tell to twenty others what they may hear of the Gospel, are certainly more suited to receive the truth than the shut up, perhaps idle and narrow-minded, zanana women of the towns.[10]

The pioneer practitioner of itinerant work among women in the Punjab seems to have been Elizabeth Clay, of the Church of England Zenana Missionary Society (CEZMS), who began her Punjab Village Mission in 1881. Starting with one Indian assistant, she soon had a staff of 50. She identified some 1,500 target towns and villages inside the four administrative divisions (or *tehsils*) of Amritsar, Narowal (now in Pakistan), Saurian, and Tarn Taran. Her aim was to "have four central mission stations (one for each *tehsil*), occupied by English workers; and connected with each a group of outstations occupied by native workers. Then may we indeed hope in God's strength to assail more effectually the strongholds of the Evil One."[11] Optimistic accounts of her work, and that of her colleagues, were published in the pages of *India's Women*. Others were keen to adopt her methods. Charlotte Tucker was most impressed when she visited from her mission station at Batala. She wrote to Mrs. Weitbrecht that

> The Hindu and Sikh villages around Narowal seem far more accessible and ready to listen than their sisters in Batala. I was struck by the difference. The villages to which we went were visited for the first time by missionary women, but in all the Glad Tidings seemed to be more or less welcomed. There was less of the prying curiosity, the utter indifference to what concerns the soul, that often saddens me.
>
> Indeed in no village was there lack of listeners. Our greatest trouble was that men wished to listen too, and their presence usually drives away most, if not all, the women.[12]

This letter and Clark's report were used by leading CMS supporter Sir Robert Cust in arguing his case for "The Female Evangelist," the title of an article he published in *The Church Missionary Intelligencer and Record*. There need be no fear, he insisted, of offending against Pauline strictures about women not speaking in the church, since Clay and others addressed their audiences in the open air! He enthused over the healthy charms of rural itineration, remembering in a veritably purple passage the years when as an East India Company officer he had been on tour in the countryside in the Hoshiarpur and Ambala districts of the Punjab: recalling the "white tent pitched in the outskirts of the village in the mango-grove,... the cry of the peacock, the cooing of the doves" and "the slanting rays of the sun shedding glory through the grove." He could conceive of "no happier life, when in the employment of an earthly ruler: how much more so when in the service of our King?"[13] Cust's article was undoubtedly a factor in the rapid acceptance of women's evangelistic work by Anglican and other missionary societies. But some doubted the wisdom of allowing women to go out and about unprotected. London Missionary Society missionary Marie Luise Christlieb, a grand-daughter of Mary Weitbrecht, began evangelistic work in the rural environs of Hospet, in present-day Karnataka, in 1893. She recalled in her memoir the disapproval of her male colleagues. "When the idea of women missionaries going to villages was first proposed, our Committee met it with unfeigned opposition. 'It is too rough for you?' 'In the district one cannot avoid getting into holes. And when a woman gets into a hole she sits down and cries.' It was 'man's work.' She silenced them with: 'aren't there women in the villages?' "[14]

EVANGELIZING IN THE PUNJAB, 1890–1920

The Church of Scotland had had a mission in Sialkot in the northern Punjab since before the 1857 rebellion, in which the two pioneer missionaries Thomas and Jane Hunter had been killed. By the late 1860s, besides the church, there were orphanages, schools, and two substantial mission houses.[15] In 1889, Isabella Plumb was appointed to work with women and children at Sialkot, the first single woman to be so appointed. Plumb was 28 at the time, and had previously worked at Poona (Pune) amongst Marathi-speaking people. On arrival at Sialkot, she found herself having to learn both Punjabi and Urdu. Her duties initially lay in supervising schools, in teaching women sewing and knitting,

Figure 7.1. Group portrait of the staff and students of the Girls' School, Church of Scotland Mission, Sialkot, Punjab. Isabella Plumb is third from the right in the middle row, c. 1910–1920. Next to her is her colleague Miss Black, with whom she worked for more than 30 years. (By permission of the Trustees of the National Library of Scotland.)

and—accompanied by Ernestina, the daughter of a local pastor, as interpreter—in visiting women in their houses. However, when another missionary, Miss Black, arrived, she took over the schools and Plumb assumed responsibility for evangelistic work.

In or around 1892 Plumb began her village itineration work. She bought a pony "as riding is the only way one can get about the district."[16] The region in which she found herself endured hot, humid summers with temperatures "from 116 to 120 degrees in the shade ... and the hot winds driving up over the Indian desert" made the land "like a burning furnace." But the cold season from October to March was delightful, and this was when Plumb regularly embarked on a branch of work she carried out with cheery competence. In addition to her pony, there were two camels to carry her tent and furniture, and a goat to supply milk. Apart from porters and servants she was accompanied by an Indian Christian woman who shared her tent at night. This appears to have been not Ernestina, but Miss Talah Singh, the only other of her Indian companions to be named.[17] Plumb estimated that the areas in which she itinerated covered about 800 villages, around 100 of which contained Christians. She took with her a "supply of books and scripture portions," but her most treasured aid was her "beautiful magic lantern." She described how, on entering a village where they were to stay, villagers would come to watch the tents being put up. She would show Bible pictures and tell them that more pictures would be shown after dark. "As soon as it gets dark they begin to come. The white screen is hung up against the wall of a house; the lantern is arranged on a table in front of it and lit; and now we are ready to start." Her task was to work the lantern while an Indian evangelist explained the pictures. "We begin with the Old Testament pictures. Adam in his sinless state, and then the coming of sin ... the life of Noah and Abraham and Moses and David and the Prophets—Then comes John the Baptist ... and so on through the Life so familiar to all of us; until its close in death and burial and resurrection and ascension [sic] to Glory. All of this takes a long time—more than 2 hours." She felt satisfied that "Christ had been preached in a way that the most ignorant of them can understand."

The following morning after breakfast, she would begin to visit the women of the village. "It was not difficult to find women to speak to; they would soon gather around us and take us into their houses and talk away about everything." To staunch the inevitable flow of personal questions, she and her companion would start singing hymns to "try to draw their minds upwards to the things of the kingdom." Next, "the headman of the village will come and ask us to go and see his wife, and we are led off to his house with a great crowd following." She was frequently asked for medicines, since the villagers assumed they were doctors "and will not believe us when we tell them it is not so."[18] On the whole, Plumb and other evangelists seem to have been received in a friendly fashion; but in this predominantly Muslim area, it is not surprising that they sometimes met with vocal resistance. Plumb's 1894 itineration diary records that as she was leaving a meeting of village women, "a woman stood up and asked me to listen while she told me about the Mohammedan religion. She said that Mohammed was the greatest prophet that ever lived."[19] In another incident in the town of Sialkot itself, the mission's school for Muslim girls was closed for a period in 1902 following a demand that the Koran be taught.[20] While reporting these and other adverse events, Plumb was never downcast and remained optimistic throughout her long service. She was content to sow the seed rather than reap a harvest of conversions. It was sufficient that people, for the most part, received them kindly and listened to their message. Confident in her race, religion, and gender, she thought such work as she was doing among women and girls "the most striking feature of the advance in foreign mission."[21]

AMY CARMICHAEL AND RURAL ITINERATION
IN SOUTHERN INDIA

In contrast with Plumb's almost unrelenting cheeriness, a much more pessimistic note is struck in the writings of Amy Carmichael. Greatly influenced by the Keswick Holiness movement, and motivated by premillenarian concerns about the thousands of heathen dying in darkness every day, she received her call to missionary service in January 1892. Styled as the first Keswick missionary, she first went to work in Japan with the Japan Evangelistic Band, but left after a brief period and joined the CEZMS, going out to southern India in 1895. Here she engaged in evangelistic work as a member of a women's itinerating band in the area around Tinnevelly (Tirunelveli), under the guidance of CMS missionary Thomas Walker and his wife. She wrote candidly of her experiences in *Things as They Are, Mission Work in Southern India*, first published in 1903 and reprinted several times.[22] The work was a shot across the bows of much of the overly optimistic missionary discourse of the period, and resonated with those who had experienced at first hand the frustrations and obstacles of evangelistic work. She recounts how on arrival at a village she and her companion would be summarily greeted, given betel, and then asked nonstop questions for 10 minutes about their caste, whether they were married or widowed, why no jewels, were they white all over, why had they left their relatives to come here, how much was the government paying them?, and so on. When she began to speak of Jesus, the women simply stared. On one occasion, an elderly lady who appeared to be paying great attention suddenly leant forward to ask Carmichael if she was a widow, since she had no oil on her hair. "All through" their visit "there were constant and various interruptions. Two bulls sauntered in through the open door ... children came and went and wanted attention, babies made their usual noises. We rarely had five consecutive minutes." Then came the objections. Christianity would destroy caste. There was no need to educate girls, since it was not their custom and girls did not need jobs in government.[23] Even before talking to the women, they were frequently quizzed by the men of the village before being allowed to proceed. On one occasion Carmichael came across a Brahmin at a rest house and begged him to consider "the question of his soul's salvation." He agreed to take some literature to read at his leisure. But then, "with a gesture expressing at once his sense of his own condescension in speaking with me, and his utter contempt for the faith I held, motioned to me to go."[24]

Carmichael averred that "neither we nor our Gospel are required" in Hindu India. The assumption "that you can distinguish between heathen and Christian by the wonderful light on the Christians' faces" when compared with "the sad expression on the faces of the poor benighted heathen" was simply not true. Some Christians might appear illuminated, but, as a whole, "the heathen are so remarkably cheerful." Then again, there was the problem that even if Christian evangelism succeeded in gaining converts, "open confession of Christ" created "disastrous divisions in families."[25] Her stark analysis offended many, but was influentially endorsed. Several noted missionaries wrote to confirm her views, including Dr. Edith Brown of Ludhiana. No less a personage than CMS statesman Eugene Stock, in his preface to her book, welcomed her account of the many real obstacles to evangelism. "Service, and self-denial and prayer" on a "different scale" was necessary, he argued, if ever the world was to be evangelized.[26] Yet despite the publication of what she called her battle-book, Carmichael herself withdrew from conventional missionary life to establish an enclosed Christian community at Dohnavur, a refuge for Hindu temple children and, as has been suggested, perhaps also for herself.[27]

BIBLE TRANSLATION AND CHURCH PLANTING:
THE TODA MISSION, 1890–1935

Ootacamund (Udagamandalam) in the Nilgiri Hills, part of the Western Ghats in southern India, had been a hill station popular with the British since the early 19th century. The summer residence of the Madras government, it was frequented by missionaries on vacation, and was also home to a CEZMS station, which in the last decade of the 19th century began a remarkable mission to the original inhabitants of Ootacamund, a hill people known as the Todas.

Very little research has been done on the linguistic work of missionary wives and single women during the period covered by this study. Such labors, particularly the composition of dictionaries, grammars, and Bible translation, shaped the careers of early Protestant missionaries such as William Carey and Robert Morrison, and a number who followed them. While Carey's second wife, Charlotte Rumohr, was said to have been "of eminent service to him in the translation of the scriptures" as was Maria Newell to her husband Karl Gutzlaff, little is known of contributions to this work by other wives or single women at this time. Indeed, for much of the period, it was thought "no more appropriate for a woman to be a Bible Translator than to be an ordained minister."[28]

Catharine Ling, working at the Ootacamund station was the first Westerner to make a study of the Toda language, an unwritten Dravidian tongue. She went on to publish a Toda version of St. Mark's Gospel, though subsequent translation work was carried out with the assistance of others. However, it is Ling's name that is particularly associated with the Toda mission, to which she devoted more than 45 years of service. As the CMS missionary Stephen Neill, later bishop of Tinnevelly, commented at the close of her career, "the creation of the Toda Christian Church is her work, the splendid achievement of nearly half a century."[29] Thus Ling was not merely a Bible translator. She is also credited with church planting, a task more usually the preserve of the ordained male missionary.

She first went out to India with the CEZMS in 1881. After four years in Tinnevelly, where she acquired fluency in Tamil, she joined the Nilgiri Mission at Ootacamund and engaged in educational and evangelistic work among both Hindus and Muslims. One Sunday in 1890, when Ling was herself in England on furlough, a Toda man turned up at a service in the Tamil Church at Ootacamund. He had come to render thanks for having been cured from illness with Christian medicine he had received from a Tamil convert.[30] This visit was interpreted by members of the mission as a clear call. On Ling's return, possibly on account of her ability in Tamil, she was deputed to begin Christian evangelistic work among the Toda people. First it was necessary to familiarize herself with the language. She began by recruiting a Toda man who could read and write Tamil through having attended a school run by the Basel Mission. She then began a tentative translation of St. Mark's Gospel. Not having a body of eminent scholars to consult, she sought a wider circle of informants, replacing the first Toda and his friends with a second group and also consulting a number of Toda women.[31]

By her own account, from these quarters she did not lack for criticism and correction![32] At length a satisfactory version emerged and was published by the British and Foreign Bible Society Madras Auxiliary in 1897.

Figure 7.2. Group of Toda women sitting in front of a traditional house, Nilgiri Hills, c. 1948. Catherine Ling had made a point of consulting Toda women when translating St. Mark's Gospel into the Toda language in the 1890s. (By permission of the SOAS Library.)

The Todas, a people numbered only in hundreds, have attracted a perhaps disproportionate amount of interest and curiosity. In her book about work in the Nilgiris, Winifred Stone, one of Ling's missionary colleagues, goes some way to explain the fascination. "They are first . . . in the estimation of the general public because of their good looks and general noble and striking appearance (extraordinarily reminiscent of portraits of Jewish patriarchs). Their picturesque dress and dwellings, their curious customs and their unique language . . . all combine to appeal to the imagination." Claiming tribute and services from neighboring tribes, the Todas styled themselves the "Lords of the Hills."[33] They lived in *munds*, small collections of huts usually including one or more dairies vital not only to their economy but also their religion. Their way of life was strictly pastoral, centering on the grazing of buffaloes and the production and sale of ghee. Their religion could be described as a "cult of the buffalo," with the dairy complexes the sacred centers of various rituals.[34] In the second of her two short books about the Todas and Christian work among them, Ling wrote of the initial aim of the mission.

> Our hope when we started this work many years ago was that the Todas would become Christians in their minds, retaining their picturesque appearance, the men with their curly mops of hair and the women with their ringlets; the men still wandering over the Downs with their cattle like Abraham and Isaac of old. We hoped that they would give up their evil customs and turn their little dairy temples into Christian houses of worship.[35]

The result as she admitted had been "far different." Most Todas had strenuously resisted evangelization, so that for the small number of converts, around 70, the act had meant "a complete severance from their own people."[36] Her uncompromising view of the schism between Christian and non-Christian Todas was not entirely shared by the anthropologist, M. B. Emeneau, writing shortly after her departure. He concluded that the Todas exhibited a "rather great degree of tolerance for the Christian converts," and that they attempted to retain "relations with them where it is possible."[37] Nonetheless, the little Christian community lived separately from the main body of the tribe, in two colonies each with church, houses, and dispensary, the men engaging in a range of agricultural and other pursuits, since they no longer had access to Toda grazing lands and dairies. An economic mainstay was the traditional Toda embroidery, worked by the women and sold through the mission, the profits helping to offset the costs of schooling and medical care.

The self-deprecating Ling tried to insist that the Toda mission had not been her work alone, yet the Christian community exhibited the deepest misgivings at her departure. While she had never had, nor could have had, a formal ecclesiastical role in the community, the Toda Christians, both men and women, had come to depend on her not only for guidance in spiritual and worldly matters, but also for protection and patronage. Even the non-Christians recognized her authority and prestige, three of the chiefs organizing a special farewell ceremony for her. "About thirty men were present, wrapped in their voluminous sheets with embroidered borders . . . and when she arrived a band of them came down the grassy slope to meet her and escort her with shoutings. They danced before her, going round and round in a circle with arms intertwined and fingers interlocked, singing the while" of her merits. A speech from one of the chiefs acknowledged her efforts in bringing the existence of the Toda people to the attention of government and requested that on her return to Britain she should ask the Queen to guarantee their property rights in their traditional lands.[38] The Christian community was right to fear the consequences of her withdrawal. In the years immediately after her departure, there was evidence both of social disintegration and also of sharp differences with the missionaries now in charge. These mainly concerned various customs, such as dancing and singing on social and religious occasions, which Ling had benignly tolerated and which her successors attempted to prohibit. It needed Ling's stately and emollient presence when she returned in 1938, in her late 70s, to smooth out the differences.[39]

BIBLE WOMEN

Underlying the evangelistic agency of Western women in both India and China lay the indispensable work of Bible women, until very recently a neglected group in mission history research.[40] Numerically, the contribution made by indigenous women agents to the Christian missionary enterprise far outweighed that of for- eign women. One historian estimates that by the early 20th century, there were three times as many indigenous women engaged in Christian evangelism as there were overseas missionary women.[41]

Bible women, so called because they frequently carried with them bibles and other religious texts, undertook the bulk of zenana visiting and other door-to-door visits, participated in rural itineration, and were responsible for much of the evangelistic work carried out in hospital wards and waiting areas. Ella Shaw, writing in 1915, outlined the work of a typical Bible woman.

> She does house-to-house visiting, teaches Sunday School classes, leads meetings for the Christians and outside women, holds station classes for teaching women to read, takes long country trips either with or without the foreign missionary, chaperones the young day-schoolteachers, visits the sick, helps bury the dead, is active in relief work, and often is one of the wise counsellors in the station.[42]

Yet despite the acknowledged importance of their work, Bible women themselves appear to have been held in little regard. They were an easy target for ridicule. A novel published in 1895 by the Indian Christian writer Krupabai Satthianadhan describes brothers mocking their sister when she wants to go on a preaching tour. "They called me a Bible-woman, and gave me a few tracts and some tattered worn-out books, which they told me to carry under my arm just as the typical Bible-woman did."[43] Usually poor widows or the product of mission orphanages, Bible women were neither well born nor well educated. Their appearance was also held against them. One American missionary remarked that when she first came to India, she heard it "said that the chief qualifications for Bible-women's work were 'age and ugliness.' "[44] On the other hand, age and ugliness might well have guaranteed respectability for indigenous women operating independently of husband and family. By the 1920s better educated women, more capable of playing an effective role in faith transmission, began to emerge from the Bible-training institutions set up in both India and China by Western women missionaries.[45] At the National Christian Conference held in Shanghai in 1922, it was declared that the "day of the semi-trained Bible woman is on the wane."[46] The 1930s brought a reduction in the numbers of indigenous women employed by churches and missions in India and China. Falling mission revenues had made some lower ranks of native mission staff, especially Bible women, redundant. At the same time, as authority in churches was gradually transferred from ordained male missionaries to local pastors, these same clergy showed no inclination to empower indigenous women evangelists. A 1938 survey found that the "younger churches ... appear to offer no great hope that women will find in them an ever enlarging place for professional service."[47]

EVANGELIZING IN CHINA WITH THE
CHINA INLAND MISSION

The CIM, like other faith missions, retained in the 20th century its commitment to evangelism as the key purpose of mission. Even in the 1880s, CIM missionaries had stood out, one none-too-sympathetic observer commenting: "The most eccentric missionaries are naturally those, many of them single women, belonging to Mr Hudson Taylor's China Inland Mission." They were, he wrote, "much given to street preaching and 'itinerating,' in which their unmarried women also take part, perambulating the streets of towns looking for invitations to enter houses."[48] Hudson Taylor, who had founded the mission in 1867, had from the start actively recruited women for evangelistic work. The original CIM party in 1865 included eight unmarried women. But he, as others had before him, found placing them problematic. The great difficulty was "finding them suitable homes."[49] In 1867 he wrote to William Berger, his London director, telling him to send no more sisters for the present. But he remained hopeful that in time they would be as acceptable in China as they were "in our city missions at home."[50] By the 1880s CIM women were once again being sent out to China. More than 260 were recruited between 1880 and 1895, 53 of them in 1887, the year of an appeal for 100 missionaries.[51] Taylor had rapidly to find a way of deploying them. Alvyn Austin suggests that the solution came via a request in 1886 from a Chinese pastor and his wife living at Hwochow (Huozhou) in Shansi (Shanxi) Province for two women missionaries to join them. He writes "this was so successful that Taylor instituted districts of 'women's stations' where the women worked under the supervision of Chinese pastors."[52] But already in that same year, Taylor was placing single women at Christian centers along the Guangxin River to work alongside Chinese colleagues.[53]

When in 1898 the German missiologist Julius Richter deplored the policy of having "whole districts of the Chinese mission field ... exclusively under the management of mission sisters," Hudson Taylor countered his censure by pointing out the advantages for male Chinese evangelists in not having to contend with the "overwhelming superiority of the European" male. It was "quite otherwise when he is associated with a missionary sister; then the whole work of teaching and preaching and representing the mission to outsiders devolves upon him; he counts as the head of the mission, and must act independently. But at the same time he is under the control of the mission sister, who is with him to advise and instruct him; and to report about him.... Of course, a great deal of tact is necessary for the sister and the catechist to maintain their mutual position."[54] Taylor did not state that there could sometimes be a benefit for the single woman also in not having to deal on a daily basis with the same superior European male! While women members of the mission were in theory on an equal footing to men, a male missionary on station would as a matter of course take precedence. Nor were women eligible to sit on the China council, which met in Shanghai at the mission's headquarters. Much depended too on their relationship with the provincial superintendent, always male.[55]

Hwochow was a city on a major trade route where Pastor Hsi and his wife had established a Christian center and an opium refuge. Their object in inviting CIM missionaries was to begin work with local women. The experimental service of the first two missionaries, a Norwegian pair called Anna Jakobsen and Sofie Reuter, was successful in its early years, but ended suddenly in 1898 when Jakobsen married an evangelist, Cheng Xiuqi. The connection was not acceptable, either to the mission or to local Chinese Christians, and she was forced to resign. They were succeeded by another pair of women missionaries, slain a couple of years later at the provincial capital, T'ai-yuan (Taiyuan), during the Boxer Rising. In 1902 a third set of women missionaries arrived—Eva French and Mildred Cable. They were joined in 1909 by Eva's sister Francesca.

The three women, together known as the Trio, were to become famous in later life for their itinerant ministry along the ancient trading routes in China's outer provinces of Gansu and Xinjiang, and for the various publications describing their experiences. One of their accounts, *The Gobi Desert,* is considered a classic. Between 1923 and the mid-1930s, when they were well on in middle age, they traversed the length of the Gobi desert five times "searching out innumerable by-paths and exploring the most hidden oases. Whenever we heard of some side-track which led to a hamlet, or even an isolated home, far from the main roads, there we went to deliver our message.... In every Gobi temple which we had touched the priests now owned a copy of the Scriptures.... A tent, a cart or an inn-room was our only home, our guest-room, preaching-hall, dispensary and bookshop." Distributing portions of Scripture as they went, they found it "necessary to carry books in seven different languages in order that the Mongol, the Chinese, the Turki, the Tibetan, the Manchurian, the Russian and the Arabic-reading *Ahung* should each be supplied with the Gospel in his own tongue."[56]

The first 20 years of their joint missionary service, however, were spent very differently. In their own words, they set aside "the free and irresponsible life of the itinerant missionary" and allowed themselves "to be tied to the numberless claims and responsibilities of institutional life."[57] Arriving at Hwochow, shortly after the bloodletting of the Boxer Rising, Eva French, the senior missionary, and Cable at first spent much time visiting local villages and listening to accounts of the slaughter. They later wrote of the need to visit every village and every home and to "spend long hours in listening to heart-rending stories." In those optimistic years, they became aware of an "extra-ordinary quickening of interest" in Christianity and felt "overwhelmed by the many openings which presented themselves on all sides." They were persuaded that bands of Chinese Christians could spread the good tidings much more effectively than ever could a pair of European missionaries.[58] Their role should be that of educators. In 1904 they began a school for girls, catering for all ages, and an institute to train Bible women, offering a variety of shorter and longer courses including "a two year course of Bible training and practical experience as evangelists."[59] They also ran a dispensary and opened an opium refuge for women. Most of their institutional undertakings required ambitious construction projects for which they first had to find funds. While most of their time was thus occupied, they nonetheless liaised closely with the Chinese pastor and his deacons, periodically also visiting local villages. Cable and the French sisters seem to have carried out their roles at Hwochow with devotion and admirable common sense. An attractive component of their published work is its infusion of humor. A typical anecdote concerned the dressmaker who lived "at the door of our mission" and who had made garments for "the three generations of missionaries" who had lived there. As she grew older, she raised her charges to take account of the fact that she sewed more slowly, so that the Trio had to pay "extra charges for inferior work." The dressmaker showed no inclination to become a Christian, confiding to a neighbor that "there seemed little inducement to repent and be saved, if going to heaven would entail associating with foreigners for all eternity."[60]

Figure 7.3. Mildred Cable stands to the right of stone tablet commemorating the erection of the Women's Bible School at Hwochow in 1909. With her are a group of students. Her colleague Evangeline French and Mrs. Hsi, widow of Pastor Hsi, study the Bible at left. (Courtesy of OMF International [United Kingdom]).

The three women occupied an honorable place in the Hwochow Christian community despite holding no formal position within the Church. If they found their role restricted, they made no mention of it. They were after all foreigners assisting, not directing local church life. But in an article published in 1922, Cable expressed her concern about the lowly status of Chinese women evangelists within the Church, arguing that it was important for the Church "to see, recognise and use the spiritual endowments of all its members."[61] That same year, the Trio decided it was time for them to move on. They felt confident that they could safely leave the work at Hwochow where its two pastors and a diaconate of 12, including four women, supervised church work, and a band of trained women teachers looked after the schools, while between 800 and 900 women had been trained at their Bible Training Institute. They had felt "the sense of a call" to the unevangelized areas further north where travelers had told them of "journeys varying from ten to forty days in duration without meeting a single witness for Christ."[62]

It took a full year for permission to come through. Given the fact that all three women had private incomes and were largely self-financing, it may be wondered why they needed CIM approval; but as they said themselves, the mission was "an authority they recognised." The permission when it finally came gave them the instruction they required to "go forward and preach, wherever God should lead them."[63]

Cable and the French sisters left their work at Hwochow just before the anti-foreign and anti-Christian agitation of the mid-1920s. Another CIM missionary, Myra (Mollie) Carpenter, arrived in China when these difficulties appeared to be receding. Many missionaries had by 1927 left China, convinced that they were no longer needed. Now they returned in large numbers, in the case of the CIM with record numbers of new recruits. Carpenter was one of 16 new workers going out from Britain in 1928—10 women and six men. An even larger number sailed in the two following years, bringing the total of CIM missionaries in China to 1,326, more than any other society. Fifty-eight percent of the intake was female, thus upholding women's numerical predominance in the mission.[64] Despite the wave of optimism as the 1920s gave way to the 1930s, the new decade proved a danger-ous one indeed. Brigands and pirates continued to control large tracts of land and ocean. There was the long-lasting conflict between Communist and Nationalist forces, periodic famine, and, from 1937 to 1945, war with Japan. Carpenter's time in China, like that of many of her contemporaries, was to be constantly disrupted. Her personal papers—deposited at the Centre for the Study of World Christian-ity, New College, Edinburgh—furnish a detailed picture of her life and work as an evangelistic missionary in China during the late 1920s, 1930s, and 1940s.

She arrived in Shanghai in November 1928 and with other women recruits departed almost immediately for the women's training college at Yangchow, where they undertook intensive Chinese language instruction and practical evangelistic training. It was difficult, she wrote, to grasp "all the unrest that is around, as we are kept in such perfect peace here, surrounded by a high garden wall on all sides." Dressed in her new Chinese clothes, wadded for winter, "bluey-green . . . with a zig-zag pattern in same colour," she, and others, emerged on fine Saturday af-ternoons to give away tracts and to practice speaking to people. Missionaries, it seems, were "the only foreigners in Yangchow. No one else has returned since the troubles."[65] By March they were waiting with some trepidation for news of which station they had been assigned to. Carpenter learnt that she had been designated to Tachi in East Szechwan, to work with "a Miss Drake and Miss Palmer," and while content that this was "the Lord's choice," she would have preferred not to be put with Anglicans. In her next letter, she was able to reveal that, most unusually, she had been redesignated. CIM Director Dixon Hoste had taken her "to a garden seat on the Compound [she was now in Shanghai] . . . and told me that he gathered from our talk at Yangchow that I wished to be in the Forward Movement to reach the unevangelised, and so he had decided to send me to the North of Szechwan [Sichuan] to Tai-ping, where there are some very needy places." She was delighted with the decision. It would enable her to be nearer colleagues she liked, doing the sort of work she felt cut out for, and to be in the mountains with their "wonderful scenery."[66] In the event, she did not go. Tai-ping rapidly became too unsafe for women evangelists. Instead she was posted to the area around Paoning, in a safer part of Szechwan, but still frequently having to move because of increasing unrest.

Her journey by steamer up the Yangtze to Paoning was hazardous. Pirates were on the river, and the boat had a military escort. Fighting detained her party for some weeks at Ichang (Yichang). Landing at Paoning at the end of May, she was pleased to find that she had been placed "with a Baptist and a Swede, instead of being with Church-y people." Here she continued her language studies, only engaging occasionally in any practical work. She wrote home that she had taken some walks "with Miss Wallis." The scenery was beautiful, but the "idols here and in some of the shrines are hideously grotesque, and it is easy to see that the peoples' religion is one of fear." They contented themselves with giving away "one or two tracts" and leaving "a gospel for the priest."[67] Paoning—in the valley of the Jialing River, a tributary of the Yangtze—is hot in summer, and in July, Carpenter joined other missionaries in making their way up to Sin-tien-tsi in the hills. In October she was still there, waiting to hear where she was to be sent. It was in that month, as she wrote in her 1930 Circular letter, "that I really began to get out amongst the people." She attended a funeral, and then a wedding of a young Christian woman. Still only able to speak a few sentences in Chinese, and accompanied by one of the senior woman missionaries, she found that "few joys can compare . . . to that of sitting in a Chinese courtyard, the family gathered round, babies and all, whilst Miss Williams or the Bible woman give forth the message." After another language examination in June 1930, in which she scored 95 percent, she was able to go on a preaching tour with a colleague, Elizabeth White, and

Mrs. Suen, the Bible woman. "We left at break of day.... It was the most beautiful walk I have ever had, the path following the river all the way.... It reminded me of North Wales, only was even more beautiful." En route, they "were unable to get a private room, so had the joy of sitting in a tea shop, which etiquette usually forbids women workers to do. Being a small market town it did not matter so much.... They are so pleased to find that the foreign lady can eat their food and wear their clothes. I hope one day she will also be able to speak more of their words."[68] Their destination on this occasion was the mountain-top village of La Chai Pa, where they were to stay with a Christian woman and her two little girls. As their little procession approached the village, there was a flurry of alarm—the area was prone to attack by brigands—followed by relief that "it was the missionaries." Their stay coincided with two market days, both Sundays, when they hoped to be able to speak to more people. It also coincided with the Moon festival. "While the heathen were worshipping the moon," the two missionaries and the Bible woman set about praising "the Creator of all things." They prayed aloud and sang and were pleased to note that "the singing attracted many and they left their worship to come and listen to ours and we had the opportunity of witnessing the Truth." Another village experience was less gratifying—"the atmosphere was very difficult," and many women said "we don't understand what you are talking about."[69]

By 1936 Carpenter's grasp of the language had much improved. She was able to lead prayer meetings and organize the winter Bible school for women at Yahsien, one of the larger CIM stations. She complained that too much time was taken up with "meetings, preparation and social duties"—she had to go out to dinner at Deaconess Liu's home, and then to the headmistress, Miss Lo. "We rather begrudge the time spent, but the fellowship helps to draw us nearer to our Chinese fellow-workers."[70] In February 1936, it was time to go on tour again, this time with Miss Lu. At one village, they held an evening service. She was amazed at how many women turned up—and some men as well. They came in the dark along "the rough, country roads" carrying "flares made of straw or bamboo." However, she and Miss Lu were displeased by the spiritual laxity in the Christian community. "Even the young man who leads the services has confessed to adultery and cannot be baptised." Another candidate was a small or second wife and also had to be rejected.[71] In March she became aware of the near-famine conditions in the area. Many of the people were "reduced to living on roots & it takes most of their time to prepare. They have to be sought for on the hillsides, brought home and pounded.... Then there is soaking, and straining, drying and reducing to powder, which is eventually mixed with a little rice."[72] In May, after seven years, she left China for her first furlough. She was more than relieved to leave her troublesome pony with Mr. Parker of the Lutheran Mission at Ichang. "He has had to deal with horses all his life and hopes to find a customer for him in due course."[73]

During her next period of service, Carpenter was given charge of an orphanage, but she continued to engage in evangelistic work when she could. She did not find much cause to rejoice, reporting in November 1940 that "the churches are in a very low state spiritually."[74] Her evangelistic work, chiefly amongst rural folk living in isolated mountainous villages, or small towns in East Szechwan, seems neither particularly remarkable nor successful. For the most part, she was interacting with struggling Christian congregations, not finding them well-led or flourishing. Her experience contrasts with those of the Cable and French sisters at Hwochow, who by 1921 felt that they could safely leave their Christian congregations and communities to embark on adventurous new evangelistic work in largely unexplored provinces. Carpenter remained in China apart from her furlough from 1936 to 1938, and again from 1947 to 1948, until the forced exodus of all missionaries from China in the early 1950s.

NOTES

1. Quoted in Sean Gill, "Heroines of Missionary Adventure: The Portrayal of Victorian Women Missionaries in Popular Fiction and Biography," in *Women of Faith in Victorian Culture, Reassessing the Angel in the House*, eds. Anne Hogan and Andrew Bradstock (Basingstoke: Macmillan, 1998), 178. The texts in the King James Bible read as follows: 1 Timothy ii 12, "But I suffer not a woman to teach, nor to usurp authority over the man, but to be in silence" and 1 Corinthians xiv 34, "Let your women keep silence in the churches: for it is not permitted unto them to speak; but they are commanded to be under obedience, as also saith the law."

2. Quoted in Clare Midgley, "Can Women Be Missionaries? Imperial Philanthropy, Female Agency and Feminism," in *Feminism and Empire*, ed. Clare Midgley (London and New York: Routledge, 2007), 119.

3. Steven Maughan, "Regions Beyond and the National Church: The Foreign Missions of the Church of England in the High Imperial Era, 1870–1914" (Ph.D. diss., Harvard University, Cambridge, MA, 1995), 277, fn. 47.

4. Geraldine Guinness, *The Story of the China Inland Mission* (London: Morgan & Scott, 1893), 384–385.

5. Extract from letter published in the *Annual Report* of the Society for Promoting Female Education in China, India, and the East, December 1835.

6. Midgley, "Can Women Be Missionaries?" 117.

7. Elizabeth E. Prevost, *The Communion of Women: Missions and Gender in Colonial Africa and the British Metropole* (Oxford: Oxford University Press, 2010), 4.

8. Society for Promoting Female Education in China, India, and the East, *Light through Eastern Lattices: A Plea for Zenana Captives, etc.* (London, 1884), 5.

9. Mrs. Weitbrecht, *The Women of India and and Zenana and Educational Work among Them* ([London]: Indian Female Normal School and Instruction Society, [1878]), 20.

10. Quoted in Robert Cust, "The Female Evangelist," *The Church Missionary Intelligencer and Record* (October 1885): 700.

11. "Appeal for Workers," *India's Women* (1884): 101.

12. Letter to Mrs. Weitbrecht, quoted in Cust, "The Female Evangelist," 701.

13. Cust, "The Female Evangelist," 702.

14. M. L. Christlieb, *Uphill Steps in India* (London: George Allen & Unwin Ltd., 1930), 13.

15. Jeffrey Cox, *Imperial Fault Lines: Christianity and Colonial Power in India, 1818–1940* (Stanford, CA: Stanford University Press, 2002), 70.

16. *News of Female Missions in Connection with the Church of Scotland* (October 1892): 167.

17. *News of Female Missions* (April 1892): 74.

18. "Village Itineration in the Sialkot Punjab Mission," Plumb Papers.

19. *News of Female Missions* (April 1894): 74.

20. *News of Female Missions* (April 1902): 31.

21. Notebook, Plumb Papers, File 16.

22. Amy Wilson Carmichael, *Things As They Are: Mission Work in Southern India* (London: Morgan & Scott, 1903).

23. Carmichael, *Things As They Are*, 7–8.

24. Carmichael, *Things As They Are*, 19.

25. Carmichael, *Things As They Are*, 278–280.

26. Eugene Stock, "Preface," in Carmichael, *Things As They Are*, xii.

27. See Eliza Kent, *Converting Women: Gender and Protestant Christianity in Colonial South India* (Oxford: Oxford University Press, 2004), 107.

28. Ruth Tucker, "Women in Missions," in *Earthen Vessels: American Evangelicals and Foreign Missions, 1880–1980*, eds. Joel A. Carpenter and Wilbert R. Shenk (Grand Rapids, MI: William B. Eerdmans Pub. Co., 1990), 273–274.

29. Stephen Neill, "Foreword," in *Sunrise on the Nilgiris" The Story of the Todas*, ed. Catharine F. Ling (London: Zenith Press, [1934]), v–vi.

30. M. B. Emeneau considers his action was likely to have been a vow, "such vows being freely undertaken by the Todas." Quoted in M. B. Emeneau, "The Christian Todas," *Proceedings of the American Philosophical Society* 81, no. 1 (May 31, 1939), 94.

31. While Ling's mission was to the whole Toda people, she rejoiced that "One of the results of Christian teaching has been a revolt of the women against their social degradation," quoted in Ling, *Sunrise*, 17.

32. Ling, *Sunrise*, 24.

33. Winifred M. Stone, *Ups and Downs on the Nilgiris* (London: Church of England Zenana Missionary Society, [1925]), 11.

34. See W.H.R. Rivers, *The Todas* (London: Macmillan and Co., 1906), a work with which Ling was familiar.

35. Ling, *Sunrise*, 53.

36. Ling, *Sunrise*, 54.

37. Emeneau, "Christian Todas," 106.

38. Winifred Stone, "A Farewell to Miss Ling," *India's Women and China's Daughters* (September 1934), 119–121.

39. Emeneau, "Christian Todas," 95.

40. But see Deborah Gaitskell and Wendy Urban-Mead, "Transnational Biblewomen: Asian and African Women in Christian Mission," *Women's History Review* 17, no. 4 (2008): 489–500.

41. Dana Robert, *Gospel Bearers, Gender Barriers, Missionary Women in the Twentieth Century* (Maryknoll, NY: Orbis Books, 2002), 13.

42. Quoted in Kwok Pui-Lan, *Chinese Women and Christianity, 1860–1927* (Atlanta, GA: Scholars Press, 1992), 82.

43. Quoted in Kent, *Converting Women*, 153.

44. Kent, *Converting Women*, 155.

45. By 1923, there were 53 Bible schools for women in China, see Pui-Lan, *Chinese Women and Christianity*, 86.

46. *The Chinese Church as Revealed in the National Christian Conference Held in Shanghai, Tuesday, May 2 to Thursday, May 11, 1922* (Shanghai: Oriental Press, 1922), 273.

47. *Interpretative Statistical Survey of the World Mission of the Christian Church*, ed. Joseph I.Parker (New York: International Missionary Council, 1938), 244.

48. Alexander Michie, *Missionaries in China* (London: E. Stanford, 1891), 53–54.

49. Quoted in Alvyn Austin, *China's Millions: The China Inland Mission and Late Qing Society, 1832–1905* (Grand Rapids, MI and Cambridge, MA: William B. Eerdmans, 2007), 296.

50. C. P. Williams, " 'The Missing Link': The Recruitment of Women Missionaries in Some English Evangelical Missionary Societies in the Nineteenth Century," in *Women and Missions: Past and Present, Anthropological and Historical Perceptions*, eds. Fiona Bowie et al. (Providence, RI and Oxford: Berg, 1993), 49.

51. CIM, "Register of Missionaries 1853–1895."

52. Austin, *China's Millions*, 239–240.

53. Valerie Griffiths, *Not Less than Everything* (Oxford: Overseas Missionary Fellowship, 2004), 101–103.

54. Quoted in Valerie Griffiths, "The Ministry of Women in the China Inland Mission and the Overseas Missionary Fellowship 1920–1990" (M.A. diss., Oxford University, Oxford, 1958), 7.

55. See Griffiths, "The Ministry of Women," 29.

56. Mildred Cable, *The Gobi Desert* (London: Hodder and Stoughton, 1942), 276–277.

57. Mildred Cable, *The Fulfilment of a Dream of Pastor Hsi's. The Story of the Work in Hwochow* (London: Morgan & Scott and China Inland Mission, 1917), 71.

58. Cable, *Fulfilment of a Dream*, 69–70.

59. Cable, *Fulfilment of a Dream*, 160.

60. Cable, *Fulfilment of a Dream*, 217.

61. A. Mildred Cable, "The Ministry of Women in the Chinese Church," *The Chinese Recorder* 54 (February 1922): 118–120.

62. "Twenty-one Years' Work in Hwochow; a New Venture," *China's Millions*, September 1923, 136–138.

63. Mildred Cable and Francesca French, *Something Happened* (London: Hodder & Stoughton, 1933), 123–124.

64. Leslie T. Lyall, *A Passion for the Impossible, the Continuing Story of the Mission Hudson Taylor Founded* (London: OMF Books, 1965), 101.

65. Letters from Myra Carpenter, January and February 1929, Carpenter Papers.

66. Letter from Myra Carpenter, April 3, 1929, Carpenter Papers.

67. Letter from Myra Carpenter, May 10, 1929, Carpenter Papers.

68. Letter from Myra Carpenter, June 16, 1930, Carpenter Papers.

69. Letter from Myra Carpenter, October 31, 1930, Carpenter Papers.

70. Letter from Myra Carpenter, January 14, 1936, Carpenter Papers.

71. Letter from Myra Carpenter, February 19, 1936, Carpenter Papers.

72. Letter from Myra Carpenter March 14, 1936, Carpenter Papers.

73. Letter from Myra Carpenter, May 23, 1936, Carpenter Papers.

74. Letter from Myra Carpenter, November 22, 1940, Carpenter Papers.

Afterword

The modern missionary movement... raised the status of women.[1]

The Protestant mission to India and China of the 19th and 20th centuries had required a high degree of participation by Western women. But there was almost continuous, and often contentious, assessment of what was thought fit or unfit for them to do. Permission to engage in the wider missionary enterprise came at a time when there was in fact little scope for women's activity outside the home circle, and the Protestant Church offered few outlets for a female religious life.[2] Western women's mission to the women of the East developed along a three-fold path: education, medical assistance, and evangelism. Yet, until the late 19th century, educational provision for girls in Britain was inadequate, medical instruction unavailable, and the notion of respectable women as evangelists unacceptable. Women's involvement in these areas was endorsed by male-dominated missionary organizations because they were seen as engaging in a mission to promote the virtues and values of Christian family life. Yet, most women missionaries were single, their unmarried state often causing perplexity to those to whom they ministered.[3] Women preferred indeed to portray themselves as sisters in what has been called a mission of sisterhood to the women of the East. But this was not, for

205

most of the period, a relationship based on equality.[4] Nor was equality a concept experienced by Western women missionaries in their relationship with male colleagues, despite their numerical superiority. Only in the 20th century, as women acquired professional qualifications as teachers, physicians, and nurses, did their status advance in the mission field. Similarly, within metropolitan mission governance, women had much ground to contest before they were able to achieve a measure of administrative equality.

Looking at the impact of missionary efforts, few would now accept an assertion made toward the end of imperial rule that "It would be difficult to exaggerate the part played by Christian missions in the emancipation of the Indian woman."[5] On the other hand, while missionary women attended diligently to the task of instilling into their pupils traditional Christian ideals of womanhood, they also, by example and precept, opened up career paths for those with the capacity to follow. Ironically, as Asian women began to acquire professional status in the 20th century, they did not experience some of the gender barriers Western women had had to face. As one woman doctor commented, women in India had not met "with the same opposition from men doctors as did their pioneers in the West."[6] There was one area, however, in which neither missionary nor missionized women were allowed equality, the area of evangelism. In her recent study of Anglican women missionaries, Elizabeth Prevost convincingly shows that "women were … central players in the spread of and indigenization of Christianity."[7] Yet, that role in the period under discussion was never an official one. No position in the Church above that of deaconess was open either to foreign woman missionary or indigenous woman evangelist. Indeed, as authority and power in mission churches was transferred to indigenous male pastors and officials in the 1920s and 1930s, the status of both further declined.[8] Only in the second half of the 20th century has that situation been reversed. Recent research among Tamil Christian women finds them active in "spreading the Gospel and sustaining and extending the Tamil Church," while in China—reckoned to have one of the fastest growing Christian movements in the world—there were, in 2005, around 8,000 women evangelists in registered churches alone.[9] In attaining full ministerial ordination, both Western and Asian Christian women experienced delays, but those in India and China achieved that status at least 10 years before their sisters in the established Church of England.[10]

NOTES

1. Kathleen Bliss, *The Service and Status of Women in the Churches* (London: SCM Press Ltd., 1952), 23.

2. C. P. Williams notes how Protestantism had reduced "very substantially the openings for women in the Church." C. P. Williams, "The Recruitment and Training of Overseas Missionaries in England between 1850 and 1900" (M.Litt. diss., University of Bristol, Bristol, 1976), 314. The mid to late 19th century, however, saw the reintroduction into Britain of sisterhoods and deaconesses.

3. World Missionary Conference (WMC), *Report of Commission V* (Edinburgh and London: Oliphant, Anderson & Ferrier, 1910), 148.

4. See in particular the writings of Jane Haggis, Susan Thorne, and Antoinette Burton. There is some evidence to suppose that relationships were more egalitarian in China where missionaries had less "standing." See C. F. Andrews, "Missions in India Today," *International Review of Mission* 22, no. 2 (1933): 194.

5. Quoted in Bliss, *Service,* 23. Also see Royal Institute of International Affairs, *Modern India and the West: A Study of the Interaction of Their Civilizations* (London, New York, etc.: Oxford University Press, 1941).

6. Hilda Lazarus, "The Sphere of Indian Women in Medical Work in India", in *Women in Modern India,* ed. Evelyn C. Gedge (Bombay: D. B. Taraporewala, 1929), 60.

7. Elizabeth E. Prevost, *Communion of Women: Missions and Gender in Colonial Africa and the British Metropole* (Oxford: Oxford University Press, 2010), 4.

8. *Interpretative Statistical Survey of the World Mission of the Christian Church,* ed. Joseph I. Parker (New York and London: International Missionary Council, 1938), 244.

9. See Valerie Griffiths, "Biblewomen from London to China: The Transnational Appropriation of a Female Mission Idea" and Beulah Herbert, "Tamil Christian Women at the Turn of the Millennium: Mission Initiatives and Gender Practice," *Transnational Biblewomen: Asian and African Women in Christian Mission, Women's History Review* 17, no. 4 (2008): 521 and 611–629.

10. The General Synod of the Church of England approved the ordination of women in 1992. The Synod of the Church of South India took the same action in 1982. The China Christian Council first ordained women pastors in 1980. A Hong Kong woman, Li Tim Oi, was ordained as an Anglican priest in 1944, but this action was repudiated at the end of the war, and Li Tim Oi resigned. Two further women were ordained in the Hong Kong Anglican Church in 1971.

Select Bibliography

ARCHIVES AND MANUSCRIPT COLLECTIONS

Angus Library, Regent's Park College, Oxford

    Letters of Timothy and Mary Richard, BMS Archive

Archives and Special Collections, School of Oriental and African Studies, London

    Archive of the China Inland Mission (Overseas Missionary Fellowship)
    Archive of Interserve, formerly the Zenana and Bible Medical Mission
    Archive of the London Missionary Society (Council for World Mission
        Archive)
    Archive of the Overseas Mission of the Presbyterian Church of England
    Papers of Derek Bryan and Liao Hongying (MS 380825)
    Papers of Gladys Stephenson, Methodist Missionary Society Archive
    Papers of Elspeth Hope-Bell, Council for World Mission Archive

British Library, London

    Papers of Dr. Clare Thomson, Mss Eur D1102

Papers of Margaret Hunt, Mss Eur F241
Women's Christian Colleges in Madras Collection, Mss Eur F220

Centre for the Study of World Christianity, New College, Edinburgh

Papers of Myra Carpenter

National Library of Scotland, Edinburgh

Papers of Isabella Plumb

Royal Free Hospital Archives Centre

Ludhiana Medical College Archive

Selected letters of Myfanwy Wood (privately owned)

MISSIONARY MAGAZINES

Chronicle of the London Missionary Society
Female Missionary Intelligencer (FES / SPFEE)
Grain of Mustard Seed: Or Woman's Work in Foreign Parts, 1881–1898 / *Women in the Mission Field* (SPG)
India's Women / India's Women and China's Daughters, 1896–1939 / *Looking East: at India's Women and China's Daughters* (CEZMS)
Indian Female Evangelist (IFNS / ZBMM)
International Review of Missions
News of Female Missions in Connection with the Church of Scotland, 1859–1897 (Ladies' Association)
News of Female Missions in Connection with the LMS, 1875–1886 / *Quarterly News of Woman's Work* (LMS)
Occasional Papers of the Ladies' Committee for Ameliorating the Condition of Women in Heathen Countries, Female Education, etc / Woman's Work on the Mission Field, 1904–1932 (WMMS / WA)
Our Indian Sisters: A Quarterly Magazine of the Ladies' Zenana Mission in connection with the Baptist Missionary Society
Our Sisters in Other Lands, 1879–1937 (PCE / WMA)
Woman's Work / Wider World (PCI / PWA)

PRIMARY PRINTED SOURCES

Balfour, Margaret I. and Ruth Young, *The Work of Medical Women in India* (London: Oxford University Press, 1929).

Bevan, Gladys M., *Twenty Five Years in India* (Great Britain: Church in the Marketplace Publications, 1993).

Brown, James H., *Frances Brockway: Memoirs* (London: Unwin Bros., 1905).

Buchan, Annie Gray, *Adventure in Faith* (Peterhead: P. Scrogie, 1973).

Burton, Margaret, *The Education of Women in China* (New York: F. H. Revell Co., [1911]).

Cable, Mildred, *The Fulfilment of a Dream of Pastor Hsi's. The Story of the Work in Hwochow* (London: Morgan & Scott and China Inland Mission, 1917).

Cable, Mildred and Francesca French, *Something Happened* (London: Hodder and Stoughton, 1946).

Carmichael, Amy Wilson, *Things As They Are. Mission Work in Southern India* (London: Morgan & Scott, 1903).

Chatterjee, Sunil Kumar, *Hannah Marshman, the First Woman Missionary in India* (Hoogly: S. Chatterjee, 1987).

Davies, Hannah, *Among Hills and Valleys in Western China* (London: S. W. Partridge & Co., 1901).

Dawson, E. C., *Heroines of Missionary Adventure* (London: Seeley, Service & Co, 1925).

Dr Agnes Henderson of Nagpur, a Story of Medical Pioneer Work (Edinburgh and Glasgow: United Free Church of Scotland Women's Foreign Mission, 1927).

French, Francesca, *Miss Brown's Hospital* (London: Hodder and Stoughton, 1954).

Giberne, Agnes, *A Lady of England. The Life and Letters of Charlotte Maria Tucker* (London: Hodder and Stoughton, 1895).

Gollock, Minna C., "The Share of Women in the Administration of Missions," *International Review of Missions* 1, no. 4 (1912): 674–687.

Herdman, Innes, *Liao Hongying—Fragments of a Life* (Dereham: Larks Press, 1996).

History of the Society for Promoting Female Education in the East (London: Edward Suter, 1847).

Hodges, A., ed., *Love's Victory. Memoirs of Fanny Woodman by Her Sister* (London: Marshall Bros., 1899).

Johnson, Lewis, *Hilda Johnson: A Memoir* (London: London Missionary Society, 1920).

Johnston, James, ed., *Report of the Centenary Conference on the Protestant Missions of the World Held in Exeter Hall, London, 1888* (London: J. Nisbet, 1888).

Lowe, John, *Medical Missions, Their Place and Power* (London: T. Fisher Unwin, 1886).

Middleditch, T., *The Youthful Female Missionary: A Memoir of Mary Anne Hutchins* (London: G. Wightman, 1840).

O'Neill, F.W.S., ed., *Dr. Isabel Mitchell of Manchuria [Letters]* (London: J. Clarke & Co., [1917]).

Pitman, Emma R., *Heroines of the Mission Field* (London, Paris, and New York: Cassell, Petter, Galpin & Co., [1880]).

Richter, Julius, *A History of Missions in India* (Edinburgh: Oliphant Anderson & Ferrier, 1908).

Salters, Audrey, *Bound with Love: Letters Home from China 1935–1945* (St. Andrews: Agequod, 2007).

Sibree, James, *Register of LMS Missionaries, Deputations etc.* (London: London Missionary Society, 1923).

Singh, Behari Lal, *The History of Native Female Education in Calcutta* (Calcutta: Baptist Mission Press, 1858).

Thompson, Jemima, *Memoirs of British Female Missionaries* (London: William Smith, 1841).

Tinling, Christine I., *India's Womanhood: Forty Years' Work at Ludhiana* (London: Lutterworth Press, 1935).

Tonge, E.M., *Fanny Jane Butler, Pioneer Medical Missionary* (London: Church of England Zenana Missionary Society, 1930).

Weitbrecht, Mary, *Female Missionaries in India: Letters from a Missionary Wife Abroad to a Friend in England* (London: James Nisbet & Co., 1843).

Weitbrecht, Mary, *The Women of India and Christian work in the Zenana* (London: James Nisbet & Co., 1875).

White, E. Aldersey, comp., *A Woman Pioneer in China, the Life of Mary Ann Aldersey* (London: The Livingstone Press, 1932).

World Missionary Conference (WMC), *Reports of Commissions V and VI* (Edinburgh and London: Oliphant, Anderson & Ferrier, 1910).

Wright, Jane, *She Left Her Heart in China: The Story of Dr. Sally Wolfe, Medical Missionary, 1915–1951* (Groomsport: Cloverhill, 1999).

Young, Miriam, *Among the Women of the Punjab* (London: Carey Press, 1916).

Young, Miriam, *Seen and Heard in a Punjab Village* (London: SCM Press, 1931).

SECONDARY BOOKS AND ARTICLES

Anagol, Padma, "Indian Christian Women and Indigenous Feminism, c. 1850–1920," in *Gender and Imperialism*, ed. Clare Midgley (Manchester and New York: Manchester University Press, 1998), 79–103.

Anderson, Olive, "Women Preachers in mid-Victorian Britain: Some Reflexions on Feminism, Popular Religion and Social Change," *The Historical Journal* XII, no. 3 (1969): 471–472.

Bowie, Fiona, Deborah Kirkwood, and Shirley Ardener, eds., *Women and Missions: Past and Present* (Providence, RI and Oxford: Berg, 1993).

Brouwer, Ruth Compton, *Modern Women Modernizing Men* (Vancouver, BC and Toronto, ON: UBC Press, 2002).

Burton, Antoinette, "Contesting the Zenana: The Mission to Make 'Lady Doctors for India,' 1874–1885," *The Journal of British Studies* 35, no. 3 (1996): 368–397.

Chaudhuri, Nupur and Margaret Strobel, eds., *Western Women and Imperialism* (Bloomington, IN: Indiana University Press, 1992).

Cox, Jeffrey, *Imperial Fault Lines. Christianity and Colonial Power in India, 1818–1940* (Stanford, CA: Stanford University Press, 2002).

Cox, Jeffrey, *The British Missionary Enterprise since 1700* (New York and London: Routledge, 2009).

Donaldson, Margaret, " 'The Cultivation of the Heart and the Moulding of the Will . . . ' the Missionary Contribution of the Society for Promoting Female Education in China, India and the East," in *Studies in Church History, Vol. 27, Women in the Church*, eds. W. J. Sheils and Diana Wood (Oxford: Basil Blackwell, 1990), 429–442.

Doran, C., " 'A Fine Sphere for Female Usefulness': Missionary Women in the Straits Settlements, 1815–45," *Journal of the Malaysian Branch of the Royal Asiatic Society* LXIX, no. 1 (1996): 100–111.

Endfield, Georgina H. and David J. Nash, " 'Happy Is the Bride the Rain Falls on': Climate, Health and 'the Woman Question' in Nineteenth-century Missionary

Documentation," *Transactions of the Institute of British Geographers* NS 30 (2005): 368–386.

Fitzgerald, Rosemary, "A 'Peculiar and Exceptional Measure': The Call for Women Medical Missionaries for India in the Later Nineteenth Century," in *Missionary Encounters: Sources and Issues,* eds. Robert Bickers and Rosemary Seton (Richmond: Curzon Press, 1996), 174–196.

Fitzgerald, Rosemary, "'Making and Moulding the Nursing of the Indian Empire,' Recasting Nurses in Colonial India," in *Rhetoric and Reality: Gender and the Colonial Experience in South Asia,* eds. Avril A. Powell and Siobhan Lambert-Hurley (New Delhi: Oxford University Press, 2006), 185–222.

Forbes, Geraldine H., "'In Search of the 'Pure Heathen': Missionary Women in Nineteenth Century India," *Economic & Political Weekly* 21, no. 17 (1986): WS2–WS8.

Gaitskell, Deborah and Wendy Urban-Mead, *Transnational Biblewomen: Asian and African Women in Christian Mission, Women's History Review* 17, no. 4 (2008).

Gill, Sean, "Heroines of Missionary Adventure: The Portrayal of Victorian Women Missionaries in Popular Fiction and Biography," in *Women of Faith in Victorian Culture: Reassessing the "Angel in the House,"* eds. Anne Hogan and Andrew Bradstock (Basingstoke: Macmillan, 1998), 172–185.

Griffiths, Valerie, *Not Less than Everything* (Oxford: Overseas Missionary Fellowship, 2004).

Haggis, Jane, "Ironies of Emancipation: Changing Configurations of 'Women's Work' in the 'Mission of Sisterhood' to Indian Women," *Feminist Review* 65 (2000): 108–126.

Hunter, Jane, *The Gospel of Gentility: American Women Missionaries in Turn-of-the-century China* (New Haven, CT and London: Yale University Press, c. 1984).

Kent, Eliza F., *Converting Women: Gender and Protestant Christianity in Colonial South India* (Oxford and New York: Oxford University Press, 2004).

Macdonald, Lesley Orr, *A Unique and Glorious Mission. Women and Presbyterianism in Scotland 1830–1930* (Edinburgh: John Donald, 2000).

Maughan, Steven, *Mighty England Do Good: Culture, Faith, Empire and World in the Missionary Projects of the Church of England, 1850–1915* (Grand Rapids, MI and Cambridge, MA: William B. Eerdmans, 2013).

Midgley, Clare, "Can Women Be Missionaries? Imperial Philanthropy, Female Agency and Feminism," in *Feminism and Empire,* ed. Clare Midgley (London and New York: Routledge, 2007), 92–122.

Nair, Janaki, "Uncovering the Zenana: Visions of Indian Womanhood in Englishwomen's Writings, 1813–1940," in *Cultures of Empire,* ed. Catherine Hall (Manchester and New York: Manchester University Press, 2000), 224–245.

Porter, Andrew, *Religion versus Empire? British Protestant Missionaries and Overseas Expansion, 1700–1914* (Manchester and New York: Manchester University Press, 2004).

Prevost, Elizabeth E., *The Communion of Women: Missions and Gender in Colonial Africa and the British Metropole* (Oxford: Oxford University Press, 2010).

Prochaska, Frank, *Women and Philanthropy in Nineteenth-century England* (Oxford: Clarendon Press, 1980).

Robert, Dana L., *American Women in Mission: A Social History of Their Thought and Practice* (Macon, GA: Mercer University Press, 1996).

Robert, Dana L., ed., *Gospel Bearers, Gender Barriers* (Maryknoll: Orbis Books, 2002).

Rowbotham, Judith, " 'Soldiers of Christ'? Images of Female Missionaries in late Nineteenth-century Britain: Issues of Heroism and Martyrdom." *Gender & History* 12, no. 1 (2000): 82–106.

Semple, Rhonda, *Missionary Women: Gender, Professionalism and the Victorian Idea of Christian Mission* (Woodbridge: Boydell, 2003).

Seton, Rosemary, " 'Open Doors for Female Labourers': Women Candidates of the London Missionary Society, 1875–1914," in *Missionary Encounters: Sources and Issues,* eds. Robert A. Bickers and Rosemary Seton (Richmond: Curzon Press, 1996), 50–69.

Stanley, Brian, *The Bible and the Flag. Protestant Missions and British Imperialism in the Nineteenth and Twentieth Centuries* (Leicester: APOLLOS, 1990).

Strobel, Margaret, *European Women and the Second British Empire* (Bloomington, IN: Indiana University Press, 1991).

Thorne, Susan, *Congregational Missions and the Making of an Imperial Culture in Nineteenth-century England* (Stanford, CA: Stanford University Press, 1999).

Twells, Alison, *The Civilising Mission and the English Middle Class, 1792–1850: The 'Heathen' at Home and Overseas* (Basingstoke: Palgrave Macmillan, c. 2009).

Williams, C. P., " 'The Missing Link': The Recruitment of Women Missionaries in some English Evangelical Missionary Societies in the Nineteenth Century,"

in *Women and Missions: Past and Present. Anthropological and Historical Perceptions,*
eds. Fiona Bowie, Deborah Kirkwood, and Shirley Ardener (Providence, RI and
Oxford: Berg,1993), 43–69.

THESES

Chatterton, Jocelyn, "Protestant Medical Missionary Experience During the War
in China 1937–1945: The Case of Hubei Province" (Ph.D. diss., University of
London, London, 2010).

Griffiths, Valerie, "The Ministry of Women in the China Inland Mission and the
Overseas Missionary Fellowship 1920–1990" (M.A. diss., Oxford University,
Oxford, 1958).

Haggis, Jane, "Professional Ladies & Working Wives: Female Missionaries in
the London Missionary Society & its South Travancore District, South India,
in the 19th Century" (Ph.D. diss., University of Manchester, Manchester,
1991).

Maughan, Steven, "Regions Beyond and the National Church: The Foreign
Missions of the Church of England in the High Imperial Era, 1870–1914"
(Ph.D. diss., Harvard University, Cambridge, MA, 1995).

Morawiecki, Jennifer A., " 'The Peculiar Mission of Christian Womahood': The
Selection and Preparation of Women Missionaries of the Church of England
Zenana Missionary Society, 1880–1920" (Ph.D. diss. University of Sussex,
Falmer, 1998).

Index

American women missionaries: comparisons with British women missionaries, 68, 71, 77, 105, 110; cooperation with, 159–60, 164; criticisms of, 173; funding by 131, 138–40, 164, 172

Anderson, Elizabeth Garrett, 152

Anderson, Rufus, 14

Baptist Missionary Society, 3, 5, 20, 47, 96, 157–60

Baptist Zenana Mission, 32, 96, 98, 157

Baring-Gould, Edith, 100

Bible women, 25n49, 190–92, 194

Billington, Mary, 123

Bishop, Isabella Bird, 39, 153, 173n1

Boxer Rising, 192–94

British and Foreign School Society, 12, 35, 90, 118

Carpenter, Mary, 125

China: Christian evangelism in, 192–99; girls' education in, 128–37; medical missions in 153–57; patriotic movements during the 1920s, 134–36; training of nurses in, 162–68

China Inland Mission: bidding farewell to missionaries at Tilbury, 49; deployment of single women missionaries, 192–93, 196–97; language tuition, 61; outfit list, 48; position of women in the mission, 109, 180; reaction to marriage of Anna Jakobsen, 80; recruitment policy, 37, 40, 43–45

Christian Medical Association of India, 172

Church of England Zenana Missionary Society: formation of, 20, 94;

About the Author

ROSEMARY SETON is a research associate of the Department of the Studies of Religion at School of Oriental and African Studies (SOAS), and co-convener of the Christian Missions in Global History seminar at the Institute of Historical Research, University of London. For 30 years, she was a professional archivist, for much of that time the head of Archives and Special Collections at the SOAS, which holds the largest accumulation of missionary archival materials in the United Kingdom. These include major archives such as those of the China Inland Mission, the London Missionary Society, the Methodist Missionary Society, and numerous personal collections. From 1999 to 2002, she was the director of the MUNDUS Project to improve and facilitate access to missionary collections throughout the United Kingdom. She has published widely in the areas of religious archives and mission history.

Lightning Source UK Ltd.
Milton Keynes UK
UKHW020753240720
367105UK00004B/75

9 781846 450174